Richard Malcolm Johnston

Mr. Absalom Billingslea

Richard Malcolm Johnston
Mr. Absalom Billingslea
ISBN/EAN: 9783743373204
Manufactured in Europe, USA, Canada, Australia, Japa
Cover: Foto ©ninafisch / pixelio.de

Manufactured and distributed by brebook publishing software (www.brebook.com)

Richard Malcolm Johnston

Mr. Absalom Billingslea

MR. ABSALOM BILLINGSLEA

AND

OTHER GEORGIA FOLK

BY

RICHARD M. JOHNSTON

AUTHOR OF "OLD MARK LANGSTON," "DUKESBOROUGH TALES," ETC.

WITH ILLUSTRATIONS

NEW YORK
HARPER & BROTHERS, FRANKLIN SQUARE
1888

Copyright, 1887, by HARPER & BROTHERS.

All rights reserved.

PREFACE.

The favor accorded to former publications by the author, and to these sketches as they separately appeared in the magazines, has led to this present collection.

In essaying to illustrate some phases of old-time rural life in middle Georgia, the author has tried to show how superior was the character to what might have been expected from the dialect of the people. Before the time of railroads, when travelling farther than twenty or thirty miles from homes was rare, simplicity, as well as activity, must have been prevalent among country folk. In this region, very fertile and almost universally salubrious, perhaps there was as little of social distinctions among its inhabitants as among those of any other in the South. The men of culture and those of wealth, as a general thing, were neighbors of the uncultured, and those with moderate or small property around them, and all were friends with one another; not only trusting and trusted, but helpful, fond, often affectionate. Among such a people—every one conscious of the freedom of his manhood—whatever was original or individual must find unhindered developments that will be multifold according to particular gifts, circumstances, and opportunities. As for the dialect, not only those who knew not better, but many of those who did, including some of the most eminent lawyers, were fond of it to the degree that they preferred it often, not only when in sportive moods, but when incensed by resentment. It will be noticed that among most of the female characters in these sketches, even of the humbler sort, dialect is less pronounced than among the men, thus proving its oft deliberate use and preference by the latter.

The author felt that it might be proper thus to preface about the people among whom he was reared, whom he has always loved and admired, and not less for some oddities of deportment and dialect with which by personal and professional intercourse he was made familiar. From this same people, of every condition of prosperity and intelligence, have sprung as many, he believes (residents not only in Georgia, but in Alabama, Mississippi, and Texas), as from those of any other region of like extent, who using the educational opportunities which their fathers were enabled to procure for them, and inheriting their loyalty to truth, justice, and all manful behests, have become eminent in Church and State, and who in social circles, whether in their own regions or elsewhere, rank with the best.

The author cordially acknowledges his thanks not only to Messrs. Harper & Brothers, but to the publishers of *The Century* and *The Catholic World*, for their generous co-operation in this behalf.

CONTENTS.

	PAGE
A Critical Accident to Mr. Absalom Billingslea	1
The Brief Embarrassment of Mr. Iverson Blount	31
Rev. Rainford Gunn and the Arab Chief	59
Martha Reid's Lovers	74
The Suicidal Tendencies of Mr. Ephrodtus Twilley	111
Dr. Hinson's Degree	133
The Meditations of Mr. Archie Kittrell	145
The Rivalries of Mr. Toby Gillam	187
The Hotel Experience of Mr. Pink Fluker	224
The Wimpy Adoptions	243
The Stubblefield Contingents	278
Historic Doubts of Riley Hood	310
Mr. Thomas Chivers's Boarder	322
Moll and Virgil	383

LIST OF ILLUSTRATIONS.

	PAGE
"'With women it's sharp's the word and quick's the motion'"	*Frontispiece*
"'I come over to see if I could borry your k'yart and steers'"	20
"He saw Martha standing on the piazza"	80
"He was becoming somewhat of an aristocrat"	82
"'Look at that Izik picked out the fire'"	89
"'You heern talk o' Aberham, hain't you?'"	93
Mr. Triplett, the Sheriff of the County	97
"'Oh, pa! pa! have you sent Madison away?'"	108
"Jodie was fond of visiting"	148
"'And I'm a-namin' o' no names'"	150
"Soft-hearted woman as Mrs. Templin was"	155
"Somehow Mr. Kittrell felt a little embarrassed at meeting them together"	161
"'Them was not only her words, but her wery langwidges'"	169
"'Missis Polly Templin vs. Missis Malviny Peevy. Debt for mone and oudacious insiniwations'"	174
"'It's like the Kittr'lls has been from everlastin' and for evermore'"	179
"A man that did half work, he contended, must expect to get half pay"	189
Harmon Griggs's	192
"'You b'lieve weddin's is made in heb'n, Mandy?'"	202

	PAGE
"'Wuz you a-tellin' o' me the fack-truth when you said you wuz done 'ith the makin' o' coffins?'"	221
"Fool who?"	225
"Mr. Fluker felt that he was becoming a little confused"	235
Mr. Marchman's pressing business with Mr. Pike	239
Mr. Solomon Pringle	250
"'Mis' Wimpy, come to ast might I cote Miss Milly, sir'"	259
The Return of the Bee-hunters	267
"'You Jes Pringle! don' you put them hands on me'"	273
Mapp and Cynthy	283
"She strolled with Wiley about the yard"	291
"'I got no physic for such a case'"	301
"'Dis Moll an' me (she's my sister, an' I'm her br'er), we ain't no free niggers; ner we hain't no runned away, we hain't'"	387

A CRITICAL ACCIDENT TO
MR. ABSALOM BILLINGSLEA.

"Were it by aventure or destené,
As whan a thing is schapen, it schal be."
The Knightes Tale.

I.

MR. ABSALOM BILLINGSLEA was a gentleman who at all periods in his career, instead of trying, like some, to disguise his age, seemed to feel an honest pride in telling it, even with circumstantiality. Having lived a bachelor, and that not from choice, it might have been expected that this pride would have been subdued after a lapse that had brought him quite into the forties. But let us hear what he had to say one day at the country store about a mile west of his residence.

"On the nineteent' o' Febuary I were forty-three, and ef I live tell the nineteent' o' this Febuary comin', I shall be forty-four; and my mother always said it were twelve o'clock of a Chuesday, and my father he always said it were the first day of his beginnin' a-plantin' o' corn that year."

The history of Mr. Billingslea prior to the attainment of this respectable age had not been specially eventful, at least outwardly. Such a history, perhaps, was not to be expected in the case of one who from childhood had been deliberate even to slowness in speech, gait, work, and other deportment. Commonly they are the quick, the vigilant, the daring, that become historic. Yet there had been as many as two times when he believed that his mind had been wrought into vast excitement, and he used to intimate what might have happened if the person who had been the occasion of that excitement had been other than a female.

"Yes, yes," he would say sometimes, in the calmness of mature reflection, " they has ben times—I don't say when nor whar—but *ef* it had of ben a man person that jes' out o' puore devilment made me feel like I did then, people would of heerd from me."

Mr. Billingslea was too prudent and honorable a man to mention names. Yet everybody knew to what he alluded, and it was some consolation to him that they did. Even if he had been disposed to conceal his views or his feelings upon any subject, he could never have found how such a thing was to be done; for he was open as the day, and as courageous as he was guileless. Slow as he had been always in his movements of every sort, he had had one dear aspiration that had suffered a double disappointment. He endured as such a man can endure, thankful that his friends and neighbors understood and respected a case allusion to which, except in vague, delicate, confidential phrase, the proprieties of social life had hindered. The whole blame for this disappointment he always had taken upon himself; and as it had been often said to him that the objects of his desire had not been attained because mainly of the want of activity in his pursuit, he had tried to become resigned to an infirmity that had cost him so dear, when it seemed too late to be worth his while to amend it, and it was only from remarks that he would make occasionally, especially when in company with young unmarried men, that inference could be drawn of his regret that he had not been swifter, at least upon two important occasions.

"Boys," he would say, blandly, yet in the confident tone often employed by kind-hearted old bachelors who are conscious that they have not lived to that period without reasonable ingathering of wisdom from experience, "you may talk about your co'tin' and your bein' of co'ted, but I tell you now that ef a feller count on makin' any headway at that kind o' business, he got to be active. With women it's sharp's the word and quick's the motion; and they want no feller, and onless they know they can't do no better, they ain't a-goin' to have no feller, exceptin' they see he's powerful anxious for them, and them only. It's so, and it's their natur' to be so. And I don't know but what in the long-run they're right, a not'ithstandin' that sech as that, in sech a game as that, leaves sech as me out. But it's more'n prob'le that sech slow-goin' poke-easy creeters as what I am had ought to be left out thar; an' ef he can't git satisfied with the sisciety of jest his lone self, to git reconciled to it the best he can. And that, maybe, he may do after a while, by goin' 'long tendin' to his own business, tellin' no lies on people, ner not meddlin' with what ain't his'n. But you boys well b'ar it in mind and 'member what I say, that 'ith women—that is, in the p'ints o' co'tin' and bein' of co'ted—it's sharp's the word and quick's the motion. I'm a-talkin' now from expeunce. Ef I had my time to go over ag'in, it might be that I might try to be peerter in some o' my gaits. But now—"

Then he would wave both hands slightly, but decisively, as if any acceleration on his own part was not to be expected henceforth, since all opportunities for its employment had passed forever; yet he would calmly smile in the satisfaction of imparting to the young among his male acquaintance, through these kind and thoughtful admonitions, benefit of a wisdom so long and so sadly hoarded.

Such was Mr. Billingslea at forty-three and the rise, when one of his near neighbors, contrary to all human expectation and probability, after a rapid decline from the flower of his manhood, deceased, leaving, among others, one who, at first a mourning, was likely to become, after decent interval, a blooming widow.

But for this unlooked-for event it is hardly probable that any biography of Mr. Billingslea would have been undertaken; and now I feel that I cannot do full justice to his subsequent career without delaying its rehearsal until I give one (as briefly as possible) of his antecedent.

II.

About three miles west of the village was Mr. Billingslea's home. His mansion, a one-story with attic, stood on an eminence near the public road, and the farm, with five hundred acres of prime upland, lay sloping in the rear, extending to the Pitman line. On the south side of the road, a quarter of a mile eastward, dwelt his sister, Mrs. Cokely, to whom this portion had fallen in the division. The Cokelys lined partly with the Ashleys, by a stream that, but for its being energetic as it was small, might never have found its way among the numerous rising grounds to Beaver Dam Creek. Lining with the Pitmans and north of Duke's Creek were the Marlers.

Between the brother and sister (the latter three years younger) had been always a very warm affection. It was only a few years back that their mother, who during her twenty years of widowhood had dwelt with the son, had deceased. Since then he had lived alone, excepting with his negroes, the sister occasionally going over to set to rights whatever things had been allowed by the bachelor to get awry.

For the purposes of this story the important member of the Pitman family was Julan, the eldest daughter. When she was fourteen years old she had the looks, the manners, the gait—in brief, a man might have travelled throughout all that region in search of her superior and not found her. Absalom Billingslea, being then twenty-four, six feet one, broad-chested, healthy as the morn, and good-looking as any man of such parts ought to ever desire to be, had been in love with Julan ever since she had been born, and many and many a time had he told her so. In his last year of schooling, which, at twenty-two, he had undertaken in order to make up for some deficiencies that he feared he had incurred during his two years' course while a boy, he used to not start of mornings to Mr. Claxton, who kept a little back of the Ashleys, until the Pitman children came on, when he carried Julan's books, and of summer evenings her very bonnet, when she would take it off in order to let her long, thick, yellow hair get all it could of the hill-side and meadow air. Then he always walked right behind her on the log that lay across the branch, except when it had swollen, if only a few inches, when either he would go before, leading her by the hand, or, lifting her in his arms, bear her across.

All this was when Julan was very young and uncommonly small for her age. In one year, from thirteen to fourteen, if anybody ever saw a girl grow and develop fast, it was that same Julan Pitman. Now so it was that from the very beginning of this nascent period Absalom Billingslea's avowals of his love became more and more infrequent, and soon ceased altogether. About that time he had ceased going to school, while Julan went a year longer. Of course they met not so often, yet they must be much together, dwelling so near, and belonging to families so friendly. What it was that had shut his mouth against the continuance of these avowals he never could understand. But the slowness natural to his being seemed, whenever he was in her presence, to come to a dead stop. Not that he did not love her more and more every day of his life. Not that he felt particularly embarrassed. Perhaps he was confused by this sudden springing from diminutive girlhood into womanhood complete. Perhaps he was ever cogitating how to piece on the old gallantry to the sober proposal to marry her, but somehow could not yet make them buckle and tongue together. He pondered and pondered; for a slow-minded man can do that as much as a quick, especially on such a theme as Julan Pitman. Indeed in such a case he does it more, and while he is thus engaged the quick may have left off that business and gone to acting. Absalom Billingslea believed, notwithstanding his late silence, that Julan knew, and could not possibly keep from knowing, that, having loved her all during her plain, spindling girlhood, he was obliged to love the very ground she walked on, now that she had developed into the round, plump, delicious thing that she was. He became fond to ruminate, especially when in her society, how she could not but rather like the adoration with which she had inspired him, and in time he began to make up his mind that he would study up a set of phrases that might go as far as human language was adequate to express the culmination of his feelings and their aspirations. It occurred to his mind that such announcement justly required words of most solemn and momentous import, and he sadly, though not very painfully, regretted that his limited education retarded their coming to his lips.

"Br'er Ab," said Mrs. Cokely one day, and that not for the first time, nor the second, "if you want Julan Pitman, you better hurry up. She's grown now, and she knows it, and everybody else knows it, and 'special Bob Marler knows it, and if you don't mind what you're about he's going to get in there before you, as he's been trying his very levellest best for six months to do."

"Why, S' Nancy, ain't I jest a-waitin' for a good, suitable chance? And as for Bob Marler, don't I know that at the school-house Julan couldn't b'ar Bob Marler? and once, when he hurt her feelin's and made her cry by laughin' and callin' her a little scrap, I took him by the collar, and told him if he done it ag'in I'd choke him tell he see stars in the daytime."

"Ah! dear, dear brother, that was a long time ago, when Julan was nothing but a child."

"'Twasn't so very fur over a year ago. Julan ain't now but in her fifteent' year, and it look like a man ought to try to be decent in the namin' to as young a person as she is sech a thing as the gittin' of married."

"Well, brother, if the worst come, you can't say I never warned you."

Such admonitions could not but exert in time some influence upon a mind even as immobile as this. The amount of cogitation done by him during the weeks immediately preceding definite action would not have dishonored the proudest philosopher who ever pondered the stars. Concluding at last that he was as near the condition of readiness as he would ever be, probably, he resolved that on the ride home with Julan from church on the next meeting day he would make the eventful announcement. He confessed afterwards, with some apparent remorse, that he not only could not tell what were the heads of the sermon on that occasion, but that he had actually forgotten the text. In this state of mind, what must have been his feelings, after the service, to find that Julan was to ride home with the escort of Bob Marler! More than that, many persons along the road said that it was talked about in the neighborhood that Bob and Julan were engaged. The very next morning he rode to the Pitmans, and knowing no better than to ask Julan if the report was true, and she knowing no better than to answer that it was, he rose immediately, went back home, and suffered as single-minded men always suffer when disappointed in attainment of the one great object of their life's desire. His sister did not scold; she only wept when she saw the pain it cost him. Some people said that Julan had gone into the engagement in a pet for his slowness, and that he might have broken it if he had tried. But he was incapable of such action, and, except to his sister, and that seldom, the subject was never alluded to by him.

Julan and Bob were married, and lived together ten years, during which Absalom was such a neighbor and friend as if nothing of the kind I have mentioned had occurred. Then Bob died, leaving her with two children. The wedded life was not thought to have been as blessed as the average; for the husband, though energetic, thrifty, and fond of the wife, was inclined to be penurious and arbitrary. Her loyalty to every behest of her condition had hindered gross maltreatment; but when he went, most of the neighbors thought, and some of them said, that Bob Marler had had quite as much as he deserved of the society of such a woman.

III.

This event affected Absalom Billingslea far more profoundly than anybody except Mrs. Cokely suspected. He had ever rather believed that the prize he so singly had desired had been lost through his own inactivity. But he was the soul of honor and justice. Though never expressing himself so to any except his sister, he had often felt indignant at what appeared on the part of her husband a lack of appreciation for Mrs. Marler and consideration for her happiness. Yet, now that he was dead, compassion for his early death struggled with the thought that Julan was again free. There are such men in the world, and they are to be found in such a country society as I am telling about as often as in any other, however more advanced in culture and refinement. This man, so slow in motion, so apparently imperturbable in mind, would have preferred to die rather than do dishonor not only to Bob Marler when alive, but to his memory now that he was dead. When he looked upon that young widow he was almost frightened to find that none of the love of his youth had gone, as he had tried to persuade himself all during her married life. Julan mourned with that strange loyalty that good women always pay to the memories of their departed husbands, however remiss these may have been in appreciation and tenderness, and this old lover admired her only the more for such conduct. At least he hoped that he did, though far more fondly did he hope that the time would come when he would be enabled to assuage her grief in a manner that would be the consummation of the highest happiness of which his own heart had ever dreamed.

Mrs. Cokely understood his case even better than he did, and after the first year of widowhood had expired she began to urge him towards what she was confident he wished and intended, if vaguely, to do whenever he could feel that he could do so with propriety.

"May the good Lord have mercy on your dear, precious old soul, Br'er Ab!" she said to him one day, after some preliminary chat, "do you suppose a woman like Julan, that's now nothing but a girl, is going to grieve herself to death or forever about such a husband as Bob Marler?"

The question staggered him.

"I—n-no, S' Nancy; I—that is, I should hardly expect—at leastways I shouldn't hope that Julan would grieve—that is, not quite forever—for—for sech *as* Bob: though Bob, poor feller, he's dead and goned now, you know, S' Nancy, and somehow I *can't* but think that maybe Bob were a cleverer feller than we ben a-takin' him to be when he were among us. And as for Julan, she—you see she war her black the same as the week after he went, and I hain't a idee Julan ever yit thought o' sech a thing as—as—"

Mr. Billingslea paused here, and actually was near blushing for the sable, sorrowing young widow.

"Yes, and right there is where you *are* mistakened. Br'er Ab, a man like you don't understand women any more than they understand babies. As for Bob Marler, he was just the man he were, and his being dead can't alter at leastways what he used to be. They isn't any doubt but what he loved Julan, as no man that had such as her for a wife could have holp doing that. But he never treated her as a man ought to treat such a wife, and you know it. Yet Julan have done what all respectable widows will always do, and 'special them that have children by a man: she's behaved herself decent, and knowing that them children is his children as well as hern, and is now orphins, she's been sorry for *them*, and *is* sorry for 'em. But Julan have too much sense, and if she didn't, she's too young, to be and keep everlastingly grieving about Bob Marler, and I *know* what I'm talking about."

It may not happen that very much delicacy finds place in beings as little cultured and as inactive as that of Absalom

Billingslea; but when it does, it is of the very best type. To make an advance towards that woman in black, who seldom was seen to smile, it appeared to him, would be an indelicacy that would not be forgiven, and ought not; and little as he had thought of her husband while living, he yet could not but feel that he owed something, however indefinite, to the memory of one whom, upon reflection, he may have undervalued. And so he continued to wait. Oh yes, he *must* wait some longer.

The death of Mr. Marler, after an interval of four or five months, was followed by that of Mrs. John Ashley, at the place aforementioned. The affliction of the bereaved husband, who was left with one male child three years old, was profound and sincere. But of course everybody knows that such as that does not last always. Absalom Billingslea was very fond of Jack, though he never seemed to care for having much to do with Wiley, his next younger brother. In his heart he pitied Jack, tried to console him by all means that he could employ, was gratified after some months to see him take rather more cheerful views of life, and, as his friend, felt almost hurt by neighborhood whisperings that Jack was already beginning to turn his thoughts towards marrying again. He even had the friendly candor to tell Jack of these whisperings one day, and he was proud of Jack for the indignant manner in which he denied that there was any just foundation for them.

"You do beat this world, Br'er Ab." Mrs. Cokely was a little vexed, and she acknowledged it. "Br'er Ab, you don't understand Jack Ashley any more'n you understand Julan Marler."

"Why, S' Nancy, the poor feller's wife have no more'n hardly got cold in her grave; and Jack told me with his own mouth that he were mad as he could be about people havin' no more feelin' than to be talkin' about his even thinkin' about gettin' married ag'in."

"Goodness gracious me! Don't you know that that's just the *ways* of them widowers when they are on the sly, as that same man Jack Ashley is now about Julan?"

"If he's arfter Julan—and which I can't believe it's so— he well fling away his weepons in that hunt, for Julan have too much respects not only of herself, but she have too much respects of her husband and Jack Ashley's wife, to even listen to sech talk. Why, didn't Missis Keenum tell me that when she hinted to Julan that Jack, to her opinions, were thinkin' o' her in a cur'ous sort o' way, that Julan cried, she did."

"And what do that show?"

"It show, in the first place, that Julan didn't believe it; and it show, in the next place, that she were hurted in her feelin's by hearin' o' her name a-bein' coupled with that kind o' business yit awhile. People, S' Nancy, is obleeged to suppose that people is decent and has feelin's, and they ought to try to have 'em theirselves."

"Ah! Br'er Ab, you let yourself get left before, and I'm much afraid it's going to be so again."

Mr. Billingslea, after his own style, waited and watched the conduct of these two bereaved. It is needless to tell the result of such behavior. If ever a man of his kind was overwhelmed with confusion and dismay, it was he, when, without public notice, Jack one morning rode over to Mrs. Marler's in his gig, was married to her, and took her and her children to his home.

"It were ruther the onexpectedest thing, I think, I ever knowed," said Mr. Billingslea to his sister when they heard the news. "I shouldn't of thought it of nother of 'em— that is, not yit, not quite yit." Then he took out his pocket-handkerchief, for the sight of tears in her eyes had moistened his own. "But," he continued, "Jack suit her, I suppose, and Jack's a good-lookin', good-hearted, and a monstrous liber'l feller. I hardly think he wanted to fool me out and out about his denyin' so positive. I suppose he found out somehow that maybe he better git Julan if he could, and the good Lord know *I* can't blame him for that. Yes, Jack's a monstrous liber'l-hearted feller. I ain't quite shore but what he's a cleverer feller—that is, in some p'ints of views—than what poor Bob were. I hope he'll be good to Bob's childern, and take good keer o' Julan and her prop'ty."

"Julan had no *business* of marryin' Jack Ashley," began Mrs. Cokely, after drying her eyes with some violence.

"Come, come, S' Nancy. I can't b'ar to hear you say anything ag'inst Julan. It were her business, and you've never been a woman as follered the practice o' findin' fau't with other people for tendin' to their own business the best they know how. Julan were a young widder, and I no doubt she were lonesome with jest them two little childern, and she see that Jack were obleeged to be lonesome with jest his one, and she knowed that all three need two parrents instid o' one, and Jack he knowed the same. And then, ag'in, they knowed, both of 'em, that it warn't nobody's business but theirn. And so they took the notion to jind and nunite together without astin anybody else's leave, and they done it, and as for me, I hope it'll turn out right for 'em both and for 'em all. And not a nary word ag'inst it and ag'inst them would I ever want to hear, and 'special from my own people."

She looked at him in silence for several moments as he walked slowly up and down in the room. Then rising, she went and laid one hand upon his shoulder.

"Br'er Ab, you want to know what I think of you? It's that slow as you are, and careless as you are about your own interests, you are the best man that lives, or ever did live, in this world."

She put her arms around him and laid her head upon his breast. He bent down, kissed her cheek, and then disengaging himself from her, left the house, and walked slowly back to his home.

IV.

"Jack, I thought you said that Absalom Billingslea and Mrs. Keenum were likely to marry. She was over here to-day, and she said that Absalom never hinted such a thing to her, and she had no reason to believe that he ever would."

"Wiley said he heard so. You know Wiley always picks up the latest news. As for Ab Billingslea, he's too slow-motioned ever to make up his mind to court any woman."

This chat was had some time after the marriage. But I shall devote brief space to the telling about that. The years came and went. The principal outward alteration in Mr. Billingslea was some dereliction in attention to dress. Doomed, as now for the second time he felt himself to be, to endless bachelorhood, there was what commonly follows such a consciousness—less care to please by attention to exterior deportment. An acknowledged old bachelor is bound to become seedy in some elements of his being. He prospered in business, however, unhasting as he was in its pursuit. He was one of those planters, in the long-run most successful, who made their most important point to raise a plenty to eat for man and beast. Such a planter usually has cash in his pocket, and can avail himself of opportunities which such a condition presents of adding to his capital by advantageous purchases. Jack Ashley used to laugh at him (for Jack and he continued on as friendly terms as ever) for his making only three bales of cotton to the hand. Yet Jack, with all his seven, was a money-borrower, whereas Absalom became a lender of more and more every year, and sometimes, in his mild way, he would give Jack a friendly warning against what seemed to him too adventurous in some of his tradings and too expensive in his way of living. Jack would always answer as to the latter that while he lived he intended *to* live. And so he did. In ten years his estate was less valuable than when he and Mrs. Marler were married. With the loss of property came the loss of energy, spirits, and health. He fretted throughout his last remaining year, leaving, besides his wife and his child by the first marriage, one by the last. The property of the Marler children, except in the wear of the land, was unhurt, but his widow's, including what she took by his will, was not equal to what she had brought upon her marriage. The neighbors tried to believe that but for Jack's decay in manliness by his misfortunes and bad health he would not have made the bequest to his wife contingent upon her remaining unmarried.

V

Now when Julan most unexpectedly had become free for the third time, Mr. Billingslea felt—indeed, he could not have told himself how he did feel. He hoped that he was sorry for Jack being cut down in the midst of his manhood, and nobody except Mrs. Cokely had ever heard him say a word against the will. Even to her he essayed by one argument and another, of course without success, to mitigate her resentment. If he tried to suppress other thoughts that rose in his mind, even at the funeral, it was but for a brief period.

Julan, now at thirty-five, was handsomer and sweeter-looking than ever. There is in young widowhood something that engages more than maidenhood, especially such a man as Absalom Billingslea, whose heart, undemonstrative as it was, sympathized with suffering of every sort. Mrs. Ashley had never in words complained of the will, and she let Wiley, the executor, manage everything as he pleased. Even a few things which she had believed to belong separately to her and her Marler children she let him, on his insisting to do so, include in the inventory.

Modest as Mr. Billingslea was, he could not but believe that if he had been more demonstrative of his feelings on the two previous opportunities, results might have been different; and now that another had occurred, he made up his mind fully that he would not have cause for blaming himself a third time. Yet it was not as a lover of their mother, but as a man accustomed to have just views about such things, that he spoke (not to Mrs. Ashley, but to others) with some freedom about the rights of the Marler children, inconsiderable as infringements upon them had been. Wiley, a bachelor himself of thirty-two, a man of powerful build, heard of these remarks, but for one reason and another did not take notice of them. As always heretofore, Mr. Billingslea visited at the house, and extended to the widow offers of assistance such as she well knew it was his habit to do in similar cases in the circle of his acquaintance. In all this there was nothing uncommon.

But what about other things? Mr. Billingslea, having seen his very fondest aspirations frustrated on two momentous occasions (first by a man in his rear, and secondly by one in his very front), now forty-three at his last birthday, destined, if he should have good-luck, to be forty-four on his next—Mr. Billingslea made up his mind to stir as he never had stirred himself before, put himself in preparation for all possible attacks in rear, front, and flank, and even make such sallies of aggression as should seem to him to be timely and practicable. He had his house newly painted; and goodness knows it needed it. He had his hair trimmed, not by Mrs. Cokely, but a regular cutter in town; and if he didn't buy a bottle of bear's-grease, I'm a liar! He got a new fur hat, and a new suit of broadcloth out and out— things he had not done in I would not like to say how long. He straightened out of his back the wrinkles that had been gathering while he was indifferent whether they came there or stayed away. He got a quickness, not to say elasticity, of step that he had never had, I may go to the extent of saying, since he had been named Absalom Billingslea. He took on a jocoseness of speech that brought to all, men and women, old and young, laughter that he had never dreamed was in him to provoke. And he did other things too tedious to mention. Ah me! such widows as Julan Ashley have made older and soberer men than he kick up their heels, or try it, in the hope of winning them, taking them back to youth, and living it over again.

There was not a soul that blamed Mr. Billingslea for any item of all this juvenility. Instead, everybody was glad to see it. Did I say everybody? Alas! I forgot that there was one exception. It was Mrs. Ashley. For you must know that all this not only had begun, but had been finished off, by the time that Jack Ashley had been in his grave some eight or nine months. Not that Mrs. Ashley had been painfully affected by the painting of the house, or the reports she had heard of Mr. Billingslea's dressiness, his activity, and his cheerfulness. For she was too sensible a woman not to know that being worried in her mind by such things would have been nothing short of foolishness. But what did hurt Mrs. Ashley I will relate as plainly as I can.

One morning little Ab Cokely, having gone on a visit to his uncle, met him at the gate, fully greased, and almost fully dressed, and that in his new broadcloth.

"Ain't you goin' to put on your kervat, Unk Ab?" asked the child.

Mr. Billingslea felt at his throat, went back into his house, folded, twisted, and tied the best he knew how a silk cravat, put his hand in his pocket, jerked out a quarter, gave it to little Ab, mounted his horse, put him into a canter, and away he went. Now the appearance in such guise at a private house, and that on a week-day, was a thing that the oldest inhabitant had never known of having been done except by a marrying man specifically and avowedly intent upon immediate, pressing courtship. Added to all I have mentioned was this, that his face was very red and his voice was husky, even while he talked with the children before Mrs. Ashley came into the house—for at his arrival she was in the garden pointing out to the cook the vegetables to be gathered for dinner. Coming in as she was, apron and all, she halted suddenly at the door, both at the sounds and the sight, as if uncertain as to whether or not she had misunderstood the messenger who had called her in with the announcement of Mr. Billingslea's visit. Then a sudden paleness overspread her face, and without advancing as usual to shake his hand, she sat down in the nearest chair and said, feebly, "Good-morning, Mr. Billingslea."

The oldest Marler child, a girl of fifteen, rose as if intending to leave the room.

"Sit down, Emily, and keep your seat," said the mother, in despotic tone.

Absalom Billingslea, with the instinct of one who is a

gentleman, however simply bred and little cultured, instantly perceived that he had made a mistake, and, as he afterwards declared to his sister, "if ever there was a time enduring every single one of his born days when he wished he had been at home and clad in his oldest old clothes, that morning was the time." Not a word was spoken for a full two minutes, at the end of which Mrs. Ashley, looking as if she felt no sort of interest in her question, curtly asked, "How's Nancy?"

Mr. Billingslea, who had been looking alternately at her plain dress and his own glistening suit, suddenly threw up his head, and with painful honesty tried to recall to his mind the person about whom it was probable that inquiry had been made.

"Who did you— Oh, you mean S' Nancy. Oh, she— she's well. That is, I—I think so. At leastways little Ab he were at my house—it were this mornin', if my 'membance don't fail—and—well, to the best o' my ricollection, little Ab he never told me that anything were particklar out o' the way with his ma. I think—that is, my opinions is that S' Nancy is about as well as common."

If Mr. Billingslea had been on the witness-stand I do not believe that he would have spoken with a more sincere, solemn purpose of rendering an answer in accordance with the best of his knowledge, information, hearsay, and belief. He sat for some time apparently waiting for further interrogations. None being propounded, he made another brief comparison of the apparels so widely differing from each other. Then, contracting his brows, and swallowing an imaginary substance of vast magnitude, he said, in tones that trembled in their efforts to show that he was not entirely hopeless of prevailing in his suit, "I—I come over—I were on my way to town, and I come over to

"I COME OVER TO SEE IF I COULD BORRY YOUR K'YART AND STEERS."

—to see if I—in fact, if I could borry your k'yart and steers."

He shuddered throughout his whole frame. The youngest of the children had to hold her nose, and the other two to cover their mouths with their handkerchiefs, to conceal their emotion. Mrs. Ashley, smiling faintly, said of course he could be accommodated in the way he desired. Whereupon he expressed the liveliest gratitude, rose, and, as well as he could, took himself away.

VI.

"Oh, S' Nancy, it were the awfullest, all-firedest lie that ary nigger, let 'lone ary white man, ever let out o' his mouth; and Julan knowed it, and so did the childern know it, and ef they'd of ben a baby thar a week old, *it* would of ben obleeged to know it were a lie o' the whoppinest kind. For they all knowed I got two k'yarts and three yoke o' steers, and they knowed I see thar one little yoke o' yearlin's right thar before the door, with thar rickety old k'yart, one spoke goned and one hub all split open, a-busy a-haulin' rails for a calf-parscher. But I *had* to say somethin', or fall dead out o' my cheer, and that was the onlest thing I could think of. As soon as I could git up, I vamished myself off. I took them store clothes home, and locked 'em up in the chiss, whar they are goin' to lay while *my* head's hot; an' I do think, on my soul, it took me a hour, with hot water *and* soap, to git that cussed b'ar-grease out o' my h'ar. I no business a-*goin'* thar on sech a arrant, because I felt like all the way thar that it were goin' to turn out just as it did."

The sister, notwithstanding her sympathy, could not but laugh somewhat at the account he gave of his discomfiture.

"Br'er Ab," she said at length, "you set at Julan in the wrong way. You ought not have went there all dressed up and perfumed up on a weeky-day without first letting her get a hint that you was a-coming, and what for. Little Ab told me you had on your broadcloth, and I thought maybe you were going to the court-house. If I'd had any notion of what you were about, I'd have gone over and told you that wasn't the way to make a set at Julan. Why, it was enough to scare her."

"That's jest what it done. But *her* skeer didn't hold a light to mine. She have that satisfaction, if she want any. If I'm any skeerder when I come to die than I were thar *and* then, them that's about me 'll see a skene cert'n. But, *Sister* Nancy," he continued, in a tone of impatience that he had never employed with her and seldom even with his slaves, " what *were* I to do? You and other people told me I were too slow both times before. And now it seem I were too rapid. The fact is, it don't lay in me to know when nor how to co't a female person, and it ain't my lot. And my opinions o' Julan is that she think she had her shere o' marryin'. At all ewents, and *in* all ewents, she don't take to me, and it would of surprised me if she did. I've always ben out, and I'm out agin, and I'm goin' to try good this time to git reconciled to stay out."

"My dear brother," said Mrs. Cokely, deeply compassionating the pain it was evident that he suffered, "don't give up that way. If Julan ever thinks about getting married again, I can't believe she'd throw away a chance that's worth both of her husbands put together. You wait a while. Julan is pestered in her mind by Wiley Ashley, who's as mean and selfish and stingy as can be, and she ain't in the condition to be courted now, at least in a—in such a—a expressing and vi'lent way, so to speak. Of course *I* can't say if she ever will be. But a man just as well wait and see."

"Oh, as for waitin', everybody have to wait for what's a-comin', includin' the time when they got to leave this country for good. But I tell you, S' Nancy, as for Julan, I'm out, like I always ben out, an' I shall never pester her any more. That ain't my lot."

Some time after this interview Mrs. Cokely made a visit to Mrs. Ashley, and from the manner in which her hints concerning her brother's feelings were received she was convinced that his conclusion to retire from the pursuit was prudent. She believed that she ought to so inform him. At the same time she felt it her duty to give him other information, which was to lead to painful consequences. The ladies had always been warm friends. Mrs. Ashley had shed many tears in speaking of the hard terms that had been imposed by Wiley Ashley, and her face had flushed with resentment while telling how, upon her rejection of Wiley's suit, he had taunted her with setting her cap with the hope of catching old Ab Billingslea, and that if he ever should court her at all, it would not be until he had given up all hope of getting the widow Lightfoot, whom every one knew he wanted. Mrs. Ashley, after giving this confidence, had requested Mrs. Cokely not to mention it; but the latter had not given her promise thereto, and so, after much rumination and consultation with her husband, who had advised against it, she concluded to obey her own impulse and tell the whole conversation, including a gross insult by Wiley in his intimation that, even during the lifetime of his brother, she had thought more of old Ab Billingslea than she had any right to. When Mrs. Cokely saw the effect this information produced upon her brother, she wished that she had withheld it.

After she had given it, he rose and said, "Wile Ashley used them words, did he, to his own brother's widder? A d—" But in a woman's presence, although his own sister, he repressed the imprecation that had risen to his lips, and walked the floor with a vigor of step that she had never seen him use.

"Now, Br'er Ab, you've got to promise me—"

He stooped, and laying his hand softly trembling upon her shoulder, said, "I promise you, S' Nancy, that I shall do nothin' but what a man that's any account can't keep from doin' in sech a case."

For a while he did not seem to hear her as she went on talking in affectionately warning language, but continued to pace the floor. After some minutes he became calm, sat down, and, changing the subject, chatted in his usual manner during the rest of her visit. When she was gone, he got his writing materials, wrote a note, read it over several times, tore it up, and began on another. Then reflecting that on the morrow an election was to be held at the store for one of that militia district's officers, he rose, called a negro man, and said to him,

"Josh, you go over to Mr. Wiley Ashley's, and tell him I wish he'd try and make it convenant to meet me at the store to-morrow mornin', as I want to see him on some partic'lar business, and fetch word if he'll be thar, and what time."

The messenger in due time returned with answer that Mr. Ashley would be at the appointed place somewhere between nine and ten o'clock.

"All right. Ast you anything about me, Josh?"

"He ax me ef I knowed what business you had wid him."

"And what did you answer him?"

"I told him I knowed nothin' 'tall 'bout it."

"Fact. Ast you anything else?"

"He said 'pear like my marster were peertinin' up jes' here lately, paintin' his house, an' gittin new broadcloff clo'es."

"And what did you answer to that?"

"I told Marse Wiley dat as for de paintin' o' de house, everybody see she need dat I dunno how long; an' as for do gittin a new suit o' clo'es, I have heerd Miss Nancy scoldin' you many an' many time for not dressin' up sprucer—young man like you."

"What did he say then?"

"No more, Marse Ab, more'n he sort o' laughed. But he war partic'lar, Marse Wiley war, to ast how all wus."

"He laughed, did he? That'll do. Go 'long."

VII.

Many had already gathered at the store when Mr. Billingslea arrived. Having dismounted and fastened his horse to one of the racks, he advanced and bade a general goodday to all.

"Ah! *you* here already, Wiley? Got somethin' to say to you when I speak a few words to these gentlemen. Gentlemen, I never 'spected to have to *talk* about such matters as I want to talk with you a little now. But I feel like it were my jooty to let my neighbors know that I has as good as co'ted Missis Julan Ashley, and that she have as good as 'fused me. Now, mind ye, I know well as ef people told me, that it ain't none o' my business how Wile Ashley ben a-managin' his brother's 'state, nor a treatin' o' his widder and poor Bob Marler's orphin childern, although I has my opinions about that and them ef he want to hear 'em any time; and I tell you all what I'm a-tellin' you now, because he have ben a insiniwatin that the said female person have ben a behavin' differ'nt from what a respectable female widder ought to berhave herself; an I'm the man ag'inst who them insiniwations is p'inted, and in your presence, gentlemen, I po—nounces 'em LIES." Then turning to Ashley, he said,

"That's the business I had with you, Wile. How shall we settle it before these witnesses?"

They were two powerful men, equal in weight, nearly so in height. Ashley had the advantage in youth by several years, and by considerable successful experience in hand-to-hand combats which his querulous, overbearing disposition had sometimes provoked, and he was as proud of his manhood as he who at Hector's funerals

"undertook
Gigantic Butes of th' Amycian stock."

The unexpectedness of the charge confounded him for a moment. Then he looked at his assailant, and answered,

"You're a good deal older man than what I am, Mr. Billingslea."

"Yes, that's so. But if you begin to cote my age on me, Wile, I shall be obleeged to believe you to be as big a coward as I know you to be a liar."

"They ain't but one way to settle it after that, sir."

Instantly throwing off his coat, he dealt Mr. Billingslea, while similarly engaged, a blow that prostrated him on the ground.

"Foul play!" cried several men, seizing hold of Ashley as he was proceeding to fall upon his adversary. The latter quickly rose, and casting aside his garment, in a tone terrific in sound and import, cried,

"Turn the hound loose, and I gives notice that any man who meddles in this fight, at leastways on my side of it, is my innimy. Turn him loose, I tell you," he thundered, as he steadily advanced.

It was a bloody, an awful contest. Several times in its midst they paused for a moment to recover breath, when the elder would renew the struggle. The by-standers at every pause besought them to cease. No answer was given by either, until, after an encounter fiercer and prolonged more than any preceding, and they were leaning against two oaks that stood near, Ashley, to these renewed entreaties, said, between his pantings, "I think myself we've had enough of it. I got nothin' in this world ag'inst Mr. Billingslea, and he ought to know it."

"Nothin' ag'inst Mr. Billingslea!" said the latter, after a loud, contemptuous laugh. "No, you got nothin' ag'inst *him* exceptin' the bein' of called a liar and a coward, which you know you're both o' them. What and who you got things ag'inst is women, and your own brother's widder at that. Come, sir, git away from that tree, and squar' yourself agin."

Then he dealt a blow that sent him staggering. Triumphant in his cause and now assured victory, he took him by the head, turned him round, gave him a push, and pursued him as the elder pursued the younger combatant in the games instituted by the Trojan hero on the Sicilian shore, when

"Disdain and conscious virtue fired his breast."

Soon the vanquished fell upon the ground, whence he had to be lifted and carried home in a wagon.

VIII.

It was some consolation to Mr. Billingslea that, although the last hope of winning the woman he had so singly loved was blasted, yet he had rendered her a service that she had sorely needed. With his old manfulness, he submitted to his disappointment as on former occasions, and when he had worn away the scars of his late combat, went forth with accustomed deliberateness to the demands of domestic and social existence.

About two months after the events last narrated, one afternoon, when the sun was nearly set, he walked over the way to the Cokelys. As he was ascending the piazza steps he was surprised to hear the voice of Mrs. Ashley as she was bidding good-by to his sister. He had not seen her since his unfortunate visit.

"Wait a moment, Julan," said her hostess, "and I'll call Jimmy to go with you all the way home, as it's rather— Just in time, Br'er Ab," she continued, turning to him as he entered—"just in good time to see Julan home. I was just going to call—"

"Oh, *now*, Nancy," said Mrs. Ashley, "it's *not* worth while to take that trouble. I'm not afraid."

She looked as if she felt deeply distressed at the enormous amount of trouble she was giving to all parties.

"No trouble at all," answered Mr. Billingslea, simply. "You oughtn't go, at leastways through the swamp, by yourself after sundown."

They went forth together, and proceeded slowly, first along the public, then down the neighborhood road that they had travelled together so often when both were at school. He talked in his usual way of one and another topic that he thought might be of some interest. She chatted with much vivacity, so much that he began to feel doubtful if he was keeping up with her fairly. He became aware somehow that she was looking up constantly towards his face, and he found himself wishing very much to look down into hers; but he knew he could not, and that it would never do if he could. On and on, until they neared the streamlet. Another log, like the old, lay in the same place.

"How often, how often," said Mrs. Ashley, "do I call back the times I used to cross that log when I went to school to Mr. Claxton!"

"Me too," answered Mr. Billingslea.

They paused simultaneously. The dusk was coming on. A cock-partridge on the fence near by whistled to his mate; two killdees were tripping along the meadow; a hoarse but affectionate croak sounded to their right, that was answered by the Indian-hen as she sped swiftly before them to her covert. They looked at each other for several moments.

"Julan," said her companion, "there's ben somethin' of a shower o' rain down here this evenin' like, and the branch banks is ruther damp."

"Are they?"

Then she put out her little foot, with its new, glistening, low-quartered shoe, and the stocking on her instep and the narrowest wisp of underskirt that appeared were whiter than the evening cloud. Oh, it would be a pity for those delicate fine things to get all wet and draggled, and that without any earthly necessity!

"Yes, ruther damp, and, in fact, I may even say ruther moist; and it and the jew has made the crossin' log ruther slippy."

"Have they?"

"Yes; and, Julan, you know that when that and sech is the case down here, I'm minded more'n common o' them old-time days."

"Are you?"

"Yes."

Then he stooped, raised her in his arms, and, as of yore, bore her across the stream and the low grounds. She laid her head upon his shoulder as he strode easily along with his burden, the while with his disengaged hand he removed her bonnet, took out her combs, and let her hair, long, fresh, abundant as ever, dishevel. When he had reached the rising ground, he let her down softly, and said, "Julan, jest as I loved you then, I've always loved you."

"And to think—to think that I never knew it! Oh, Absalom!"

He folded his arms around as if he would first comfort her. After a little while he lifted her head, and said, "Julan, we mustn't complain now. *I* say, blessed be God! What do you say?"

"I say," she answered, beaming with grateful tears and smiles, "blessed be God!"

"And, oh, boys, it were a accident, my gittin' of her at last." He was talking to a knot of young men in a corner of the room on the night of the wedding, while his eyes followed Julan moving among her guests. "I never knowed how to go about a-co'tin', and I'd 'a' never of got her in this wooden world but for me—jest her and me, jest accidental—we was by ourselves at the medder branch, whar I had toted her a many a time over the crossin' log when she were a little girl a-goin' to Mr. Claxton; and somehow thar—I don't know agzactly how it come about, but I shall always believe it were a accident."

THE BRIEF EMBARRASSMENT OF
MR. IVERSON BLOUNT.

"If thou dost perform,
Confound thee, for thou art a man."
Timon of Athens.

I.

Some reflections habitually indulged by Mr. Iverson Blount, from a certain period in middle down to the end of old age, were so calm and sweet that I feel as if I ought to relate a few of the circumstances to which they owed their origin. The older he grew the greater the fondness and circumstantiality with which he would enlarge upon a very embarrassing duty that he once had to perform, and his satisfaction with the results of his endeavors in its behalf. However regretful of the necessity, I must abridge much of a history that, to him at least, was ever extremely interesting.

When a young man of about five-and-twenty, he had married Miss Mary Jane Kitchens, with whom he lived reasonably happy for eighteen years. At the end of this period, of the offspring that had been born were living Susan, sixteen, and Josephus, ten years old. Besides these children of her own, Mrs. Blount for the last ten years had had charge of a little girl whom its own mother on her dying bed had consigned to her. Of this child, Mahala Herrindine by name, she had been most tender withal, and many a time she had been heard to say that, wrong as it might be, she was obliged to confess that the difference in her own heart between Susan Blount and Maly Herrindine was so little that she was always pestered in her mind whenever she went about trying to find it. This, of course, went to show what a good, docile, thankful child Maly always had been.

Mr. Blount, a hard-working, economical, and during this early period generally considered a rather close and cold man, had consented reluctantly, and only after much affectionate persuasion, to this adoption; but he managed with discretion the child's little property, and had always tried to partake to some degree of his wife's fondness for her. Yet he had often expressed the hope that as soon as poor little Maly, as he always called her, should be old enough, she might make an alliance that would leave to him and his wife the sole care of their own family.

At this period Maly was fifteen years old, and was as smart and as industrious, though she might not have been thought by most young men as pretty, as Susan.

A great affliction now befell this interesting family. But I do not propose to try to harrow up people's feelings by giving in detail the events of Mrs. Blount's long sickness and death. I must not omit, however, to say that before her departure she asked and obtained from her husband a promise to persist in the care that had been taken theretofore of the orphaned girl. Mr. Blount, full of grief at the loss of so dear a companion, and somewhat remorseful in the reflection that he had fallen short of his full duties in this and in other respects of her wishes, gave the promise, although he could not but foresee that it must devolve much responsibility.

"When sech a woman," he would say afterwards, with

what softness he could employ—"when sech a woman as Mayjane Blount dies, and have been the wife she have, it ain't every man that have the heart to deny her dyin' words. Ah, law me! And yit, what I'm to do with that po' orphing child in the fix I'm in—well, I must natchelly supposen that the good Lordamighty know. *I* don't, certain *and* shore. Ah, law me!"

Everybody pitied the family. Mr. Blount, following the instincts of self-defence against too excessive grief, indulged the melancholy consolation of speaking constantly in terms of unbounded praise of his late companion's excellent goodness. There was comfort of its kind in trying to call to mind occasions wherein he may have been more or less regardless of her feelings even in unimportant matters, and in resolving to do henceforth with punctilious fidelity things that he now sadly remembered too often to have postponed. The late Mrs. Blount was a remarkably neat person, and perhaps the most serious complaint she had ever felt like bringing against her husband was his carelessness in that behalf. For, good man and good husband as he was, it had to be admitted that, as a general thing, he was what was called rather slouchy in the matter of his dress, and by no means scrupulously careful in that of his manners. When the girls had grown large enough to be noticed by young men, Mrs. Blount would gently remonstrate, and as for Susan, she would get to downright scolding at such lapses. But the fact of the business was, Mr. Blount used to contend, he had too many things to attend to of his own and other people's to be kept everlastingly shaving, brushing himself up, and minding every step he took. Maly, knowing the trouble she must be to her pa, as she called Mr. Blount, never had joined in these complaints, either in words or in spirit.

Yet at the funeral Mr. Blount let Susan persuade him to put on his best things, and otherwise deport himself as becomingly as possible to one who in the matter of studied grave demeanor was rather a new beginner. Continuing even after the funeral in this course of conduct, he could not but be thankful for the far more comfortable feelings that he had now merely in his physical being. The almost prostrating grief he had endured at the beginning of his bereavement was thus made to assume some dignity that contributed its own part to his relief, and sometimes he would sigh gently to think how he often had disregarded what at last would have induced a higher enjoyment even to himself.

"Ah, law me! a man never know what sech a wife is tell he lose her. Then he know."

II.

Everybody who has ever received or imparted sympathy knows how sweet it is. It was touching to see how this benign influence went forth and back, back and forth, between Mr. Blount and the girls. Maly, poor child, suffered evenly with Susan. As for the sympathy from outside, that actually poured in upon all the bereaved. People said in most compassionate dismay that they could not see how that family was to get along without such a wife and mother. In particular, Mrs. Juliann Truitt, an excellent, comely young woman of, we will say, twenty-eight years of age, whose husband, dying some four years before, had left her with a snug little property, though childless, was prompt to say that if she did not know how to feel for people in the condition of that family she would like to know the person who did. Then there were two young men, Cullen Banks and Williamson Poole, whose deportment during the first period of mourning, though not as demonstrative as that of

Mrs. Truitt, was probably more soothing, at least to the orphaned girls. Indeed, the relations between Mrs. Truitt and the late Mrs. Blount unfortunately had not been altogether and uniformly as pleasant as those between the latter and several other ladies in the neighborhood. The plantation of Mrs. Truitt joined that of Mr. Blount, a nice bit of meadow-land lying on the border. It had been absolutely impossible, without keeping them penned all the time, to hinder the two flocks of geese from frequent intermixture; and more than once, at feather-picking times, Mrs. Blount had had her feelings hurt. Not that in her heart she blamed Mrs. Truitt for anything more than listening too credulously to her negroes, who always claimed for their mistress more of every spring's produce of the flocks than Mrs. Blount considered entirely just. At such times Mr. Blount would become quite angry, and but for the influence of his prudent wife might have made serious ado. I mention this circumstance, apparently trifling, partly because of the fact, well known in primitive country communities, that geese, in one way and another, give occasion to more disputes among women who reside in close proximity to one another than any other domestic animal, and partly to account for the less soothing influences of Mrs. Truitt's visits upon the girls than those of the young men. Mr. Blount determined, it seemed, that all resentment he had ever felt towards this excellent woman should be buried in the grave, and sometimes he would gently chide Susan for the way in which she would speak of her. Susan's face would flash at such rebukes, but she would at once become silent, and afterwards extremely anxious.

Now, people may say what they please about second marriages, and the heartlessness of widowers in suffering themselves to be led into them with indecent haste. In extenuation of what seemed levity in this particular case, I plead only that Mrs. Juliann Truitt was an uncommonly good-looking woman, with a handsome property immediately adjoining that of Mr. Blount, and that now, upon mature reflection, Mr. Blount was obliged to acknowledge in his heart of hearts that he could not feel sure in his mind that she had ever put any deliberate wrong upon his family on the goose question or any other. The fact is, people ought to try to be fair in the judgments they pass upon others. Worse men than Iverson Blount have waited longer, but I will say also that some even better have not waited so long as he did, before trying to repair a great loss. I hope, also, that in spite of the blame that may be put upon his action, some allowance will be made for the earnest desire he continued to feel to discharge the trust he had undertaken in the care of Maly Herrindine, conflicting as may be the opinions regarding its results.

It was not very often that Mrs. Truitt came to the house; but she positively must come sometimes, in order to do what she was sure in her mind the late Mrs. Blount would have done in reversed circumstances.

Both the young men seemed to understand well how to time their visits and their conversation. Williamson Poole was a cousin of the late Mr. Truitt, who had brought him up from boyhood, and upon his death-bed commended him to his wife as one whose services to her would become more and more valuable as he should grow older. At the present period he was approaching his twenty-first year. For at least three years he had been the main manager, and in a way entirely satisfactory, of his cousin Juliann's plantation business. Everybody, old as well as young, spoke well of Williamson Poole.

Cullen Banks was a year or so younger, and was not

altogether as settled and industrious as Williamson. But then he was not under the necessity of being so; for besides a snug property already, he would be entitled to much more at the division of his father's estate, which was to take place at the death of his mother, who was now advanced considerably beyond sixty. Other young men were residents in the neighborhood, some of them quite promising in most respects, but these two were the nearest neighbors and the most frequent visitors of the Blounts.

I have already intimated that during his wife's lifetime Mr. Blount had hoped that Maly might make an early suitable alliance, that would relieve him of the painful responsibility he had always felt in her behalf. If anything, he now indulged this hope more anxiously than before, and he did so the more, perhaps, because he noticed the increasing aversion of the girls for Mrs. Truitt, especially that of Susan. Not that he ever felt the slightest temptation to forget the promise which he had made about Maly. Iverson Blount was an honorable man, and he knew that an honorable man must ever be bound by promises, especially those that were as solemn as the one that he had undertaken. Now, in regard to Susan he had no great anxieties, for he knew that she was pretty and good, and that, with already a snug property, he was making more with ease and rapidity, and he had no doubt that Susan would do well, all in good time. But Maly—there was Mr. Blount's embarrassment; and there is not a particle of doubt that for a while—I cannot say exactly how long—that gave him much concern. Many a widower, though having lost as good a wife as Mr. Iverson Blount's, had been less anxious about how to fulfil all his duties and wishes than he was now, with these young children on his hands, one of them an orphan.

It will not be doubted, I trust, that Mr. Blount felt sincerely the loss of the good wife with whom he had lived so long. Yet when in Susan's presence he was more forbearing of expression to his grief than when alone with Maly. Indeed, he did not think it right to harrow his daughter's feelings by a too frequent allusion to their great affliction. This was one reason. Then he had not been slow to perceive that Susan's hostility to Mrs. Truitt, in which he could not join conscientiously, had subtracted somewhat from her confidence in the sincerity of his expressions of his sense of bereavement. Yet when alone with Maly he would dwell upon the theme to the degree that — well, the good girl would declare to Susan afterwards that to save her life she could not keep from crying to see how pa missed ma. At such times Mr. Blount would repeat the solemn promise he had given, and add that if he did not keep it, it would be only because his life was not spared.

"And as for that, Maly, you know I'm a man of remarkable good health, and ain't so ageable but what a body that's tempert and keerful of hisself might be expected to be liable for a right smart stretch o' time yit, more'n some that's younger. And as for Missis Truitt, she's of course a very fine woman; and if I was in Susan's place, I wouldn't be quite so severe on her, though the child may think she know more about her than what I do. Ah, law me! it's a world of trouble, and yit—" But here Mr. Blount would stop, take out his handkerchief, and cover his eyes.

Now, the fact was that Maly liked Mrs. Truitt as little as Susan, though of course she did not feel that she had the same liberty to express or otherwise exhibit to her pa the resentment that she believed she owed to her ma's memory, at least in secret, to indulge. But Maly had always been a prudent girl, and now she forbore giving to her pa any expression of opinion regarding the widow.

III.

It is interesting to see how soon sometimes a girl becomes a woman. Not long after her mother was laid away, Susan, feeling the responsibility of her position, went to the work of domestic affairs, and showed apace how she had profited by good examples. Maly also, at becoming pace, followed in all duties, and many a man younger than Mr. Blount might have brought himself to some reconciliation for his loss by the contemplation of so much that had been spared. To Susan there was some consolation in her sorrow from the ever-increasing deference that her father paid to her and Maly both, speaking to them generally as if they were grown women, yet with a tenderness to which in other days they had not been accustomed; and there was partial relief to Susan's anxieties on account of her father's persistence in dressing himself with unwonted care, in the fact that his habits while at home were the same in this respect as when he made visits to Mrs. Truitt.

"These old widowers do beat the world," Susan would say in confidence to Maly. "Ma never could make pa take any pains with his clothes, hardly even of a Sunday, and now he dresses up even for me and you and Josey. There's some satisfaction in *that*, and some hope—at least I hope so."

The young men, Cullen and Williamson, after a decent interval, began to visit as before, sometimes separately, but more often together. And now it was interesting to see the conduct of Mr. Blount when, remembering his promise to the dead, he felt it to be his duty to bestow upon the intercourse of these young persons the attention that used to devolve entirely upon his wife. After he had seen them together several times, Mr. Blount smiled inwardly at something which he had seemed to consider his duty to study closely. Maly's prospects for a suitable alliance appeared to be brighter than for some time he had been apprehending. For there was no manner of doubt that his desire was to get Maly's case off his mind as soon as possible, when he would feel perfectly free for any other movements he might choose to make. As for Susan and Josey, he knew he was their father; but in Maly's case there was some delicacy which even the rudest could not forbear to consult. So one day he said to Susan,

"Glad to see Cullen and Maly like one 'nother so powerful much."

"Cullen Banks, pa!" said Susan, laughing, yet with some redness on her face. "There's nothing in the world between Maly and Cullen, except that they like each other well enough as friends. Why, what upon earth put that notion into your head?"

Mr. Blount looked as if he felt much disappointment. However, he calmly answered,

"I don't know, but I notice him right smart about Maly here lately."

"No more than Williamson Poole, pa, and—I'm not certain—if—quite as much."

"I know them boys in gener'l hunts in couples; but I some ruther s'picioned—ahem—you think Williamson have any particklar hankerin' arfter Maly?"

"I don't know about *hankerin'*, pa, as you call it; but I know he likes Maly first-rate—that is, I am pretty certain of it in my own mind."

"Um, hum. You do; and what's your 'pinions as to how Maly like Williamson?"

"She likes him very well, as well as Cullen, if not some better."

Mr. Blount nodded his head several times extremely ominously, but said no more to Susan. That night at the supper-table he discoursed at some length upon the subject of marriage. Among other things he said,

"Young people, 'special' females, owes it to theirselves to be monst'ous, streenious keerful and particklar who they take up with in that kind o' style; and 'special' in the p'ints o' prop'ty. For it's a heap easier, and it's a heap convenanter, and it's a heap comfortabler to *start* with some prop'-ty than it is to have to work an' projeck, and deny a body's self the lugjeries, and the comforts, an' sometimes the very needcessities o' life, which, in course, a person 'd like to have 'em, but which, when they *starts* po', by marryin' of po', they has to wait for 'em, and which, ef they'd wait and look around keerful, the chances is some of 'em might do better than what they been a-expectin'."

Mr. Blount did not say so in those words, but he was decidedly opposed to Maly's marrying as poor a young man as Williamson Poole, and he meant to tell her so, if, upon further study, he should suspect that there was likely to be any understanding between them. Susan might fret herself about Mrs. Truitt if she wished, but her father, whatever might be his hopes and intentions regarding that fine woman, was not going to abate one jot of his care for the child of his wife's adoption.

That night when Susan and Maly had gone to bed, to sleep together as usual, Susan said,

"Maly, think pa didn't suspicion that there was something between you and Cullen?"

"You don't tell me so," answered Maly. "That's why he praised Cullen so high to me this evening then, while you were getting supper, and he and I and Josey were out on the piazza."

"No; for I told him not an hour before that there wasn't."

"That so?"

"Yes, indeed."

"Why, he praised Cullen to the skies, and said he were altogether another sort of man from Williamson, but that he wouldn't for the world Mrs. Truitt should hear he had used such words about her cousin."

"Mrs. Truitt!" said Susan, with disgust. "*She* must come in! However, it was rather natural for her to come in there. Say, pa rather run down Williamson?"

"No, not exactly *run down*. I couldn't say that. But he lifted up Cullen sky-high, and he said pointedly that a girl with little or no property would make a great mistake to—to take up, as he called it, with a poor young man like Williamson."

"That, indeed," said Susan, thoughtfully. "Yet, but don't you know, Maly, that to-day, talking to me about them boys, he praised Williamson more than he did Cullen? You didn't let on that there was anything between me and Cullen, did you, Maly?"

"Certainly not."

"I—almost wish you had—but—what does pa always want to drag in Mrs. Truitt for? He knows very well that ma never liked her, and pa owes it to ma, and he owes it to me and Josey, and he owes it to you, too, Maly, not to be so afraid of hurting Mrs. Truitt's feelings. The reason why he talked to you so about Williamson was because I told him Williamson liked you uncommon well."

"You didn't!"

"Yes, I did. The fact is, Maly, I thought I ought to. He promised ma, you know, to take care of you, and do his best for you, and his ideas are to see the way clear before you. That is very good in pa, I think, and if he could just leave Mrs. Truitt out of the case I'd think it was all right."

Maly drew a long breath. Williamson Poole had never courted her in set words; but she did not know what he might do some day, neither had she determined what she would do in certain contingencies. So all Maly could do now was to draw a long breath.

"Maly," said Susan, after some pause, "that woman is after pa, and she's been after him ever sence poor ma was put in the ground. It does look like some people have no decent feelings. And if pa was to marry her, the day he done it would either kill me or throw me into conniption-fits." Then Susan nestled her face in Maly's bosom and sobbed, and Maly had to sob too, as she tenderly patted her beloved sister's head.

The next morning Mr. Blount said at the breakfast-table,

"I thought I heerd some laughin' first and then some cryin' among you two last night, arfter you went to bed. What were the funny things, and what were the deficulties?"

Never had Mr. Blount looked better in all his life. It was believed in the neighborhood that no man had lived at any period who had learned so fast, after beginning so late in life, to tie his cravat so deftly, and dress himself in general so well. As for cinnamon and bear's oils, it would be useless to speculate upon the quantity that man put upon everything that came in contact with himself.

"Oh, pa," answered Susan, sadly, "just some little talk I and Maly had made me laugh, and then I got to thinking about poor ma, and then we both cried."

Then Susan and Maly cast down their eyes.

"Poor dear Ma'y Jane!" said Mr. Blount, sympathizingly. "It ain't easy to see how her place is to be filled."

"Why, pa!" said Susan, looking up with reanimation, "I

think we are getting along right well—me and Maly—attending to things."

"Oh yes, indeed," replied Mr. Blount, "toler'ble well for the present time bein'; but supposing you, and supposing Maly, was to take it in your heads to go away and leave a feller, what then?"

The girls looked at each other and again cast down their eyes.

"Ah, ha! Um, hum!" said Mr. Blount, rising. "Well, ef anybody ever missed another like I miss your poor ma, all I got to say, I'm as sorry for 'em as ever I were for a po' lame duck with one broke leg and one broke wing to boot, and got nothin' upon top o' the blessed ground to do but to go about a-hoppin' and a-floppin' with the tothers; and the fact is, *I* can't stand it. But I tell you, Susan, and I tell you, Maly, that I don't intend to be rash, and I don't intend to be brash. As for you a-marryin', Susan, I were jes' a-runnin' on about that, and it's in course onuseless for you to be even a-thinkin' about sech a thing for, lo and behold, these many years; and I don't supposen that Maly 'll have sech a idee tell *she* can see her way cler to gittin' as good a home as the one she been allays used to."

Then Mr. Blount retired with dignity, ordered his horse, and rode over to Mrs. Truitt's.

"What *does* such talk mean, Maly?" said Susan. "Looks like pa's losing his senses. When he talks about my not marrying in years and years, don't he know that I couldn't live in this house with that woman? I wish you'd speak out positive with pa, Maly, and tell him it wouldn't do to bring her here."

"Why, Susan, what could I do with pa? It wouldn't look like it was my business to tell him he oughtn't to marry again, and, besides, it wouldn't do any good. He's a young man yet, that is, tolerable young, and—the fact is, Susan, pa misses ma perfectly dreadful, and I can't but be sorry for him the way he talks about her when him and me are by ourselves. I wish myself that Mrs. Truitt wouldn't be quite so—well—insinuating is what I'll say as for her. But I tell you now that fussin' and frettin' with pa will do more harm than good."

"Well," said Susan, mournfully, "I'm going to try to put my trust in the good Lord to save us all from that woman."

"That's just the place where we'll have to put it, Susan," answered Maly, who, if anything, was even a more religious-minded girl than Susan.

IV.

Mr. Blount, knowing that he had matters on his hands that required both caution and despatch, in a comparatively brief time did an amount of thinking that might safely be said to have been enormous. The Blount and Truitt plantations adjoining, he and Williamson Poole must often meet near the border and have a friendly chat while sitting on the division fence. On the same day of the table-talk at home, Mr. Blount, although he had had, only a few hours before, a comfortable visit to the widow, yet designedly rode out into the meadow, and not seeing the young man, hitched his horse, climbed the fence, and walked to the rise in the field. Williamson, who was a quarter of a mile distant, observing him, left off his work, and joining the visitor, the two walked back to the fence. There they had a long, long talk; for on occasion, and especially with his juniors and inferiors, Mr. Blount was not at all wanting in volubility of speech. Just before parting he looked with much kindness upon Williamson, and said,

"Williamson Poole, I tell you now, right here, betwixt

me and you and this fence, that when a young man, and special a good-lookin', industr'ous young man—I'm a-namin' o' no names, for people oughtn't to be a-namin' o' names right in the presence o' them they talkin' about, because the flatterin' o' people is what I allays dispised, so fur as *I'm* concerned; but yit when sech a young man *start* with his nose on the grindstone, it's in gener'l his own faut't, and it's obleeged to be long before he can git it off, ef ever. Not as I should adwise a feller out an' out to go for prop'ty, and nothin' but prop'ty, and no female a worth havin' to be flung along with it. Yet prop'ty's a monst'ous good backer-up to a feller, and it's allays been strange and cur'ous to me when a feller, special them that's industr'ous, and good-lookin' to boot, don't try to marry into it when he's a-thinkin' about of settlin' of hisself for good. Well well, well! But, bless my soul, Williamson! what a sple-splendid 'oman is your Cousin Juliann! A beautifuller I should never desires to lo and behold, and it is my desires that you give her my best respects, though it ain't been more'n three hours sence I seen her."

Williamson Poole was a young man of excellent character and sense, though not quick to understand any other than conduct and conversation entirely direct. But he thought he was not so dull as not to comprehend the meaning of Mr. Blount's present deportment. He sat upon the fence and looked thoughtfully at him as he rode slowly away. When Mr. Blount had gotten out of sight, he said,

"You be dogged. You think you can beat creation, old man. Want me to help you to git Cousin Juliann, do you, by makin' out like you willin' for me to git Susan if I can? We'll see."

Now, Mrs. Truitt had not remained a widow thus long for want of opportunities to change her state. Yet within the last year or so she had been growing apparently more bright and cheerful than during the previous years of her widowhood, and notably since the death of Mrs. Blount she was becoming a different woman altogether. People knowing the plantations adjoined saw how natural everything was, and they blamed neither her nor Mr. Blount for their inevitable and rather rapid approximation to each other. In spite of Mr. Blount's age and the incumbrance of children, he had great vigor and activity of body, and, already with a good property, was getting more faster than any other man in the community. In a very few months, therefore, after his wife's departure, Mrs. Truitt had discarded every particle of black except a very narrow white ribbon, which, to prevent too much talk, she wore round her neck when abroad. To Williamson Poole she had always been very kind, had paid him reasonable if not high wages for his services, and Williamson knew that his cousin Juliann wished him well, because she had often told him so with emphasis and entire sincerity.

The same night after his talk with Mr. Blount, while at supper, he delivered the latter's message, yet not with great heartiness.

"Sent his respects, did he? Much obliged to him. Say anything about me, Williamson?"

"Oh yes'm; complimented you high."

"Ah, indeed? Said I look tolerable well for one of my age?"

"No'm, not that, by no manner of means. He said you were the youngest-looking woman of your age he knewed of."

"Oh, ho! Say how old he thought I was?"

"He allowed he thought you might be somewhere between twenty-three and twenty-five."

"I *was* married very young," said Mrs. Truitt, thoughtfully. "Did Mr. Blount say how old *he* was, Williamson?"

"Yes'm; he said he disremembered whether he was thirty-eight or thirty-nine."

Mrs. Truitt laughed.

"A right spruce-looking gentleman, isn't he? and a nice man, a very nice man, indeed." Then Mrs. Truitt drew a long, sweet breath.

"Which you think is the finest girl, Williamson, Susan, or Maly? I think myself that Susan Blount is one of the finest girls I ever knew. Of course I include property, which Maly has little of, and may have none if Mr. Blount—what of course he has the right to do—should charge her for her board, though the poor child is a very good, and indeed I think an excellent, girl."

His cousin Juliann having answered her own question, Williamson could think of nothing to say more than that he thought both of them very fine girls. That night he could not get to sleep, oh, I suppose, not before midnight; and he lay in his bed and turned and turned himself over and over, pondering. Even when he got to sleep he dreamed endless and most curious things about Mr. Blount and his cousin Juliann, the two girls and Cullen Banks. Considering the want of celerity in Williamson Poole's habitual mental operations, few young men ever did a greater amount of thinking in the same length of time than was done by him during the next few weeks.

Time went on. Mr. Blount seemed to grow younger and younger. When the young men would ride over in the afternoon, sometimes he would challenge them to jump and leap with him, and he would beat them both fully two inches. Both knew better than to accept his banter to wrestle, or even run a foot-race. So Mr. Blount would absorb most of the talk during such visits, and sometimes he was suspected by all of managing to couple together as much as possible Cullen with Maly, and Williamson with Susan. As for Susan, she had a double trouble: one, her father's unbecoming juvenility and evident growing partiality for Mrs. Truitt; the other his apparent disregard of Cullen in the relation that her heart had been set upon. Her father, noticing her want of proper cordiality towards himself, allowed some coolness to grow, and it was all that Maly could do, in going between, to keep them on even reasonable terms with each other. To Maly he spoke without reserve upon whatever subject he happened to think of. They were never together that he did not talk of his departed wife in a way to make Maly cry; and though at such times he seldom mentioned Mrs. Truitt's name, kindly avoiding disturbance of Maly's affectionate thoughts of her benefactress, he would get upon the subject of Cullen Banks, and, while scarcely mentioning Williamson's name, praise Cullen to the very skies, and intimate what a fine thing it would be for a girl with little or no property to get him for a husband.

"But, pa," said Maly, one day, "Cullen does not care particularly for me, nor I for him. I thought you knew he liked Susan better than me, and that she likes him better than I do."

"That so?" said Mr. Blount, with some darkness on his brow. "I knowed, Maly, that if it were either of them boys you liked the best, it were obleeged—or ought to be obleeged by good rights—to be Cullen. For, to save my life, I couldn't see how—well, my dear Maly, there is subjects that people can't help from thinking about. As for Susan and Cullen—ah, law me! That weren't adzactly—but time enough to think of that for many a year yit. Susan need adwice if she only knowed it. As for me, I s'pose even *I* mout need adwice sometimes well as she. But look like me and her can't talk together to much satisfaction, and you too prudent I know to repeat over to her all I say. Of course, I think Mrs. Truitt one o' the finest and beautifullest women anywheres, and if I should ever take it in my mind to marry again, it don't look reasonable to suppose I'd ask Susan for her consents. And besides, you know yourself, Maly, that I'm a young man, a reasonable speakin', and can outrun, outjump, outlift, and fling down other Cullen or Williamson, and outlast 'em at whatsomever we mout go at. Though, matter of course, I shouldn't desires for Mrs. Truitt to hear of all I said about Williamson, for I should hate it dreadful to hurt her feelin's; but I know you prudent enough to know what to tell and what not to tell."

Many such chats these two had together. When the girls would go to bed, and Susan, as always, would get upon her own troubles, Maly would comfort her the best she could, and the two would go to sleep in each other's arms. Of course, Maly did not tell Susan of how her pa had spoken comparatively of Cullen and Williamson, partly because she knew that he expected her not to do so, and partly because she would not for the world that Susan should suspect for a moment that her intention or desire, even with the powerful assistance of her pa, was to supplant Susan in Cullen's regard. To tell the truth, Maly Herrindine was one of the most honest-hearted girls in this world.

V.

Meanwhile Mrs. Truitt was growing younger and younger, to all appearance, although people said that, in the circumstances, it would be more becoming for her to try to look a little older. But circumstances are rare when women at any age do that. She visited freely the girls, not without suspecting that neither of them liked her. But she knew that appearances had to be kept up, and so she visited them often, and was as motherly in her deportment, especially towards Susan, as one so young could be. Susan, of course, treated her with proper respect while at the house, but after her departure, and as soon as she could find an opportunity, she would pour out her griefs on Maly's sympathizing breast.

Mr. Blount began soon to make his visits to his fair neighbor more and more frequent. The coolness grown between him and Susan seemed to make him resolve to push matters to a settlement. He and Williamson continued to have their chats at the fence, in which the property question always came up, and was dwelt and dwelt upon by the man of experience. Of late Williamson had been growing somewhat resentful, or at least sullen in his feelings, towards Mr. Blount. He had found that Cullen and Susan were in love with each other, and he suspected that Mr. Blount knew it. Then he thought with pain of Maly's apparent indifference to his having been thrown of late so often in Susan's special company. Now, of the two girls Williamson admired Maly the more; but he knew what his cousin Juliann would say if he told *her* so. Then he knew he was poor, and he could not but reflect that Mr. Blount's repeated allusion to the contact of a poor young man's nose with the grindstone, if unkind, was not altogether inapposite. When his mind had come to the conclusion, or almost there, that Mr. Blount would not be willing for him to get either of the girls, Williamson felt and thought—but the fact is, it would be difficult, and would require an extended analysis of human motives in such a case which I do not feel competent to make, to tell all of what Williamson Poole did feel and think. I can only narrate actions. On one point he became fully convinced, and that was, that all Mr. Blount's pretended kindness to himself had a selfish motive, and that was to prevent hostility upon his part to the suit of his cousin Juliann.

One afternoon Mr. Blount, while at the fence, after his usual homily on the nose and the grindstone, and then suddenly branching off to the extreme youth and beauty of Mrs. Truitt, and what a fine property she had, and what a splendid plantation the two would make if they should ever be united into one, spoke regretfully of the changes and separations such an event would necessarily effect.

"But, I tell you now, Williamson Poole, that I shall never forgit what a fine, pleasant, good neighbor Williamson Poole used to be, although a not of ownin' o' the plantation nor no great deal o' property of no sort."

"Made me that mad I couldn't hardly see."

This last remark was made in a presence wherein, if as excellent a young man as Williamson Poole had had more time for reflection, he might not have made it. Mrs. Truitt smiled, and then, looking intently at him, said, in a gently chiding tone,

"I hope you didn't get mad, Williamson, because Mr. Blount said I looked so young and—and all that. I hope I don't look so very old to *you*."

"Law bless my soul, Cousin Juliann! in course not. You look a thousand times too young for—"

But there Williamson knew he was going too far, and he saw his cousin Juliann's eyes opening wide. So he left off abruptly, and did not return for an hour. He was gratified to find no trace of resentment in his cousin Juliann's words or manner. The fact was that Mrs. Truitt knew too well what a faithful relative and friend Williamson Poole had been to her, to resent a hasty remark that in the circumstances was possibly natural. Other talk they had, and when Williamson went to bed he could not but feel in his heart that he ought to bear no malice against Mr. Blount, so kindly had his cousin Juliann spoken of him.

Cases of the sort I am telling about generally culminate fast. Young as both Mr. Blount and Mrs. Truitt felt, they were obliged to know that they would never be any younger. Susan found herself growing more and more in love with Cullen, and was beginning to take some comfort in the thought of the reliance she knew she could place on his faithful heart; for she had made up her mind that when "that woman" (as she called Mrs. Truitt) should come into that house, she would leave it, with her father's consent or without it. But then what about poor Maly, whom Susan had been observing to be very thoughtful at times, and even sad?

"I'm ashamed, Maly, after what pa promised ma on her very dying bed, for him to go on in that way, and bring that woman here to hector over you. But never mind, precious, they *sha'n't* abuse you. You shall live with me and Cullen."

Then Susan would take Maly to her bosom, and Maly would hug Susan and sob. The good girl did need comfort from some source, she thought. Yet Maly Herrindine had much strength of character, and though without saying so to Susan in the latter's present frame of mind, she had been seriously considering what she ought to do, and what she would do in given contingencies. Then, in her private chats with her pa, he had solemnly assured her that whatever should happen he would do his best that she should not suffer from any change in his circumstances. So Maly, though often thoughtful and sad, would sometimes look quite calm, and occasionally try to look moderately cheerful, especially when in the presence of her pa, to whom, after all, she knew that she ought to be grateful for all that he had done and said. Not unfrequently, when Mr. Blount was away, in town or at Mrs. Truitt's, she would repair alone to Mrs. Blount's grave, and sit there quite a time, musing and shedding tears. "Poor little Maly!" the affectionate Susan would often sigh.

The event came on even sooner than had been expected. One morning at breakfast Mr. Blount, looking, if anything, younger than he had been in six months, and redolent of cinnamon and bear's oil, with a business, yet somewhat embarrassed, air, said,

"You all's invited next Chuseday night to Missis Truitt's. I'm goin' to town to-day, and would want one of you to go with me and help me choose a present for a—for a person o' the female wocation o' life; ahem!"

Mr. Blount simply *had* to look down. Susan turned perfectly red, and said, disjointedly,

"It's come, pa, is it? Well, pa, under the *circumstances* —under *all* the circumstances, I don't — no, I should *not* think you'd expect *me* to go with you."

Then Susan rose and left the table.

"All right," said Mr. Blount, recovering himself. "Get ready, Maly. Be in a hurry. Sharp's the word, and quick the motion, now."

Maly regarded Susan with deepest, tenderest sympathy; nevertheless she rose instantly and went to get her things.

"Oh, Maly, Maly," said Susan, while assisting her to dress, "it's too bad. I do hope you'll make pa buy the meanest, ugliest thing in the store for that woman."

"My dearest Susan, I do think you are too hard on Mrs. Truitt. Let us all hope it will all turn out better than we —may be, we may all be afraid it will."

"Bless your soul, Maly! you've got a forgiving heart, and a great deal better one anyhow than me. If it wasn't for you—and Cullen, of course—I should just lie right down and die—I know I should."

Left alone, except with Josephus, Susan had but little to say during the forenoon, even to him. She told Josey, resignedly, that he was a boy, and therefore could stand it, but that he owed to the memory of his mother not to be run over every day and every hour of his life by that woman; and Josey said that if that woman would let him alone he would let her alone, and that if she did not there would be a fuss. Susan wished that Cullen would come. But the day before, unknown to her, Mr. Blount had told Cullen that if he would meet him at the court-house this morning he would answer definitely a question that Cullen had put to him some weeks before. The question pertained to Susan, and Mr. Blount had said to Cullen that Susan's marrying him with her father's consent, and getting any of his property to take with her, would depend upon her conduct in circumstances then too many and too tedious to mention. The county-seat was about twelve miles distant.

About the middle of the afternoon here came Cullen galloping to the gate. Susan had just time to give her hair another turn and tie a fresh ribbon around her neck when he came running into the piazza.

"Why, Cullen, what in this world makes you so rapid and so red in the face?"

"Let me get my breath—and—I'll tell you. Now, Susan," said Cullen, when he had gotten through with his news, "mind what you do; everything with us depends on it."

To her dying day Susan Banks (*née* Blount) would declare that she did not know which she did most, crying or laughing, on that momentous occasion. She would cry awhile, and then scream with laughter. Finally, when she could compose herself, she said, in a religious tone,

"Oh, Cullen, I'm so thankful that I put my trust in the good Lord, and I'm going to do it now more than ever."

An hour afterwards the gig came on leisurely; Susan and Cullen, hand-in-hand, met it at the gate.

"How dy', pa? good-evening, ma."

Then Susan, crying and laughing, again rose upon the step, hugged the bride in the very gig, and all the way out of the gig, and into the house. And the bride hugged Susan, too, though somewhat in irregular spasms, for she trembled the same as an aspen-leaf, and her face was as red as any beet.

"Oh, pa!" cried Susan, at last pouncing upon him. "You sly, good, deceitful, glorious old — dear old coon, and fox both! How come you to fool me so, and make Maly fool me so?"

For the bride was Maly.

"How long have you had Maly in that old head, pa? I thought you was going to bring here that woman over yonder."

"Look at me, Susan. Didn't I promise your ma on her dyin' bed I'd take keer o' Maly?" Mr. Blount spoke solemnly, as if he were in the very presence of the dead. "To the best of my ricollections I did make her that very promise, and I'm a-goin' to keep it."

"And what about poor Mrs. Truitt? Have you gone and fooled her, pa?"

"Not so bad but what Williamson 'll make it all right and straight next Chuseday night."

"What!" screamed Susan.

"Yes, indeed. I see Williamson could git her ef he only knowed how to go about it, and I knowed he were a fool to let sech a chance slip; and I teched him up, and I teched him up, tell I got him agin me and kinder jealous o' me, and he at last pitched in, and the poor old feller was jes' natchel 'stonished outer all his senses when he found that he didn't have to open his mouth but wunst, ner hit but jes' one lick."

"Well," said Susan, "my solemn opinion is that this world is *bound* to come to an end some time or another. Oh, you Maly, you Maly! Do you know, Maly, that my belief is that my angel ma is this minute a-lookin' down on you and a-smilin' on you?"

"Oh, you think so, Susan? I was afraid ma's feelin's—" And the tears streamed from Maly's eyes.

"Certainly. Certain-*lee*. I've not a doubt about it."

And they went again into each other's arms.

"Susan," said Maly, between her sobs, "I wanted all the time to tell you about it all, but pa, he thought best—best not. I hope you'll forgive me, Susan."

"Forgive? Nothing to forgive, you darlingest darling, but all to be thankful for."

"You see, Susan," said Mr. Blount, calmly, "my feelin's was obleeged to be a little hurted by you a-spicionin' that I had eler forgot how your ma's feelin's was hurted about them geese."

Then turning to Cullen, he said,

"Cullen, she's yourn, a-prowidin' her and you keep in the idee of jindin' together."

"Thanky, Mr. Blount," said Cullen.

"Thanky, pa," said Susan. "But, pa, I do want to ask you one question, and that is: Did you ever think Cullen wanted Maly?"

"I'll answer that, Susan, a-prowidin' that'll satisfy you, and you'll promuss not to ast no more. Will you?"

"I suppose I'll have to, pa."

"Well, then, no, I didn't."

"Oh, you dear old, cunnin' old pa!" She patted him on the forehead for a moment with her finger, then flew consecutively to the smoke-house, the kitchen, and the pantry, in order to have prepared a supper as fit for the occasion as the brief notice would allow.

"Hit's been now a'most forty year ago," Mr. Blount, when very aged, would often say in the midst of his friends and numerous progeny, "ner nuther have me, ner nuther have Maly, been sorry for what we done. You mind, I had give a promuss to a dyin' person, an' I were *bound* to keep her. An' as to how she were to be kep', I don't 'member ner ricollect, as I never were more nonplushed in my mind, ontil one day she jest natchell flashed all over me, and that all of a suddent. It tuck some time, an' it tuck a heap o' pains, an' it tuck a powerful sight o' managin', for her to flash on to Maly the same an' likewise; but when she did, and the child could see whar her jooty p'inted, she give it up, and she done it fa'r an' squar'; and my believes is, and allays has been, that that were a weddin' that were made in heb'n."

REV. RAINFORD GUNN
AND THE ARAB CHIEF.

"And prove their doctrine orthodox
By apostolic blows and knocks."—*Hudibras.*

The Rev. Rainford Gunn had a small farm, the income from which was supplemented, to a varying but always moderate degree, by the pay that he received from the two country churches to which he rendered stated monthly service. Admitting himself to be of quite limited education and other advantages favorable to an eminent public career, he contended that nobody could have been taken by greater surprise than himself when the call came to him to preach the gospel—a call, however, that had been heard too distinctly to admit of hesitation to heed it. His success had been beyond any expectation. He was a man of good presence, tall and erect, of excellent common-sense, of sincere piety, and had acquired in time a stock of words that he could employ with some effect.

Mr. Gunn's forte as a preacher was not considered, even by those who admired him most, to lie in the eloquent elaboration of doctrinal points, although he would not forbear, when he believed it necessary or proper, to wrangle with the knottiest; and he would generally emerge from the scuffle in a plight that seemed reasonably satisfactory to the brethren. He might have been, it was probable, a speaker of considerable unction but for a peculiarity of his pathos, which, when at its highest, had to be excited to it by ire, instead of sympathy and compassion.

"I ain't no great hand at cryin', bruthern," he would say, "'ithout I git mad. I don't often git mad, and that's when I start on a cryin' spell; because cryin,' ev'y sence I knowed myself, makes me mad."

Yet more than one revival had attended his ministry in which several men far superior to him in culture had been brought into the church. His modesty, approximating humility, his industry and his stanch integrity, in spite of his homely phrase, obtained for him the respect of men of every degree. A devoted family man was he, yet people used to suspect that among all his children, about half a dozen in number, he was rather fondest of his daughter Lizy Ann, who, at the period told of in this sketch, was about nineteen years old, tall, fair-haired, peachy cheeked, cheery, industrious, affectionate, pious, and admitted to be the very best singer of religious songs among all in both her father's congregations. In the last revival that had taken place in the church nearest their home Lizy Ann Gunn's voice in the various singings was argued by many, especially among the younger men, to have been very nearly, if not quite, as effectual as her father's preaching in the ingathering. More than one or two, or, for all I know, three in that class had tried their hands to induce her to change her name, but she had always answered about thus:

"Not yet. I'm not ready, quite yet, for such as that, Mr. Blank."

Mr. Gunn had been in the ministry about a dozen or so years when he received a call from the church at Raysville, a village of a population numbering about three hundred, situated in an adjoining county, beyond the Oconee river, about ten miles distant from his residence. This call was almost as unexpected to him as the original, for there were several wealthy and some considerably cultivated persons residing therein or in the near neighborhood. Few of this class, however, were members of any church, especially that which had sent an invitation to Mr. Gunn, though they, as was the case with all classes, habitually attended the monthly Sunday meetings.

On this invitation, notwithstanding the cordiality, and he might say the liberality with which it had been extended, Mr. Gunn had to ponder before accepting, and advise with some of the brethren, and with his family, especially Lizy Ann; and I will candidly state why. Raysville had long been noted as an uncommonly wicked town. They fought chickens there; there they raced horses; there they played cards, all with impunity, even the last, which was forbidden by the laws, but which the solicitor-general never could get at, because so many of the Grand Jury habitually practised it themselves. The fact was that matters had become so discouraging to this officer and even to the presiding judge that for their consolation they would occasionally take a moderate hand themselves in these games. But that which had imparted to the town its greatest notoriety was the existence of a secret band of young men, styling themselves Arabs, who often at night, after the rest of the people were in bed, went about the streets singing songs, beating tin pans, removing wheels from vehicles and gates from front yards, building fences across the street with rails taken from contiguous cattle pastures, and making such and similar pranks specially marked in the case of any who were unusually pronounced in their words of condemnation. The resignation of the late pastor of the church was suspected to be due to the fact that shortly theretofore his horse, while standing in Brother Mullen's stable, had had his tail shaved. Not only so, but he had received an anonymous letter intimating that not only his horse but himself would fare worse if he were not more guarded in what he had to say in his Sunday sermons about the behavior of certain persons in the meeting-house and elsewhere.

Another matter Mr. Gunn pondered over and counselled with his friends and his family. This was how a plain countryman like him, with his country ways and country clothes, was to get along before a town congregation. Yet, it was urged in the counsellings he held that calls of that kind, the same as the first he received to the ministry, come from Heaven. Then the stipend (for the brethren at Raysville thought it almost certain that among themselves, with contributions from outsiders, they could count upon sixty or seventy dollars) was not a thing to be despised by a man with a family of the size of his. So he concluded to obey this new, unexpected call. His country congregations, gratified at the Raysville indorsement of their estimate of their pastor, went so far as to raise, extra of their usual pay, a sum enough to buy several yards of nice satinet, together with thread, buttons, lining and binding, and these by the deft hands of Mrs. Gunn and Lizy Ann were cut and made up into a suit that everybody in the neighborhood who saw it said was decent enough for anybody, not even excepting the governor.

The meeting days of the Raysville church were the third Sunday and the day before. On Saturdays very few besides the members attended service, though there was always a sermon preceding the "conference," held for purposes of discipline and general business. On Sundays, however, the house was usually filled; for chicken-fighters, horse-racers, card-players, and Arabs were near as punctual as the best, partly to see, be seen and amused, and partly to show that they, though not professors, were as good respecters of religion as there was any reasonable need to be.

The embarrassment of the new preacher, on his first Saturday's appearance, did him no disservice, for there is something always respectable in the persistent endeavors of a single-minded man who is as modest as he is earnest. All, especially the older members, felt and so expressed themselves, that Brother Gunn's work was destined to give general satisfaction and be productive of good.

That night he tarried at the house of Sister Aikens. This pious and otherwise excellent woman, among other much chat about the church and about the village ways, enlarged upon the orgies of that "gang," as she styled the Arab club. It had been started, she explained, by one Tom Rogers, a young man of about thirty, who had been brought up in the city of Augusta and had settled in Raysville two years ago.

"He's one o' the desperest men, Br'er Gunn, anybody ever see. He have some prop'ty, and some people say that what make him so Gallio-like in his ways, and set sech a example. He don't git drunk, and he even don't play keards like some, an' in the daytime he's gene'l tolerable decent in his behavior, though he's got a tremenjuous temper; an' anybody make him mad, there's a fuss and a fight, a-providin' the man don't back out, for he's a puffec' Julus Cæsar about fightin', an' they say he can whip anybody that'll fight him, an' he had the imperdence to tell Br'er Pilcher that if he weren't a preacher he'd whip him for what he said about the gang, though he didn't 'peach that he been one of 'em, nor that he knowed any of 'em, an' so, lo and behold! they shaved off poor Br'er Pilcher's hoss's tail off, an' people say, some of 'em, that Tom Rogers driv him off. An' yet, if you'd believe me, Br'er Gunn, Tom Rogers is a perlite an' a obleegin' sort o' feller, a-notwithstandin' his wildness, an' he give free not only to poor people, but he put his name liber'l to help paint an' new weather-board the meetin' house."

Mr. Gunn felt that the situation was grave. He lay awake that night much beyond his usual hour after retiring to bed and ruminated.

The house on the next day was crowded. The Arabs were in unusually full force. Their purpose, it soon appeared, was to test the metal of the new preacher. He speedily recognized many of them, especially their leader, by their inattention to his words, their whisperings and giggling among themselves, and other unbecoming behavior. Such conduct, so unlike anything to which he had been accustomed in the simple-minded people of his country congregations, pained and embarrassed him much. Several times he remonstrated in a homely but not offensive manner against what he styled unorderly behavior in some of the congregation. The Arabs would suddenly come to order, for a brief while appear to be almost painfully attentive to the sermon, but upon a mute signal from Rogers, a very stout, well dressed, and rather handsome man, they would speedily relapse into pranks so patent as to be plainly indicative of their meaning to be insulting and defiant.

The confusion of the speaker at last became such that he foresaw that he must cut short a discourse the threads of which he was fast losing. Stopping suddenly, he covered his eyes with his hands for a few moments, then removing them, and closing the great Bible before him, he said, in a tone which it was evident that he was striving with much difficulty to control,

"Brotherin and sisters: I have took charge of this church in the good hopes of the doing of some good in a place where it's mighty plain that some good o' some kind is monstous bad needed to be done by somebody. But you'll have to be disappinted of a sermon from me to-day. I ain't been used to the behavior that's been carried on 'mong them back benches, and I'd have to git used to it, unless it can be stopped, before I can do even what little preachin' lays in my power too preach. I ain't denying that my feelin's has been hurted, not only as a minister o' the blessed Gospel, but as one lone, singuil, poor man by his lone self. And they'd of been hurted a heap worse exceptin' that I've notused that some o' them onorderly people is nuthin but boys, and is led on in their mischief by older heads. Now as for me, I nater'lly loves young people, and special boys, because they got to be men some time if their lives is spar'd, and I've in genil notused that when they're oncommon bad, it's because they're led off by older heads that keers nothin' for God, ner for man, ner for— I come a mighty nigh sayin' for who else. I ain't mad, brotherin an' sisters; for if I was to git mad I should go to cryin' first. I ain't mad, but I'm sorry, and I'm disappinted. Let us pray."

This homely remonstrance, delivered in tones that sometimes became tremulous, impressed all. Everybody looked at Rogers, some reproachfully, others amusedly, and his followers sympathizingly and interrogatively. He was evidently in a rage. When the congregation was dismissed, he had a brief conference with his set at the back door, after which all except himself went away.

The last to leave the church was the preacher and his hostess. As they reached the edge of the building the former, casting his eyes down the side that now came within view, saw Rogers standing just by the corner of the farther end.

"Sister Aikens," he said, "you go on; I want to step back a little while in the meetin'-house, and pray. I feel bad, an' I jes' know that a little prayin' right now 'll help me. You go on. I sha'n't keep your dinner a-waitin' too long."

Saying which, he turned and went on back.

"I'd of some ruther," soliloquized Sister Aikens, "that Br'er Gunn 'd of come 'long o' me. He mout meet up 'ith that Tom Rogers, an' he, mad as he is, an' big man as he think hisse'f, wouldn't dasn't to give Br'er Gunn much o' his sass before me."

When Mr. Gunn had entered the house, he straightway ascended the steps of the pulpit and kneeled, his face, as on occasions of public service, towards the farther end. In a very few moments Rogers, who had re-entered by the back door, walked rapidly up the aisle through the men's side, his walking-cane in hand, and when he had gotten within a few feet of the pulpit said, bluntly,

"Wish to speak with you, sir."

"Can you wait a few seconds, sir, ontil I can get through with a—"

"No, sir; right now, sir."

The preacher deliberately rose, saying first audibly these words:

"Now, 'member, good Lord, what I ast you."

Then descending to the floor he stood before his antagonist and said, mildly,

"Now, sir."

"When you was noratin' all that meanness an' foolishness, sir, I want to know who you was a-meaning it at, an' if you was a-meaning it at me?"

"I shall first stick a pin right thar, sir, whar you names

the preachin' o' the blessed Gospel, er ruther the tryin' to do it. You names it meanness an' foolishness, an' I'll now ast you your name, although I hain't a doubt but what it's Rogers. That so?"

"My name's none o' your business, sir. Answer my question."

"Umph, humph! Well, you know, Mister—Rogers—I'll call you that jes' for the sake o' the argiment, so to speak, that when one man astes a question, sometimes before he can git his answer he's liable to have more'n one question ast of him hisself. I'll put you another. Wern't you or wern't you not the one that chawed paper an' rolled it in a wad, and looked at me, an' flipped it from your fingers, an' a leetle more an' it would have struck one o' the female persons o' the congregation; an' done it more'n wunst at that?"

"I sha'n't answer that question, sir, neither. None o' your business, nor the business o' no other clodhopping, deceitful old cuss."

The preacher's eyes moistened as he said, in low, measured tone,

"Young man, when I see you a-standin' out yonder at one o' the back cornders, I knowed whut you was arfter, an' I let Sister Aikens go'long on home by herself, so as me an' you could settle it betwix' ourselves; jes' you an' me, us two."

Here Mr. Gunn made a brief pause, in order, it seemed, to snuff the air. Then he proceeded:

"I come back in here determ'd in my mind to ast you, like Abner ast Asahel, to turn to the left, or turn to the right, anyway you choosen, so as to not be a fullerin' arfter me; and I've jes' a minute ago made my pra'ar to Godamighty to not let me cry 'ithout were His will, an' ef it were to let me cry good; and, bless His holy name, He have heerd me, an' I feel 'em a-comin'."

They were, indeed, coming drop by drop, quicker and quicker, though his face was wreathed with smiles.

"Now I ain't o' keerin' not so mighty much about the names you named me, but did you mean to say, sir, that the preachin' o' the blessed Gospel is meanness and foolishness?"

"I did, you old—"

These were the last words of the chieftain then and there. The preacher took a step rearward, doubled his fist and dealt upon the assailant's breast a blow that prostrated him upon his back at the foot of the pulpit. Snatching his cane as he was falling, he raised it aloft.

"Now try to rise if you dare," cried Mr. Gunn, whose eyes were floods of tears, "an' I'll scatter that pulpit with your brains."

"My God!" cried Rogers.

"Them's the words, sir; them's the wery words. Before I let you up I'm goin' to make you beg Godamighty's pardon; an' ef you don't do it 'ithout, I'm goin' to git down on you an' choke you tell you do."

"You got the advantage of me, sir."

"I know I has, an' I'm goin' to keep it. Come, sir. I got no time to tarry long. Out 'ith it! You sorry for your impudence to Godamighty in His own house? No mealy-mouthin' 'bout it. Out 'ith it. Sorry or not sorry, whach?"

The prostrate man looked up, and he afterwards declared that if he had ever seen the Bad man, it was on that occasion, in the weeping eyes that were bent upon him.

"I'm sorry, Mr. Gunn."

"All right so fur, sir; but tell me, now, is it a godly sorrow, or is it you're sorry because you're knocked flat on your back, an' ain't quite shore you ain't goin' to be beat into sassage meat?"

"I—I—I—reckon, Mr. Gunn, it's—it's—a—some o' both."

"That's jes' what I 'spicioned. Howbenever, I'm thankful you got on that much gainin' ground. Know the Lord's pra'ar?"

"Of course I do, Mr. Gunn."

"Say it."

Rogers hesitated.

"Say it, I tell you."

"Won't you give a man time to think it up?"

"I thought you knowed it. Said you did."

"I do, Mr. Gunn, but it's been so long since—"

"Blaze away, and go as fur as you ken."

"'Now I lay me down to sleep,
    I pray—'"

"Stop it, sir!" cried the preacher, with almost a shriek. "Call that the Lord's pra'ar? My goodness of gracious of merciful Heavens! Look at me, Tom Rogers; I heerd o' you some time back. You 'n your gang betwixt you driv Br'er Pilcher away from the pastorship in this church, an' shaved his horse's tail off."

"I didn't, Mr. Gunn, God knows I didn't."

"Very well, maybe you didn't; but you know who done it, and you know you could ov perwented it. But let that go. You ain't goin' to shave my horse ner let him be shaved. I got no anexity on that pint o' the case. But now you look at me. Look straight at me. I ain't goin' to tell 'bout this here fracus here a perwidin' I hear that you've broke up them Arabs, as you call yourselves, or done your level best a-tryin', and arfterwards you'll try to behave yourself when you are in the House of God."

Then drying his eyes, he continued with softening voice: "Pity, pity, pity! You've got money, Mr. Rogers, and they tell me you're liberal with it. Sister Aikens say you put down wery liberal to new weather-boardin' and repaintin' this here meetin'-house, and you gives free to poor people if they don't cross you. I wonder you picked me out, that's a poor man hisself, that never done you no harm, nor never would of wished to do you any harm, and jes' try to hurt my feelin's when I'm a tryin', in a mighty poor way, I acknowledge that, to preach the blessed Gospel. Has you got any parrents?"

It was now time for the Arab chief to shed a tear.

"My father died when I was a child, Mr. Gunn; my mother not long before I moved here."

"Was they Christian people?"

"My mother was, sir, a very prayerful one."

"Well, it's to my hopes and my opinions that her pra'ars ain't to allays go 'ithout a anser. Now git up and go 'bout your business. I hope the Lord'll forgive you. I do."

The vanquished man rose from the floor, sat down upon the front bench, and covering his face with his hands, sobbed aloud. Mr. Gunn had already turned and gotten as far as the door when, hearing the lamentation, he walked back, sat down by the weeper's side, and taking one of his hands away from his face, held it within his own. And then they had a talk together, lasting full half an hour. Sister Aikens had already grown uneasy about him, and especially so when, going out of her house and looking towards the church at the end of the street, she saw the two coming along side by side. Just before reaching her gate they parted, and Rogers, who had come some distance beyond his own boarding-house, turned back and repaired to it.

"'Pon my word, Brother Gunn, I were that oneasy about you, an' 'special' when I see that Tom Rogers along o' you, that I—well, I didn't know what to do. What did the creetur have to say?"

"Oh, well, Sister Aikens, we had a little chat, an' I conwinced him, I think, that I were nigher right than he were. We quit friends. But, Sister Aikens, I owe this people a sermon, because they ain't no a-denyin' of it, I broke down to-day, an' I'm a man that in giner'l tries to pay up as I go up, as the sayin' is; and I'll thank you to tell the brotherin, and to let word be sent around that I shall preach, God willin', in the church to-morrow night, at candle-light."

He lingered only to eat his dinner, answering his hostess's suggestion that she should send for some of the brethren, that it would be near night when he reached home, and he must have a good rest after the day's experience. The brethren, surprised but gratified by this mark of persistence and fidelity in their new pastor, gladly sent the notice to all in the village.

Some time before sunset on the following day Mr. Gunn returned to the same hospitable mansion, but this time in his gig, and accompanied by his daughter Lizy Ann.

"I brought her 'long, Sister Aikens, because I wanted her to see the people that her pa is to go in and out before; and—and then Lizy Ann's a right good singer o' hymes, an' somehow when I can hear her voice in the singin' it 'courages me up, an' so I told her ma, if she could spare her for this evenin' and to-morrow, to let her come along 'ith me. She ain't goin' to give you much trouble, and she's willin' to hep you 'bout anything you want."

"Why, bless the child's heart! trouble! Sher! I'm proud you brung her, Br'er Gunn."

The house was nearly full again, for the breakdown of the preacher of the day before had created considerable interest in him. Rogers had not been seen on the street the whole day until late in the afternoon, when he had interviews singly with quite a number of his class, all of whom afterwards attended the night service. During the singing of the first hymn a voice, new, and of marvellous sweetness, was heard, and many turned to notice whence it proceeded. The preacher taking for his text the parable of the Prodigal Son, spoke with a fluency and unction that had not been believed to belong to him, and when he was through, to the astonishment of all, he announced that while the next hymn was being sung he should descend to the space in front of the pulpit, where he would be glad to take the hand of any one who might thus express a desire for interest in his prayers and those of the brethren and sisters. As he descended he said,

"Will the brotherin and sisters please sing "Come, humble sinner, in whose breast?""

The first distich was scarcely sung when, from the very last bench, Rogers rose, walked rapidly along the aisle, gave his hand, and weeping aloud, laid his head upon the preacher's shoulder. Murmurs rose into cries, into shouts, when in a few moments the Arabs, by ones, by twos, by threes, then sprinklings even of the chicken-fighters, the horse-racers, the card-players came rushing up. Indeed—but how could I describe that scene and the great revival that followed? Sister Aikens, laughing and crying the while, used to say, among multitudes of other things,

"That first night, me and Sister Little, we hugged an' hugged, we did, so that Sister Plunkett used to laugh, an' say we look the adzactly like we was a-wrastlin'. The rewival it lasted two weeks, an' we gethered in forty-three, an' which the most of 'em had done been giv' up for lost. An' as for Lizy Ann's singin', if I didn't consate sometimes it sounded heb'n-like. An' then to think that nobody ever heerd o' that kyarin' on in the meetin'-house betwix Br'er Gunn and Br'er Rogers ontil the night, six months arfterwards, when him an' Lizy Ann was married, an' bless your soul, you would of laughed to hear Br'er Rogers say how skeered he was, special when he found he couldn't even say the Lord's pra'ar, an' he weren't shore but what Br'er Gunn, he cried so and were that mad, were a gwine to scatter his brains all over the meetin'-house."

MARTHA REID'S LOVERS.

"Call me not fool till Heaven hath sent me fortune."
As You Like It.

I.

IF Madison Crowder was not mistaken, Martha Reid was the finest girl in all the region round about Ivy's Bridge. Now Martha Reid herself was obliged to know that she was a fine girl, just as well as Madison Crowder did; for although only sixteen years old, she had heard from him and several other boys, and at least one grown man, words that were very peremptory in the line of the present argument.

Yet Madison, tall, fair, stalwart as he was in contrast with Martha, petite, brunette, and slender, had little hope to win. The oldest of three boys — only children of a widowed mother — he was managing only tolerably their little farm, whereon was a working force of three or four hands besides the white boys. People said that Jasper, the next brother, was a better farmer than he, who, as was known generally, had some ambition to be a clerk in a store preparatory to becoming a merchant, and that it was owing mainly to Jasper's good judgment and steadiness of purpose that the crops made were not even smaller. Still, Madison was so polite in manners and so obliging in all neighborly offices that everybody liked him and wished him well.

The Crowders were sandwiched between two large plantations. The wife of Josiah Reid having died when Martha, her only child, was an infant, he had married Miss Crowder, an aunt of Madison's, and everybody said that the child could not have been reared more discreetly or affectionately by her own mother had she lived. The father, poor in his youth, had remained a bachelor until over forty. A good man in the main, the too high value that his mind had always set upon the possession of property became higher and higher as his own accumulated and the time drew nearer when he must part from it. He loved his daughter dearly, and he was reasonably grateful to the wife who had been continuously faithful to both sets of her duties. He honestly believed that his own career was the very best exemplar for poor young men; and the older and richer he grew, the more resolute his purpose that nobody but a man in possession or expectation of property equal to or approximating his own should wed his daughter. He was obliged to know that Madison Crowder wanted her, and whenever the youth's name was mentioned in the family his manner evinced the hostility that would have been much more pronounced but for the young lover's relationship to his wife.

Knowing old Mr. Reid as he did, Madison would never have fallen in love with Martha if he could have helped himself. But I have noticed more times than I could recall that where such a girl as Martha Reid is concerned, no amount of sense or observation stops a young man on that line of march. He had never asked Martha if she returned the feeling he avowed; that is, not so fully in words as in tones of his voice, looks of his eyes, manners of his every service. She treated him like the rest of the beaux—with that sort of politest cordiality which is most discouraging to an ardent lover. His aunt, to whom he could not but mention the subject sometimes, ever warned him against the indulgence of hopes which, whatever Martha's feelings might become in time, could never be compassed during the life of her father.

The plantation on the other side, extending to the Ogeechee River, and including the store at the bridge, was owned by the Fittens, mother and son, the former apparently sixty and the latter thirty-five years of age, who, removing from somewhere in South Carolina, had purchased this property, and been resident thereon for five or six years. The store, built by the former owner, had been enlarged somewhat, and being on the highway leading from the court-house of the county to that of the adjoining county east, and about equidistant from both and from Dukesborough, had lately been honored by having a post-office. The mother, a pale, plain, reticent woman, seemed to render to her son entire subservience, which it was believed that he exacted in return for having raised the family, as he claimed, from very humble beginnings to its present exalted state. They had a gang of rather unlikely negroes, with whom the son ran the plantation, and in spite of the diversity of occupations he succeeded abundantly at both.

Madison Crowder, in all of his dreams about a clerkship, had never thought of Mr. Fitten in that connection, for, among other reasons that he believed he had for not liking him, was an assurance of his mind that his intention ever since his first removal to the neighborhood had been to marry Martha Reid if he could. Within this last year she had sprung into womanhood, and there was little doubt upon anybody's mind that at this particular time Mr. Fitten was soliciting her with the full consent of her father. Madison, therefore, was much surprised one day when the merchant, on his way home from Mr. Reid's, drew up his horse, and calling him from work in his field, informed him that he had discharged the clerk he had had; and then he offered to him the position for a wage that was quite above what the youth had hoped to get at first anywhere.

"Why, Mr. Fitten, I — I never thought you — I never dreamed of such a thing."

"Ah! Somebody told me, leastways my 'membrance is *somebody* told me, you had a idee of learnin' to be a merchant, an' were a-tryin' to git a place in a sto' in town. Maybe I were mistakened."

"No, sir, you were not mistaken. I mean to say that I was not expecting *you* to— I didn't, in fact, know that you expected to part with Will Evans, Mr. Fitten, and—"

"Will's a good boy, a good 'nough boy, but I don't think that Will have the—I'll say the *talons* for to be a merchant. What I want in my business, Madison, is for my clerk to have *talons* for the business, an' in perusin' around, my mind have fell on you; that is, a-powidin' *your* notions is that way. Ef not, why, in co'se."

"When must I give you my answer, Mr. Fitten?"

"In co'se you want to talk along 'ith your ma, an' possible your aunt, Missis Reid, and—well, we'll say four days, or you may make it five if you want. Say five. Your crop's laid by, you know, an' Jappy, if he git pressed in getherin' it, why, you know, Mad's'n, we can all help him pull through."

After some further conversation, it was agreed that by the fifth day next succeeding Madison was to give notice of his decision. If such an offer had come from any other source he would have accepted eagerly at once. As it was, the first feeling, as Mr. Fitten rode away, was a poignant pain at the thought of assuming towards him a relation of admitted subordination. Yet for some time past he had been almost without hope to win Martha Reid, for even if she should return his feeling—a result she had never given him reason to expect—he well knew that she would never wed without her father's consent, and that could never be gotten for him—at least so long as he continued so poor in the matter of property. As for thanking the man who had just made the offer to him, which he ought to have done, he was very far from that. Instead, as he went on slowly to his mother, he felt some resentment, he could scarcely have told for what. His mother, after some reflection, said that perhaps it was best for him to accept. It would be a start in the way of his long-indulged ambition, and if, upon better acquaintance with the man, he should not grow to like him, he at all events would be learning the new business and becoming qualified for a satisfactory position elsewhere.

"I don't know what to say about it, Madison," said his aunt on the next day. "Me an' Marthy were both took by surprise when Mr. Reid told us last night that Mr. Fitten was going to make you an offer."

"What did Marthy say, aunty?"

"She said—that was when me and her were by ourselves, for she said nothing before her pa; but when he went out she said that ef she was in your place and wanted to go to clerking, she'd believe she'd go farther from home. But she took that back immegiate, and she hasn't named your name to me sence. You know I've freekwent told you, Madison, to not set your heart too much on Marthy, but go 'long and do the same as ef they wasn't no sech a girl. I love the child the same as ef she was my own child; but you know as well as I do that in this family Mr. Reid's words is the law. Your ma and Jappy think maybe it's best, and maybe it is."

The interview with Martha, two days afterwards, was brief. Not that she was wanting in cordiality; that on her part, though always polite, was never very pronounced; but he thought he could see that she recognized the humbling inferiority to which the contemplated change was already beginning to subject him. He rather hoped that she would mention the subject first. As she did not, he said,

"I've been thinking of clerking for Mr. Fitten."

"So ma tells me."

"Yes, Jappy can manage now at home very well—better than me, I must say, an' I've been thinking for some time that I'd like to get into some other business, in town, or Augusta, or somewhere."

"Yes. Had you made any effort that way, Madison?"

"Why, no; that is, not much. I thought I would this fall. And so here comes Mr. Fitten's offer. It took me by surprise. For somehow I didn't think Mr. Fitten— Well, the fact is, the whole thing surprised me."

She smiled so faintly that he was sorry he had mentioned the matter. Then he rose.

"Are you going?" she asked, evidently not expecting so speedy a departure, yet as evidently not disappointed.

"Well," he soliloquized, after leaving the house, "it's hard to be poor. If I had half, or a third, or even a quarter of the property of that old fellow, he *shouldn't* have her. It's all old man Reid's doings anyhow; but good-by, good-by, good-by."

Three times he said these last words; and then, as he

"HE SAW MARTHA STANDING ON THE PIAZZA."

was about to descend the hill, turning for one more view of the mansion he had just left, he saw Martha standing on the piazza where he had taken his leave of her. At that moment she also turned and entered the house.

II.

"'N'a-las: n'an dad: h'my Save-yer bleed:
N'an dad: h'my Sov-ring d—'

Humph! Dah boy done put me out an' my hime out, bofe un us."

Such conversion into spondees of the iambics of this sweet old hymn, and such abrupt breaking down of the last word in the opening distich, need explanation, of course.

Shortly after Madison Crowder had set in with Mr. Fitten, the latter had hired from Mr. Reid, for the purpose of waiting about the house and the store, a negro lad named Isaac, who, though good for little in the field, was fond of waiting, specially on white people. The daily putting to rights the store and the shed-room attached had hitherto devolved upon the clerk. But Mr. Fitten said that a young man raised like Madison should have a negro for such work, and as he owned none exactly suited to the purpose, he offered for Isaac a price that Mr. Reid, notwithstanding some humble remonstrance of the boy's father, indorsed by Mrs. Reid and Martha, accepted. In this new rôle Isaac delighted, and advanced in the arts of his business to that degree that he was becoming somewhat of an aristocrat, not only among the Fitten negroes, but the rest in his neighborhood. The store was on the first rise from the bridge, and the mansion on the second, about three hundred yards distant. Isaac waited on both.

On the occasion of his first visit home, Greene, his father (it was a Sunday morning), was sitting before his cabin door, under the shade of a mulberry, his Bible in his lap, and the hymn-book "Mercer's Cluster" lying on a stool by his side. He let his son pass with only a simple salutation into the cabin, and about an hour afterwards called to

"HE WAS BECOMING SOMEWHAT OF AN ARISTOCRAT."

him, "You Izik, I speck by dis time your mammy an' dem got 'nough er your qual'ty talk; en' ef dey is, step out here, en' less me 'n' you swap a few words."

He looked at his son's well-carded head, his white not overworn shirt, and other evidences of his rise.

"'Spected you las' Sunday. Leastways your mammy did. Whyn't you come?"

"I were dat busy, daddy, I couldn't. You know I has to 'tend to de house en' de sto', bofe."

"Ah, well, den; ef dey needs you, your business to be on han' at all times. Whar you git dat sto' shirt?"

"Mis' Fitt'n gin it to me."

"How you gitt'n' on, anyhow? an' how Marse Mad's'n gitt'n 'on ?"

"Oh, jes' splendid, daddy."

"Who splendid?"

"Why, Marse Mad's'n. Mis' Fitt'n praise him 'way up yonder, en' so do his ma. Dat ter young man he wait on hisself, but now I waits on Marse Mad's'n."

"Umph! humph! Ant'ny en' Neel tole your mammy las' week dat when dey seed you, as dey was a-comin' fum de mill, you wuz a-braggin' what fine qual'ty victuals dey feeds you on, en' how big you is in genil 'mong dem Fitt'n niggers."

"I jes' a-runnin' on wid dem boys, daddy."

"Jes' runnin' on? Den dey don't pomper you so mons'- ous pow'ful? As for dem Fitt'n niggers, dey show fer dey- selves; *dey* ain't fed like marster's niggers. But *you* does look fat en' greazy, so to speak."

"I waits 'bout de house, en' in co'se I gits de moest plenty."

"Umph! humph! En' dey trusses you to sweep up de sto', does dey? Well, now, sir, you be mons'ous pittickler, en' de furder white folks trusses you, de pitticklererer you git, en' don't you let nothin' stick to you dar."

"Daddy, I wa'n't fotch up to steal; you 'n' mammy—"

"Let 'lone me 'n' your mammy. Don't you 'pen' on fetchin' up. You 'pen' on ketchin' de cowhide, en' mars- ter bein' broke up payin' you out o' jail, en' den my takin' whut hide de sheyiff en' de ter white people leff on your back. You ken go 'long now. When dey ken spar' you uv a Sunday like, I want you come home. Not as I can't eat my 'lowance o' victuals fer grievin' atter you, but your mammy want to see you sometimes, en' I wants to hear how you gitt'n' 'long en' behavin' yourself to white en' black. When you git back, 'member my 'spects to your Marse Mad's'n."

"En' Mis' Fitt'n too, daddy?"

"No; I got nothin' to do 'long Miss Fitt'n, en' I got no use fer white folks what pompers ter people's niggers agin dey own. Go 'long off wid you."

It was here that old Greene, as above recorded, failed in his musical endeavor.

Several weeks passed. The mouth of Mr. Fitten, especially when at the Reids', where he now visited frequently, had been for a while full of praise of the new clerk. If it had been less so of late, this might be attributed to the theme having gradually become trite. Madison now seldom visited there. What he had come to recognize as hopeless, with the strength of youth he had ceased to pursue. But now he was seized with a too ardent desire to get money. The contemplation of what such a man as Mr. Fitten, whose coarseness and ill-breeding he exaggerated, could accomplish by the possession of money, and of what such another as he considered himself must fail to obtain for the want of it, induced a resolution to get money at the sacrifice of some things which heretofore he had held much more dear. Disguising the disgust, the full extent of which he must have been aware that he had no right to indulge, he yet went diligently to all his work, and discharged it to the full satisfaction of his employer. If the latter penetrated his disguise, he yet persisted in the confidence he bestowed, and it seemed, if not to Madison, at least to his friends, as if he was trying by kindness to overcome a repulsion which he could not but recognize in the circumstances to be natural. Madison could hardly have said himself whether it was with pain or a sort of pleasure that he noticed the want of affection between Mr. Fitten and his mother, so thin, pale, and apparently so unhealthy, who seemed as though she had suffered many griefs, but had not lost thereby, as he soon discovered, either energy or will. Her house was decently kept, and the negroes were provided for as humanely as the penuriousness of her son would allow; more so, indeed, for sometimes secretly and sometimes openly, silently taking his rude complainings, she supplied them with things that he had refused.

With the instinct of one brought up as Madison Crowder was, he treated this woman with every becoming deference, that grew to be more marked as he noticed the indifference of her son to her feelings and general welfare.

"The old lady is old and sickly," he would say to Madison, "an' them make her fretful an' hard to please. I got so myself I done quit tryin' to please her, I has. When people git that way, they ain't no tellin' what's best fer a feller to do."

The woman received Madison's deferential services with some apparent gratitude, and sometimes when they happened to be together alone she would talk with him, though without allusion to her griefs or mention of her son's name, yet as if she was beginning to feel an affection for one from whom kindness had come to her unexpectedly. Lately he had observed that occasionally, after mother and son had been holding private conversation, her eyes seemed as if they had been weeping. Estrangement of these men, gradual at first, became more pronounced, though never leading to hostile words.

On several occasions the cash, though in quantities inconsiderable, was found to be short in the till; but both agreed that in some periods of omission on Madison's part Isaac had gotten the key and taken it. Madison repressed as well as he could the indignation he felt in the changed looks and manners of his employer, meaning, as he believed, a suspicion that the money had been appropriated by himself. This indignation was increased when, at the end of the year, on Madison's claim of additional wages for the last three months, which Mr. Fitten in the beginning had partially promised in case his services should increase in value as expected, the merchant refused to allow it.

"Never mind, sir," said Madison, soliloquizing, but aloud, as Mr. Fitten went out by the door leading into the shed-room, "I'll be even with you yet."

A few minutes afterwards Mr. Fitten, who he supposed had gone to the mansion, appeared at the front piazza steps, and calling, said, in a tone of entire confidence and friendliness, "Mad's'n, I spected a letter from Stovall and Simmons this mornin' 'bout buyin' some wool fer 'em. None nuver come, did they?"

"If any had come I should have told you of it, Mr. Fitten."

"So I knowed, 'ithout you'd a-forgot it. Nuver mind: it'll come to-morrow, I reckin." Then he turned again and proceeded to the house.

The mail, carried by a boy on horseback, came shortly after breakfast, and was usually opened by Madison, who was wont to be at the store before his employer. On several of the following mornings Mr. Fitten received the bag himself. Madison did not ask if the expected letter had come. Indeed, none except necessary, and that the briefest, conversation was now held between the two. A sense of fear, a sense also of something like that of the losing of manhood, took possession of Madison. So a few days afterwards he said, abruptly, to his employer, "Mr. Fitten, I think we better part, sir."

"Don't know but what you're right, Mad's'n. Things here haven't been goin' to suit me lately somehow. I made up my mind to send Izik back to his marster, an' by good rights they ought to be a investigashin o' some *few* things befo' us all parts. All right—all right: people lives in the world to larn an' meet up with dis'p'intments. Tommy Wheeler want a place. Wonder how *he'd* suit? I'll step over to his mother's house to-night an' have a chat with her 'n' him."

This was a Monday evening. Madison had been at his mother's the day before, and while there she said to him that he owed it both to Mr. Fitten and himself not to stay there with the feelings which he admitted to entertain towards him. After supper, before returning to the store, he lingered a short time with Mrs. Fitten, her son having gone to the Wheelers'. Her manner seemed more than ever soft and affectionate.

"I just as well tell you good-by to-night, Madison," she said, with a trembling voice, as he rose to go. "I mayn't be to breakfast in the morning, as I feel now so bad. Good-by—good-by. You've been a great deal to me since you've been here, and I sha'n't forget you. May God A'mighty bless you, Madison!"

With eyes overflowing she turned from the steps, whither she had followed him, and going to her chamber, knelt by her bed and sobbed aloud.

"Mistiss," said her woman, Rachel, of about her age, then coming into the room, "for de Lord's sake git up an' stop some o' dah cryin'. Look like you gwine grieve yourself to death 'bout dah boy."

"Oh, Rachel! Rachel!" she said, suffering herself to be raised up, "you don't know all he's been to me. Help me to bed."

III.

Half an hour before breakfast-time next morning, while Madison was arranging his clothes in his trunk, and Isaac was chopping wood preparatory to making a fire in the stove, Mr. Fitten, accompanied by young Wheeler, whose service he had engaged the night previous, came. Proceeding into the store, he called Madison, and in a low tone said, "Mad's'n, I wouldn't of thought you'd of done what you done about the deffernce betwix' us. Our ric'lections was deffernt 'bout my raisin' o' your wages; but I were determined to let you have it your way ruther'n have feelin's too bad hurted; but you oughtn't to of tuck it jes' so."

His manner was compounded of the mildly complaining and the kindly admonitory.

"I don't understand you, Mr. Fitten," answered Madison, turning pale.

"Not so loud. Look at that Izik picked out the fire in the shed-room."

Madison took the paper, which was a half-consumed letter. Enough was left undestroyed to see that it had been sent from Stovall and Simmons, and purported to enclose a fifty-dollar note, which the writers had marked so as to identify it if lost or stolen. The young man shuddered.

"That negro lies, sir."

"You Ike," called Mr. Fitten, "come here. Now you, sir, put down that axe, go to the house, bundle up your rags, take yourself home, and tell your marster I sent you for stealin' fifty dollars, an' then tryin' to lay it on a white man."

"For de Lord's sake, Mis' Fitten," cried the negro, "kill me ef you 'n' Marse Mad's'n wanter, but don't sen' me home wid dat messenge. For ef marster don't kill me, daddy will.

"LOOK AT THAT IZIK PICKED OUT THE FIRE."

Marse Mad's'n been 'cusin' me to you a-cons'ant. But he know I nuver got dat money, en' he know whar 'tis dis minute."

"You lying scoundrel!"

As he started towards him the latter took to his heels.

7

"Mis-ter Fitten," said he, "I don't understand this business. I've packed my things in my trunk, except what I have on my back; but come in here and I'll take them out, and we'll search this place through and through."

I pass over this painful scene, during the search and after, when the money was found carefully concealed beneath the paper with which the bottom was lined, the angry dismay of the unhappy youth, the vast but unpainful surprise of young Wheeler, the contemptuous pity of Mr. Fitten. Laying the note calmly on the table, he said, "Tommy, now don't you make no blowin' horn o' sech a little matter. Mad's'n thought—he honestly thought I owed him the money. That's all right, Mad's'n. We'll quit even. Keep the money."

Madison gave bewildered looks at the money, at Tommy Wheeler, at Mr. Fitten. He seemed as one just awakened from a dreamful sleep. Suddenly he said, "Good-by, Tom," then immediately went from the place.

"I'd 'a' nuver b'lieved it," said the new clerk. "I knowed he were proud, an' had a mons'ous ambition for money, but I'd of nuver of b'lieved that of him."

"Now, Tommy, whatever you do, don't you peach about this business, an' 'member I 'cused Mad's'n Crowder o' nothin'—'member that."

Profound as appeared Mr. Fitten's regret for the disappointment of his hopes regarding Madison, there is little doubt that he had some of the satisfaction that such a lover must feel in view of the ruin of one who would have been, if he had dared, his rival. Then there was the consolation that Isaac had cleared himself of the suspicions that had been put upon him. For he would not have been willing, related as he was to the Reids, to have any enemy, of whatever rank, in that household. Only a few weeks before he had addressed Martha through her father, and though she had asked time for consideration of his offer, he knew that her father was his constant advocate, and he hoped that whatever partiality Martha might have had for Madison would now disappear. Upon the whole, therefore, he was not sure but that he ought to be gratified rather than troubled by his miscalculations. Isaac was more than restored to favor. The very next Sunday a negro on a neighboring plantation, returning from a meeting some miles on the other side of the river, reported that he had met him there with a brand-new suit of store clothes—coat, breeches, hat, shoes, and, bless your soul, a striped waistcoat; not only so, but that he was perfumed all over with cinnamon.

A matter so grave could not be concealed. Mrs. Crowder, notwithstanding her son's avowal of innocence, remembering his dislike and his threats towards his employer, had doubts so apparent that he talked as if he would go off and never return. It was several days before he had the heart to go to his aunt, and when he went did not ask for Martha, and hoped that he would not even see her. To his great relief he found that Mrs. Reid, who had heard the news that very afternoon, expressed full confidence in his integrity.

"Madison," she said, "Greene don't have even an idea, so he says, but what Isaac took that money, and getting scared about it, put it in your trunk, and he says if God spares his life he means to find out the truth."

They had been together but for a short while when Martha, opening the door without knocking, entered the room. Her step was firm, but her face was crimson.

"Madison," she said, without extending her hand, or making other salutation, "you told me several times before you went to Mr. Fitten's that you loved me. Is the fact of your ceasing to come here owing to that of your finding that you were mistaken in the feeling you thought you had, or that it is gone?"

Her lower jaw trembled, and her eyes were fastened upon him, as he rose and stood in silence before her. "Because," she continued, advancing slowly—" because if either of these is not the reason, I want to tell you in the presence of your own aunt, who has been more than a mother to me, that I did not know how deeply I loved you until I saw your spirit breaking down under the coarse rule of that man. I've prayed that your connection with him might not hurt you, and I shall blame myself as long as I live for not warning you, as I wanted, and ought to have done, against him. Oh, Madison! Madison!"

She threw her arms around his neck, pressed her cheek to his for a brief moment, then turning, fled from the room.

The next day, about ten of the morning, Greene repaired to the spring at the foot of the hill, and near the road leading towards the bridge. From the thicket near by he cut several young hickories, and seating himself on a washbench, carefully trimmed them. As the season was not one for providing props for pea and bean vines, one might have surmised that he was getting a supply of ox-goads. In a few minutes Isaac, for whom, partly at his suggestion, his master had sent, was heard advancing. As he was about to pass, "You Izik!"—spoken in sepulchral tones—was heard. Turning himself towards the spring, and seeing his father, he climbed the fence and went to the spring.

"Howdy, daddy? Gitt'n' steer-poles?" he asked, with an unconcern of manner that he had not in his mind.

"Nuver you mind 'bout whut I gitt'n'. Ole Marse Aberham's Izik nuver axed *him* whut he gwine do wid de sticks he made him kyar. Sposen you got 'bove him, ef he wuz a white boy. Ben sech a stranger here lately, 'low'd maybe you mout come dressed up in dem fine close Harrell's Ned tole some un 'em he seed you in a Sunday at Elom. Leas'ways I ben smellin' de cinnimum on you evy sence you got on top o' de fench dar. Sposen you'd bring dat 'long anyhow,

"YOU HEERN TALK O' ABERHAM, HAIN'T YOU?"

but couldn't 'ford to w'ar your qual'ty close jes' 'mong jes' common niggers. Shoulder dem poles, en' come 'long wid me in de thicket dar."

The boy had well learned the terror of his father's ire, and he ruminated rapidly as they advanced towards the spot where they were to stop.

"Dar, now," said Greene, drawing a rope from his pocket; "cross dem han's, en drap down on dem knees."

"De good Lord, daddy, whut all dis 'bout? Whut *is* I done?"

"Name o' God, boy," answered the old man, as he slowly wrapped the rope around his wrists, "*I* don't know. Dat whut I gwine fin' out, er w'ar out every hick'ry in dis thicket on your hide. En ef you goes to hollerin', as I see you gittin' your mouf ready, Ill beat you to death befo' marster, er your mammy, er any un 'em, ken git to you. You heern talk o' Aberham, hain't you? Well, I'm him, en ef de Lord 'll gim me strenk in de arms, I'm gwine to fin' out whar you got dem close, en whut fer."

Then he raised aloft with both hands one of the rods.

"Fer God A'mighty's sake, daddy, stop, en' I'll tell you de blessed troof!"

He lowered his arm, and ten minutes afterwards father and son were walking leisurely and peacefully together up towards the mansion.

IV.

In spite of the delay of Martha Reid's answer to his proposal, and the unhappy fall of his late clerk, Mr. Fitten was in reasonably good spirits, especially after the return of Isaac with news of how forbearingly he had been dealt with at home for the part he had acted. The distress of his mother, instead of subtracting from his contentment, added to it, perhaps; for he was resentful in contemplation of his rival's superior manners and the grateful influences which they had exerted upon her to whose happiness he was so selfish as to be ever indifferent.

"Look like you been cryin'," he said to her on the evening of the day succeeding that of Isaac's visit home. "Had the right feelin' for your son, you'd be glad, instid o' goin' mopin' about because that feller's out o' my sto'."

"I have, or I try to have, the right feelings towards you and everybody, William; but I can't help feeling as I do about a boy that was as respectful and as kind to me as Madison Crowder was, going away as he did; and to my opinion, William, that case is going to make more trouble than you've been counting on."

"What do you mean?" he asked, angrily.

"I mean that if Madison Crowder is not guilty, or if he says he's not guilty, of stealing that money, the end of the business has not come yet."

"Jes' like you. Always a-prophesyin', an' 'special' agin me. Nobody ever 'cused him o' stealin' of it. The money were found in his trunk, an' Tommy Wheeler 'll b'ar witness that I nuver opened my mouth with the word *stealin'*, ner nothin' like it, an' I've nuver told not a human, exceptin' o' you, that he did steal it. His actions speaks louder 'n my words, even ef I'd a-said 'em, which I didn't."

"Ah, well, William, we'll see. That family of people is poor, but they're proud, and they've got connections that have money. That young lawyer, James Mobley, that they all say is the fastest rising young man in all this part of Georgia, is kin to him. You didn't know that, did you?"

"No, I didn't. What's that got to do with it?" He asked this defiantly, but his face discovered anxiety.

"*I* don't know, William — *I* don't know. But if he thinks there's a fly in the lock, he'll try hard to find it. I got nothing more to say."

She rose and went to her chamber.

On the next day, an hour before sunset, the afternoon, though in the midst of winter, being balmy, Mr. Fitten was sitting on the piazza of his store. He was in such deep meditation that he did not observe that a horseman had ridden to one of the racks, hitched his beast, and alighted. Hearing advancing footsteps, he started, and the more visibly when he discovered that the comer was Mr. Triplett, the sheriff of the county. Ascending the steps slowly, as was his fashion, the latter, saluting in friendly words Mr. Fitten, took the offered chair, and said, "Fine weather for breakin' up ground an' mendin' o' fences, Mr. Fitten."

The merchant looked at the officer as if he knew just as well as he did that the state of the weather or plantation-work was not the matter to which he owed the honor of this visit.

"I've got a paper for you, Mr. Fitten."

The paleness on the man's face at the mention of the paper deepened into that of the dead when he read on the back the statement,

"*Madison Crowder, by his next friend, William Mobley,* v. *William Fitten. Case, etc.*"

"Mis-ter Triplett," said he, appealingly, "what *do* it mean?"

"I know nothin' about it only what I heerd the clerk an' Squire Mobley say, Mr. Fitten."

"*I* nuver done nothin' to Mad's'n Crowder to be harasted an' tried to make pay money for. Whut did Squire Mobley say? Like to know what *he* know about the case more'n I know, an' more'n Tommy Wheeler know, an' which he's back thar in the sto', an' I'll call him out here, an' you may ask him."

"Needn't do that, Mr. Fitten," answered Mr. Triplett, kindly. "I got nothin' 'tall to do 'ith the case exceptin' to serve the papers that's give me to serve."

"What did Squire Mobley say?"

"Well, now, I ain't a man that make a practice o' totin'

MR TRIPLETT, THE SHERIFF OF THE COUNTY.

news, onlest it's that that's good. But Squire Mobley say the case are a bad one, an' he got it dead on you, an' he told me I mout tell you so."

"Umph! humph!"—with quasi contempt. "Want, I s'pose, two hunderd, er maybe three hunderd, dollars, an' him take half of it fer his fee."

"Ef you'll read the writ, Mr. Fitten, to the eend, you'll see that the damidge ain't laid at nary one o' them figgers."

He read, in a low, mumbling tone, as far as through the words "to the damage of your petitioner of," when he almost screamed, "*ten thousand dollars!*" and it was pitiful to see his dismay.

"Did that—did that lawyer tell you, Mr. Triplett, that he spected to make me pay sich—sich a damidge, or the—or the hundith part of it?"

"Well, now, Mr. Fitten, Squire Mobley told me that of you ast me, to tell you that he have tried to 'bout size your pile, an' he have laid the damidge to jes' about kiver it. William Mobley's a ter'ble feller in the cote-house, young as he is, an' they ain't none o' them big lawyers ken turn him down when his dander's up, as it are now, Madison a-bein' o' his kin. It seem to me, though 'tain't none o' my business, but it seem to me that ef I were sued to that figger o' damidges, I'd—ruther'n I'd be tore up in my mind, an' have to stan' William Mobley's tongue when he's mad like he are now—I'd try ef I couldn't git a compermise, Mr. Fitten."

"I've done nothin', Mr. Triplett. Whar's his witnesses? I've done nothin'; but I'd like to know whar's his witnesses."

"Well, in co'se, Mr. Fitten, *I* don't know; but I *did* hear William say that he spected to prove *somethin'* by your ma."

"By ma?"

"Yes, sir; bes' o' my riclection he said your ma."

A sense of relief was evinced in Mr. Fitten's face. Yet when the sheriff rose to leave, saying that he had to go by the Crowders' to carry a letter from the lawyer to his client, he sent a request to Madison to come to see him.

"Not as I nuver done the young man any harm, that is, intentual, ef I knowed it, but I wouldn't wish him to be my innimy."

Immediately after supper the new clerk was dismissed to the store, and as soon as the table was cleared, mother and son sat down together for a conversation. The former had seen the sheriff as he rode by the house on his way to the Crowders', and her suspicion of his business became assurance when she saw the perturbed state of her son's mind.

"It hasn't come much sooner than I expected," she said, mildly.

"Beginnin' on your prophesyin's ag'in, eh?"

"No, William; we're talking now about some of 'em coming true. I told you you'd hurt yourself in trying to ruin Madison Crowder, and it looks like you've done it."

"It's a lie. You put that feller agin me, an' put him up to—put him agin me."

She did not seem more excited than in the beginning.

"I'll be back in a minute," she said, rising and going to the back door, from which she almost immediately returned, and resuming her seat, she said, "No, I've never tried to put that boy against you, William. It was because he was so kind and good to me always, and so like a gentleman, that I hoped he would not fall into the trap that I knew you set for him; but I never tried to put him against you."

"What trap you talkin' about?"

"The trap you set for him when you brought him here

because you believed that he stood between you and Mr. Reid's daughter, and who I told you always you'd no more get than you'd pull down one of the stars."

Resentment and fear were both plainly visible upon him.

"You've been agin me all my life — agin your own son."

"No; God knows I have not. I've saved you before now, as you well know, from things — not quite as bad as this, but bad enough, and I tried to save you from this, but I couldn't."

"Talk about makin' a man's own mother a witness agin him! You know nothin' 'bout the case, an' ef you did, an' ef they was any case, which they ain't, an' you did know anything, you know you ain't a-goin', an' no 'oman that's a mother an' got a heart under her ribs ain't a-goin', to the cote-'ouse an' try to ruin the onlest child she's got."

"William Fitten, when you brought that boy to this house I knew what it was for, because I know the spirit that's been in you ever since you were born; and I made up my mind that he should *not* be ruined while under my roof if I could help it, and 'special' since he showed to me in the time he was here a respect you never showed in all your lifetime. I know more about this matter than you think; but I'm not going to any court-house if I can help it."

"I should think not — I should think not."

He fastened his teeth together, and looked warningly at her.

She returned his gaze calmly. Many a time before had he tried to frighten her.

"I said that I was not going there if I could help it. Suppose I can't, and then they ask me to tell what I do know?"

"You know nothin', an' you'll tell 'em so; an' ef you did

know anything agin me you know you daresn't stand up thar and ruin your own son. You *daresn't* do it."

Either she did not understand or she ignored the deadly gaze that he bestowed upon her.

"If I am to put my hand on the Book of God, I shall answer the questions that are asked me like I'll be glad to remember when I stand before the Judgment. You know that, William Fitten; and you know that the fear of God with me is before any other fear, no matter how much cause I've got to be afraid of you, especially now when my body is broken down, like my spirit's always been."

She placed her hand upon her forehead, raised her eyes upward for a moment, then looked upon him with deepest sadness.

There is that in maternity that to some degree must awe the most reprobate in filial love and duty. This with her solemn invocation made him lower his eyes.

"The thing for you to do, William Fitten, is to try to settle this case without going to court. Madison Crowder wants to get back his name more than he wants what property you've got. And let me tell you *you* can't settle it, but I believe I can."

"How?" he asked, eagerly. "They ain't nothin' to settle, but how?"

Then, as she paused before answering, he bethought to hide his eagerness, and asked, contemptuously,

"Didn't know you got so smart in your old age as to know how to settle men-folks' business better'n they do theirselves. You needn't be a-tryin' to git me to pay my money, or 'knowledgin' I been tellin' o' lies."

"I think I can settle it without either. I must think on it to-night. I'll let you know in the morning what I think is best to be done."

She rose, and in much feebleness retired to her chamber.

When his mother had gone, Mr. Fitten went out to the kitchen and called for Isaac, who was not to be found. Demanding of the woman Rachel where he was, she answered,

"I 'clar', Marse William, I don't know whar dat boy gone."

"You old devil, whyn't you tell me he wasn't here?"

"Marse William, I can't keep up wid dat boy. I nuver knowed but what you sont him somewhars."

"Ma," he asked, loudly, at his mother's door, "that Izik ain't to be found. Know whar he is?"

"Please, William, don't disturb me to-night about Isaac, I suppose he's stepped over home. Let me rest to-night, and I'll tell you in the morning how I think this matter can be settled, and that without your losing any of your property, or anything else you've got."

He sat up until a late hour, alternating between the mansion and kitchen. Finally, seeming to have abandoned hope of the negro's return, he went to bed.

V.

The next morning Mr. Fitten had just risen from breakfast, to which his mother had only then seated herself. He was walking on his piazza, pondering the continued absence of Isaac, when Mr. Triplett rode up to his gate, accompanied by Madison Crowder. Doubting how to account for this visit, yet strongly hoping for a satisfactory settlement, he cordially invited the visitors to alight. When they had done so, and entered the piazza, Madison not having spoken the while, the sheriff, laying his hand upon Mr. Fitten's shoulder, said, "I arrest you, Mr. Fitten, on this summons, and I has one fer the old man Reid's nigger boy Izik—both for conspurricy. Mawnin', Missis Fitten," he continued, as she appeared at the door, pale and trembling. "I've got a suppeny fer you, ma'am." She would have fallen, but that Madison went to her relief, and tenderly seated her in a chair. Her son looked alternately at the three in silent dismay.

"Madison," said the woman, when she had sufficiently recovered, "I was intending to go to your mother's to-day and try to settle this case with you. But that can't be done now except in town. I'll be ready to go in a few minutes. William, you and Mr. Triplett can ride on. Madison, I know, won't object to going with me, and I can talk to him by the way."

This was arranged. While she was in her chamber preparing for her departure, her son, having gotten leave to enter, said to her in tones just above a whisper, "You mind what you say to these people, and on that stand. *You mind!*" And she never forgot the look he gave.

The sheriff had reached the court-house with his prisoner, and turning him over to his deputy, had gone to the office of Mr. Mobley to report this fact and his inability to find the negro boy on the premises.

"All right, Triplett. This one will do for the present. Yonder comes Madison with the mother."

The two latter rode on. Passing the court-house, they alighted at the horse-rack nearest the law-office, and proceeding at once to it, entered, when Mrs. Fitten asked the sheriff to bring her son there.

"William," she said, when all were seated, "I sent for you because I wanted you to hear the terms I'm going to offer to Madison."

The abundant tears that she had been shedding during the ride were gone from her eyes, and she spoke with composure. Addressing herself mainly to Mr. Mobley, she said,

"It wouldn't do any good to tell you and the others here how William Fitten has been doing ever since he knew the difference between right and wrong, nor how he's treated me in all this time. When that boy there," nodding towards Madison, "came into my house, I soon saw that he was one of a kind that any woman, if she had any heart, would try to save from being ruined. And when the child treated me with the respect, and even with the affection, it seemed to me, like that he had for his own mother, then I determined, and I made a promise to God Almighty that, with His help, he *shouldn't* be. That money," she continued, after a brief pause, "that was found in Madison's trunk was put there by William Fitten."

"Ma," said the prisoner, rising, a fearful picture of wrath and fright, "that's a d—"

He checked himself as the men all rose.

"Sit down, gentlemen, sit down—please sit down. I've been used to such talk as that. Please sit down."

She kept beseeching them until they had resumed their seats. Then she narrated in detail the reception of the letter from Augusta by her son several days before his mention of it to Madison, the boy Isaac being set against him because of being told that Madison had avowed belief in his dishonesty, and the penetration of confidence between the two by the woman Rachel, at the instigation of her mistress. Then she told how she had sent off the negro the night before, as she had intended to inform her son on the next morning of her knowledge of their joint transactions.

Haggard, abject, yet with eyes fixed upon the speaker, the prisoner sat during this circumstantial narration.

"And now," she said, addressing herself to Madison, on whom she tenderly looked, "I'm going to make an offer, Madison. I'm an old, sickly, friendless woman, without husband, without parents, without brothers or sisters, without relations, except what are far off in home and in kin, and without— I didn't tell you *that* as I rode along to-day; I've always thought until now that I'd carry that with me to the grave." She blushed, wrinkled as was her cheek, and turned away from view of the prisoner, whom she never saw again. Pointing her finger backward where he sat, she said, " When I married his father I knew that he had been engaged to a woman who was his cousin, but I did not know until some months after my marriage, when that woman died, leaving that creature who is now in the hands of the sheriff, how far that engagement had gone. Shortly afterwards my husband died, begging me on his death-bed, and getting my promise, to take and raise his child."

The prisoner shrank in his chair aghast, for although he had never even dreamed of such a thing, he doubted not its truth.

"Madison," she continued, after a brief pause, "that poor man has no property except the goods in the store, and they not all paid for. The land we've been living on was bought with money from selling part of the negroes in the neighborhood we moved from the last time. If you'll let him off to go clear away, I'll give him two thousand dollars, which he knows is more than his goods are worth, even if they were all paid for. I'll tell you what I'll do then. Oh, Madison, Madison, don't refuse my offer. I've always longed— if I couldn't have somebody to love me—at least to have somebody about me that I could love. For years and years I've prayed for direction what to do, and somehow when you came into my house, and treated me as you did, and my heart went out to you as it did, I felt a hope that the good Lord was going to send the answer that He had kept from me so long. Madison, I know I can't ask you to take up your home altogether with a forlorn creature like me; but if you'll stay there part of the time, and will take the management of my business, I'll give you everything I've got, and I'll give it now, and Mr. Mobley may draw up the papers, and I'll sign them before I leave this office. Here's the money for William Fitten, and he may have the horse he rode here to-day besides. But he must go away from here. After what's passed, he and I couldn't live in the same neighborhood. Oh, Madison, Madison, don't—don't—"

She could say no more. Leaning her head upon the table near which she sat, she wept aloud.

A few months after the occurrences just related, Mr. Reid, sitting in his piazza, looking after Madison Crowder as he rode away from his gate, called to his daughter.

"Marthy," he said, in the tone of a man imparting dismal information, "I ain't shore in my mind — in fac', I hain't a idee—that you know that that feller ridin' off yonder on one o' Missis Fitten's horses is other a fool, born so, or los' his mind for the present time bein'."

"Oh, pa! pa! have you sent Madison away?"

"I has; an' you want to know the reason why? It's because he's a born fool, *er* a lunacy, an' it make no odds which, an' not while my head stays hot shall the onlest child I've got marry any one o' them kind o' folks. To think he, po' as he is, would 'a' 'fused that ole 'oman's offer o' every blessed piece o' prop'ty she have, an' work on wages fer her, though I'm not a-denyin' that he's a-managin' better'n I ever thought were in him. Yit to ruther work fer her on wages than to take her prop'ty, when the po' creeter got nary kit, nor b'ilin', nor generation o' kin, he—he's a fool, I tell you, er he's a lunacy, an' it make no odds which."

"Pa, Madison is doing with Mrs. Fitten what he believes

"OH, PA! PA! HAVE YOU SENT MADISON AWAY?"

to be right, and what I believe also. If you refuse to let me marry him, I'll marry nobody."

"You! you got no more sense 'n—" But he loved her too well to finish this sentence.

After that Madison seldom came to the house.

Greene was deeply concerned about the troubles of his young mistress.

"Miss Marthy," he said to her one day, "why can't Marse Mad's'n, if he 'shamed to take all, why can't he take part o' de prop'ty de 'oman want to give him, en leave her de balance?"

"Oh no, Uncle Greene, Madison wouldn't be willing to do that, and I wouldn't be willing for it either."

"Umph! My sakes! De Lord bless my soul! Well, den, Miss Marphy, couldn't Marse Mad's'n—couldn't he sort o' *let on* to marster dat de prop'ty were his'n—er leasways a part un it?"

"That would be still worse, Uncle Greene. I'm surprised that a good Christian like you should advise such as that."

"Well," he said, not noticing the rebuke, "ef de 'oman —she ole en 'flicted anyhow—ef in co'se it was de will o' de Lord—in co'se a body'd wish she mout go in de triump' o' de faith—en den leave to Marse Mad's'n whut she got—"

"Uncle Greene! Uncle *Greene!*"

"I done wid you, Miss Marphy."

Colloquies similar to these two last mentioned took place at varying intervals during the next two years, in the which Mr. Reid grew more and more strengthened in the belief in Madison Crowder's incurable malady of understanding, while old Greene revolved the tardiness of death among those who were as ready and fitted in all respects to depart as Mrs. Fitten. At last one day, full of peaceful hope, she expired in the arms of him who had been as the son of her old age. Then William Mobley propounded her last will and testament, wherein, theretofore unknown to all except the testatrix and her lawyer, her property of every description had been bequeathed to Madison. The legatee, in Mr. Reid's judgment, was restored to sanity as instantaneously as if he had been dipped in the pool of Siloam, and just exactly such another wedding had not been in that neighborhood for, oh! I couldn't now say how many years.

"En, oh, Miss Marphy," Uncle Greene used to say, with what resignation was possible in the regrets that he hoped he had felt for the departed—"oh, young missis, I'm dat tankful—as de po' 'oman *had* to go when her time come, *in* co'se — I'm dat tankful she went in de triump' o' de faith."

THE SUICIDAL TENDENCIES OF
MR. EPHRODTUS TWILLEY.

"Aspice, quam sævas increpat aura minas!"—PROPERTIUS.

I.

THE emigration of the Twilleys from South Carolina ended at our village by the breaking down of the horse that drew the wagon bearing them and their property. A small house just out of town on the east being without a tenant, they took it. The family, after the death of the horse, comprised only Mr. Twilley, his wife, and their daughter, Simanthy. Their dress and general appearance suggested that either such poverty was not their normal state or that they were not without ambition to improve: the man, somewhat above middle height, slender, mild, though inquiry-looking; the woman, rather low in stature, quick of motion, and studied in speech; the daughter, now ten years old, seeming to have inherited her father's physique and the rest from her mother. All got early notice from the villagers, the earlier perhaps from the fact that very shortly after their arrival they were known to be members of the religious denomination to which a large majority of the former belonged.

Even the Christian name of Mr. Twilley was made known

as early as the second day after their arrival, he, while his wife and daughter were engaged in stowing in the new residence their household goods, having walked up-town and seated himself on a chair in the piazza of Mr. Bland's store. This name was originally meant for *Epaphroditus*. But his parents, being persons of limited education, contracted it to *Ephrodtus;* and the bearer, whose literary advantages, for some reason, had not been better, though a somewhat aspiring person, never laid claim, if he knew of it, to the proper elongation.

It was not difficult to see that pride in the possession of this distinguished name had existed long before Mr. Twilley's removal to Dukesborough. It was said that at one time he had claimed direct lineal descent from the historic character who had transmitted it; and not until repeatedly assured that this bearer of the Epistle of St. Paul to the Philippians was, in all probability, a Jew, did he rebate this claim, and become content with other inheritances besides mere blood. These were weak health of body, demonstrative love of the members of his religious denomination, proper hostility to those of all others, special devotion to church officials, and a notable fondness for bearing letters and other messages among them. Superadded to these was an apparent preference for rendering such service as what he styled his "ofting infirmities" allowed to others than his own family — a trait not very uncommon with some sorts of men.

As people became more and more acquainted with the new-comers they joined in various degrees in the surprise which Mrs. Twilley occasionally, at some proper distance, intimated to have been felt by herself, that such a woman should have taken such a man for husband. She was not, however, a high-tempered nor a gloomy-spirited person in general. Necessity for the activity that was born with her, the practice, in the line of business, of arts, some of which made decency, cheerfulness, even studied softness of manner, indispensable to success, had hitherto kept off everything like desperation. Her face had the signs of having once been handsome; her dressing, poor as she was, was not only scrupulously neat, but stylish to a degree quite beyond what Dukesborough had been used to; and her language, though usually conducted on a subdued key, gave evidence always of being formed with careful regard to the selection of words and the pronunciation and intonation that would be of every possible advantage. Her gait was as stylish as her dress and speech; perhaps more so, for Mr. Twilley often said, and she never denied, that she was related to the Plummers, who, in former prosperous times, were as good people as any in all that region of Carolina.

The occupations of Mrs. Twilley besides domestic, when she had become well known, were various, but mostly pertained to the peculiar wants of persons of her own sex. She did indeed cut and make clothes for men and boys; yet feeling what a delicate person she was, this was not one of her favorites, but done incidentally during those intervals wherein her professional duties of which she was fondest slackened, and because, as she often declared, she could not bear to be idle. She was an adept at making and fitting ladies' garments, and the trimming of their Leghorn bonnets and green silk calashes. As for the repairing of the former, and restoring the golden sheen with which they had first come out of the store, she obtained in the very briefest time the monopoly of that business. Then she iced cakes beautifully, and her cuttings of paper-hangings for syllabub stands were said to be perfect. Further yet, Mrs. Twilley, though not claiming to have had a professional education (for, indeed, there was in those times no such thing for the sex), yet had united in her the qualities of physician and nurse to a degree that some of the ladies used to call excellent. Doctors' bills, then as now, were subjects of complaint, so that such as Mrs. Twilley, though none so often and with so satisfactory results, used to be called, particularly to women and very young children.

These, as in the matter of outward decoration, were her preferred patients. Yet to men and boys, notably in cases of rheumatism, fits, burns, and boils, she would have considered it wrong to refuse to prescribe (though always with utmost delicacy) what, with taking accentuation, she called her tinctions and dequoctions. In time she was believed to know about some cases as much as the doctors, if not more. Ladies with extremely young children found in her a physician skilful as there was commonly any need to be, a perfect nurse, a pleasant companion, sometimes a cherished confidante. Calls for her at length came even from the country. At a Saturday conference, the first she had been able to attend for some time, Mrs. Byne, who dwelt three miles south, near the hither bank of the Ogeechee, said to Mrs. Leadbetter, wife of the leading deacon,

"How I'd of ever got through what I've been through, Sister Leadbetter, and come out a live woman, hadn't been for Sister Twilley, goodness only knows. And as for my baby, its little stomach had got that wommacked up with the doctor's medicines, when it had the hives, that Mr. Byne and me give it up to die; when Sister Twilley took it, and soon as she took it, look like the poor little thing knowed who were its friend, and it hushed and begun gitting better that very minute. And Mr. Byne say hadn't been we called in Sister Twilley, the doctor's bill would of took a whole bag o' cotton. And he say furthermore, Mr. Byne do, that she's as ejicated a person as they is in Dukesborough, and I believe it, because she used a many a word that *I* didn't know the meaning of 'em. And what do Br'er Twilley do, Sister Leadbetter?"

"When," answered that lady, "well as I can gether, Sister Byne, when he ain't a-kyarrin of messenges and a totin' of news, he's a-settin' in Mr. Bland's peazer."

II.

Inactive as was the career of Mr. Twilley, it was not wholly uneventful. No valetudinarian, it is probable, except among uncommonly saintly persons, ever made less angry complaint, at least in public, against infirmities of health, than did Mr. Twilley against those which he had inherited from his renowned namesake.

"People," he would often say, "that is a everlastin' complainin' about their bad healths can't expect in reason to have enjoyment of theirselves. I've always been ag'in sech as that, 'flicted as I am, and so were Ephrodtus in the Bible thar, who my father, an' he done it o' purpose, named me arfter. *He* were sick nigh onto death, so the 'postle writ, an' yit he never complained, nor went about a-complainin'; but he got up, took the 'Postle Paul's epistle, and kyarr'd it straight to them Phlippians, who he writ it to, straight as he could go."

"Well, but, Mr. Twilley," Mr. Bland might interpose about here, "your Bible namesake got well and went at something else, didn't he? He didn't jes' confine hisself to kyarrin letters, did he? and do not a blessed thing for his livin', I hope."

"The Bible don't say so, Mr. Bland. You read it. It don't say he got well ever complete, an' never got laid up. He went on to his jooty, an' it's what I tries to do. I jes' natchul can't help from lovin' to fetch the glad tidin's, an' 'special' 'mong my brethren an' sisters, an' as for goin' reg'- lar to meetin', I'm goin' to do that long as I can git there, makes no odds if them fitty spells does come on me, an' Br'er Leadbetter and Br'er Hall has to take me out twell I can rewive an' come back."

"Were he a married man?"

"The Bible don't say so."

"Because I thought if he was he could of found something else to do besides of kyarrin letters."

"You can't put in the Bible what ain't thar already, Mr. Bland."

"Oh, I'm puttin' nothing in it. I were just a-inquirin'."

The spells alluded to by Mr. Twilley were of so frequent occurrence that the boys, and even some of the girls, were disappointed when a Sunday meeting passed without the stir they produced.

"Look out!" one would whisper, "Mr. Twilley's goin' to have one of his fits."

These occurred during the sermon, and were usually preceded by a most felicitous expression on his face, as if the unction poured down by his pastor was so abundant and sweet that he must be carried into the outer air to be relieved of a portion of its redundancy. After a few moments he would return to his seat, when, bestowing a look of thankfulness all around, he would lift up his head and begin to take the remaining supplies. It had gotten so that neither preacher nor congregation was much startled by these spells. To the younger portion of the latter they served to make the sermon appear of more endurable length. In time, however, the deacons became wearied, not that their true hearts were without sympathy, or their stalwart arms without strength, but that they were not willing, unless unavoidably, to lose any, especially the very warmest part, of their pastor's discourse. Mr. Leadbetter, the older of the two, after some reflection, thought he would appeal to Mrs. Twilley's medicinal skill for relief to all parties.

"I wonder, Sister Twilley," he said to her one day when she was visiting at his house, "that, as you helps other fitty people, you don't try an' see what you can do on Br'er Twilley."

"Laws of mercies, Brother Leadbetter!" she answered, with an indifferent smile, "them egzitements of Mr. Twilley is nothing in the world but little sprasm-fits that comes on him in meeting when he have the ideases that he is too full to hold no more. They are not paryoxims at all. If they was paryoxims, I could do somethings with him; but, as it is, you notice that when he have them I never goes a-nigh him, but sets an' listens to Brother Swinney the same as if no accident, an' which they isn't, just betwixt me and you."

Mr. Leadbetter reflected, and then said, "But, Sister Twilley, couldn't you — ahem! — couldn't you fling him — ah! what you say them tother things wuz?"

"Paryoxims, Brother Leadbetter. They are a kind of fits that *is* fits indeed, and requests clos' managings and attenchings. I has had *sometimes*, but not ofting, to throw childern into paryoxims to get those out of the whooping-cough; but it is resky, an' with grown people it's dangersome. An' as for Mr. Twilley, his case ain't a case for *females*. *I* can do no more with him than you can, and, in fact an' truth, not as much. I've tried persuadings an' adwisings, but that only fret him an' make him go to threatening. But that is dimestics matters, an' belongs to the mere little sprasm-fits that's his kinds of pets, an' which *I* can't manage no more than you can, an' not as much, an' the dilicacies of my sitooations keeps me from being prepeered to say how."

Mr. Leadbetter frowned, yet with full respect, upon the lady, but did not press either the suggestion he had made or the solution of her remarks, which were far from being satisfactory to his mind. But a few days thereafter, while Mr. Twilley was on a visit to him, and they were sitting in the piazza, he said, in a tone that, if remonstrative, meant to be regarded as affectionate also,

"Br'er Twilley, ef them fitty spells of yourn is obleeged to take you in the meetin'-house, I wish it could be so that they could be put off untwell after Br'er Swinney git through with his sermont; because, as we don't hear him but oncet a month, it stand to reason that it go ruther hard on me an' Br'er Hall to have to be a-totin' you out right in the wery hottest part, an' a-havin' the young people o' the congregation—you know how young people is, Br'er Twilley. Ahem! Now, of course, I know that 'flictions is 'flictions, an', as the 'Cluster'* say, is oft in mercy sent, yit my hopes should fain be strong that you could, as it were, you may say, brace yourself ag'in 'em, at leastways for the present time a-bein', so we can all git all we can outen the messenges Br'er Swinney fetches us."

"Br'er Leadbetter," answered Mr. Twilley, with a humble smile, "it's because I gits that full o' consolation at them messenges, that I jes' natchelly feels like runnin' over, an' *then's* the time the fits gits me."

"Jes' so, an' *ef* you could jes' only hold on an' hold in ontwell Br'er Swinney was done, it would be *sech* a ricommendation to you an' us all, Br'er Twilley, an' 'special' to me an' Br'er Hall."

"I'll do my best, Br'er Leadbetter," said the invalid, after a sad pause. "*I* no doubt Ephrodtus, that the 'Postle

---

* "Mercer's Cluster," a hymn-book used among country people.

Paul used to send his 'pistles by, tried his levellest best to git well, ef not for hisself, for his other brothrin, an' I means to do the same. My father named me arfter him, Br'er Leadbetter, an' I ben a-tryin' to foller the egzampul he sot; but I'll try harder yit from this day an' date."

"That's right! *That's* right!" said Mr. Leadbetter, with a cordiality that was gushing; "an' I no doubt you'll be thankful for doin' of it. I know me an' Br'er Hall will."

It went to show what virtue is in earnest purpose and resolute endeavor that Mr. Twilley's very next fit was postponed even until the congregation was dismissed.

"Sher!" said little Tom Beach, "sech fits as that ain't worth a copper to look at."

Said Mr. Leadbetter, "The brothrin was all gratified, thankful, 'special' me an' Br'er Hall."

III.

As if he noticed the diminution of sympathy for his belated spells, Mr. Twilley's cheerfulness in and out of church seemed to decline. He punctually, as before, continued to take his wall end of a bench near the lofty pulpit, but it began to be observed that, instead of ecstasy upon his face (pleasant to see except for the scene it used to forbode), he now regarded the preacher with a stern intensity during the first half of the discourse, and when the unction had begun to fall fairly he rested his head sometimes against the wall, more often on the bench in front, and had precisely the appearance of a person asleep. Tom Beach maintained that he *was* asleep, and, in the manner of a person resentful for an injury, said, frequently,

"Sher! them sprasm-fits he used to have, he had 'em to keep his eyes open when Miswinney was a-preachin'. He may fool Misleadbetter; he can't fool me."

The very last public prostration of Mr. Twilley took place in the front yard, and was so uneventful comparatively that Tom Beach said that if nobody would ever mention the name of old man Twilley again where he could hear it, he would be much obleeged to 'em.

But consequences quite beyond the mere diminution of cheerfulness were destined to follow the change thus brought about by so extraordinary efforts at the control of an unfortunate malady. Formerly it had been remarked that Mr. Twilley's highest pleasure in reading the newspaper published by his congregation was derived from the obituary notices of pious brethren and sisters who had departed. Acquaintance with these when in life was not at all necessary to the sweetness of the recital of their last hours. At such readings he would softly and brokenly express the request that, when he should go, some of the brethren would write to the paper, telling, among other things, how he had gone in the triumphs of the faith, especially that branch of it in which he had always been located—if he could so speak. But now even these harmless transports became more and more subdued, and whenever the subject of death in any form was mentioned in his hearing his countenance wore an expression more and more gloomy, even threatening. Mr. Hall one day mentioned to the leading elder his apprehension that Mr. Twilley was in danger of backsliding.

"Oh, I hope not," answered Mr. Leadbetter; "at least, no very fur ways. I've told Br'er Twilley ef he could find something to do besides of walkin' about an' settin' about, ef it were only a-weedin' out his wife's g'yard'n, er cuttin' wood, er fetchin' water fer her, in my opinions he'd be better off in body an' mind. He say he broke hisself down a-workin' when he were young. I hain't—jes' betwix' me an' you, Br'er Hall—I hain't been witness to his hurtin' hisself that way sence he ben here. But I hain't been afeard o' his *backslidin'*, that is, to no great extents. He have a too good of a egzample of a wife for that."

"But there it is. They tell me that here lately she ben a-tellin' him it's a shame he won't work to help support his fambly, an' that he got mad as a wet hen, an' ben a-threat-'nin' ef she didn't hush both'rin' him about work he'd— well, the words *I* heerd was, he threatened to make a widder of her."

"M-m-make—make what of her, Br'er Hall?"

"A widder."

"A wid—you mean, make a widderer of—of hisself?"

"No, *sir*. The word I heerd was *widder*."

"Why, what — why, don't the man know he couldn't make no widder of—of his own wife, no marter ef he was mean enough to try to? 'Bleeged to be some mistake some'r's o' some kind, er else the man *have* backslid, shore, an' that rapid. Something have to be done to— You cert'n in your mind, Br'er Hall, that the man use the word *widder?*"

"That's the word I heerd, Br'er Leadbetter, with my own ears, in town."

This was portion of a conversation between the deacons at their meeting in the road as Mr. Leadbetter was return- ing from a visit to his country place. His wife met him at their gate, confirming the news.

"An,' Mis' Leadbetter, ef such as that is let go on, we'll jes' have to 'bolish the church an' t'ar down the meetin'-house."

"But the question is, my dear Ninecy, what the man mean? *I* don't understan' it."

"Ner neither do me; but which make the case worse, an' make 'pear like—I come mighty nigh a-sayin' like a murricle."

"That's egzactly what it do *sound* like. I would like to know whut Br'er Twilley a-drivin' at by his remarks; but my ricommendation to you, Nineey, is to be very prudent in what you say to—to Sister Twilley."

Mr. Leadbetter had not been deacon for thirty years without finding out some things about the starting of inquiries concerning matters of importance. The more he cautioned his wife about keeping herself away from the Twilleys, the more detremined, as he foresaw, she would be to go among them. So that night, as Mrs. Leadbetter talked and talked, he sat and said little except to warn her about the repetition of his own remarks to Mrs. Twilley, while she grew more and more sure in her mind that on the very next morning, as soon as he should leave the house, on her head her bonnet should go, and straight as her feet could take her to the Twilleys there she would travel.

"And, Sister Twilley," she said, after a brief sorrowful salutation, "ef I was to tell you the truth, I don't honest think I got more'n three good fa'r winks o' sleep the blessed night last night, a-layin' awake a-thinkin' not only about you, but the case in gen'l, an' how any man person 'ith any conscions in him would want to make a widder outen his own lawful kimpanion, an' then, ef so be the case, how he 'pended on goin' about it. Mr. Leadbetter—an' he's a-readin' man, you know—he say sech a thing *can't* be 'ithout a man jes' set in an' kill hisself—jes' on'y so, out an' out."

Mrs. Twilley, remembering the ancient connection of her family with the Plummers, deliberate, careful, calm, neat in speech as in the icing of cakes, the trimming of bonnets, and the spreading of poultices, thus answered:

"I were perpeered, Sister Leadbetter, to be requested about Mr. Twilley's performans, for sech performans in the courses of times cannot be hid under bushels. The life I am now living for the present times is not of that blissful kinds that is fashionable with your families and other families in this delightful—I would fain call it city, such is my predergices for its inhabitants and populations. As for Mr. Twilley, ever since we were joined and, I may say, united in the banes of matermony, he have done nothings I can remember in my mind to help support hisself even, let alone his family. Now the not being useded, in the families I was raised, for men to do nothing whatsomever, and women do everything whatsomever for the support of rising domestic families, I have sometimes told him so in waruous words, languages, hintings, and suspishings. He at first, Mr. Twilley did, he brought up the case of the good brother in the Scripters of the Aposchil Paul, arfter whom, and I have always thought since I have knew Mr. Twilley intimate, that it was a great pity his parrents named him arfter him. When he see *they* didn't convince me, he went into the consequences of having of very small sprasm-fits. But by that time, Sister Leadbetter—for, Sister Leadbetter, I feel like I can talk to you *as* a sister—I had studied and edjecated tinctions and dequoctions to that that I never had the least ideas that them little sprasm-fits would ever come to a paryoxim, and at lengthwise I said so, or languages according to it. And now lately Mr. Twilley have been going into still more consequences, and them are that he threatened one day that if I didn't mind he would make a widow of me. Of course I were surprised, just like you was when you first heard the interesting news; and to tell the truth, I was affrightened with fears, a not understanding Mr. Twilley's meanings. But this was in foreign days, and 'special' when Brother Leadbetter requested him about putting off his emoshings in church until after the sermont, which of course he knewed, in all the circumstances of the cases, he could not unoblige and deny Brother Leadbetter, a-knowing he were the deacon, and the oldest deacon of the congregation; but which that had made him mad, and 'special' when he notussed that I were glad for the change. At first I were affrightened with fears, as I repeated to you; but when Mr. Twilley explained his opinions, and I found that he was a-talking and a-speaking of killing hisself, my mind got becalm, because I knewed that were *un*possible excepting he were to meet up with a accident. The truth is, Sister Leadbetter, Mr. Twilley is nowheres nigh being the despert and voilent man that might be supposened from such voilent and interesting remarks. But a few, a very small quantity of days ago, when I had got fatigued with my trying to get him to rise from his slumbering positions and kinditions and go to work at *some* business and ockepations as would, if no mores, feed and clothe and wash his own self, his remarks was yit more interesting; and he spoke with that voilence that Tommy Beach, when he were a-passing by our door, he were obleeged to hear him, and that is the way the news spread, I have not a doubts in my own nor any person else's minds.

"But, oh, Sister Leadbetter!" she continued, with a sad, soft smile, "one time, in former days, I were affrightened by Mr. Twilley's first open attempts, which I can now calmly call interesting, because my experiences is there never was anything in them, and never will be, excepting, as I before repeated, by a accident; but yet one day I heard a groaning in the backyard at a most *important* rate. I run to the solemn sounds, though affrightened, like the deer. There set Mr. Twilley, with a end of a rope h'isted over a chainyberry tree, around his neck, and a end in his hands, and which he made the remarks that his strenkt had give out just at the last jerk, when he wanted it the mostest, an' that he would have to stay in this vale of tears a while longer, until some other opportunities. I were a small somewhat affrightened, I acknowledge, betwixt me and you, Sister Leadbetter, but I amejiate saw the kinditions and the sitooashins. Besides, I were already at the time a-mixing of the brimstone and other ingregiencies for Sister Hall's bonnet, an' I jest could *not* afford to tarry at any such a childless scenery. The times is positive not sufficient"— the lady ended with tones and expressions indicating incipient slight fatigue — "to information you about Mr. Twilley's a-drinking, instid of the dequoction of jimson-weeds he *said* he had perpeered, from a bottle of rum and allocampane which I had tinctioned for Missis Plunket's weak stomach, and then agoing to bed a-requesting that it shall be said when he were gone that what killed him were his heart were broke, and then, when he waked up the next morning, to have to say to Simanthy that it did seem like he had as many lives as a cat, and that in my very presons, but which I set silent as the very tombstone, and that an' varous other performans in which you see how I've been fooled, though, of course, a-knowing always, both now an' in former times, that nothing is never in them, nor won't be, excepting, of course, a accident of some kind."

When Mrs. Twilley had ceased, her visitor rose abruptly.

"Sister Twilley, it *do* beat! And it's a pity but what some kind o' ac—"

But right there Mrs. Leadbetter saw that as a Christian woman she ought to restrain the words that were burning on her tongue. She sat down again, and as strictly confidential as Mr. Leadbetter had been with herself, she repeated to her hostess some of the words that had been employed by that sagacious and excellent man relating to the subject-matter now in hand. When she was about to go, and Mrs. Twilley said, "Oh, Sister Leadbetter, if it was not for my respects for thee and my love for thee," and then broke down, Mrs. Leadbetter broke down a great deal farther; and when she next saw her husband, after repeating as well as she could Mrs. Twilley's history, she said: "And you think, Mr. Leadbetter, the blessed good woman didn't call me *thee?* I *told* you she were as edjicated as the best of 'em, and now I tell you she's a saint. She could a-never of used them words to me 'ithout of bein' of one. And I set and listened to her woice for nigh on to two hours, which I think, on my soul, is sweet a'most as singin'."

"Very fine, very fine indeeds."

"It's jest another case, Mr. Leadbetter, of a man a-dissip'intin' of his lawful wife, and a-gittin' out of it with threatenin's that has nothin' in 'em but laziness."

"He have not been flung in a parrysism yit, I suppose," remarked Mr. Leadbetter, thoughtfully and rather distantly.

Mrs. Leadbetter laughed.

"The laws! Mr. Leadbetter. How you can git things wrong! They ain't parry-*sisms*, they're parry-*sosms*. And as for that, he may be flung there sooner'n he's a-expectin'. The fact is, somethin's *got* to be done to stop these proceedons, or the deacons 'll have to fetch 'em up before the Confer'nce."

"Nothing is ever made by hurryin', Nineey. My opinions is that for the present, ef Sister Twilley—I don't mean anything that's *too* projecky—but *ef* Sister Twilley could fling Br'er Twilley into say a mod'rate size one of her parrymoxums, or whatsomever she mind to call 'em, for you know she acknowledge that she know what to do with them— But all sich talk is, in course, jes' betwix' me and yon, Nincey. You understan' that, an' I want you to. It ain't—not for the present—it don't seem to me it ain't a case for the Confer'nce. My hopes is on Sister Twilley, an' her—whutsomever the things is."

Other remarks were made on this occasion by Mr. Leadbetter, in that strict confidence warranted between husband and wife.

IV.

The mind of Mr. Leadbetter was, indeed, much perplexed, mainly for the sake of the honor of the church of which he was leading deacon. The scandal of a member threatening to commit suicide was of course a matter of painful contemplation, the more so as some of the other religious denominations had been reported to be much amused at the state of things. Yet a mere threat—and that generally regarded as idle—to commit a crime was far this side, even when serious, of its perpetration. For it might be prevented by the offender's return to better thoughts, or, as now seemed Mr. Leadbetter's hope, by fortunate accidents in the case under present contemplation. So Mr. Leadbetter concluded, if not to wait, at least to hasten slowly.

One night, after a very long, burning drought, the village was visited by an abundant and most refreshing rain. On the next morning, after a plain but bountiful and excellently cooked breakfast, Mr. Twilley looked cheerful, and as if he was grateful for the sweetness shed all around.

"Mr. Twilley," said his wife, as mildly as she could to save her life, "I wish you would go in the garden and set out some cabbage-plants and potato slips, as I am busy, ockipied with Missis Taylor's cap, which I promised her she should receive by dinner-time to-day."

"I'm not well enough, and you know it," he answered, with a threatening frown.

"You are well enough for that very small vocation, Mr. Twilley," she replied, and, I must admit, with more positiveness than was her wont, for it is more than probable that after several recent interviews with Mrs. Leadbetter she had been already revolving a change of schedule in the run of her domestic life.

"Lookee here, female," said Mr. Twilley, fiercely, with that stern courage so habitual in his family, "you've come a-mighty nigh bein' made a widow many a times. You want to be one before your time come?"

"I've been a-thinkin' on the exper'ences of widows, Mr. Twilley," she answered, with restored mildness, "and a-seeing in my mind's eye how much comfortabler and pleasanter some of them passes their days away than some others that has the names of being married, that I don't know, and am not quite certain that I am perpeered to make a changing expeer'ment, if so be it—it should be my lots."

Then she rose, opened her cupboard, took out a carving-knife, sharpened it upon a whetstone that lay near, felt with her fingers the edge of the blade, soliloquized, " I think that will preform the business ;" then said, yet calm, but with awful solemnity,

"Mr. Twilley, you has put those threat'nings on me several times for lo those many years, an' you has tried to carry them into performance for lo those several times, with hanging yourself with ropes and strings of several size, with taking a various and deffer'nt kind of tinctions and dequoctions, an' a-running heads-foremost against the back garding fence where the palings was off, an' you had, of course, to merrily go through the gap, an' other var'ous intentions which did not peduce your desired effects. I have now sharpened this knife, an' you may both see and feel for yourself that the aige is keen, an' one single wipe across your th'oat will make the widow it seem your desires to see, an' I'll promise you to not raise a finger to pervent it."

By this time Mr. Twilley had risen, and as she advanced, proffering the instrument temptingly before him, he backed to the front door, down the steps to the gate, kicked it open from behind, backed through the opened space, wheeled, then fled amain.

Mr. Leadbetter sat in his piazza; his open Bible lay in his lap; his spectacles drooped far down on his nose; his eyes were closed. For the grateful rain had invited first to read in the precious volume, and in the midst to sleep.

"Distracted, Br'er Leadbetter! ravin' distracted!" cried Mr. Twilley between breaths as he ascended the steps.

"Distracted? Who? You?" repeated Mr. Leadbetter, roused from sleep, and rising to his feet.

"Me? No, sir!"

"Well, ef you shore it *ain't* you, set down and tell me about it."

When the story was through, ending with a plaintive appeal for advice, Mr. Leadbetter, after a few moments of rumination, said, "Seem to me, Br'er Twilley, ef it was me, I'd go back home, and in as gentleman'y way as I knowed how I'd go to settin' out them cabbage and potato slips, and arfter that I'd never much as fling out a hint about my wife bein' of a widder in no shape nor form. To be honest with you, Br'er Twilley, sech news as you've brung wouldn't of took me by sech surprise exceptin' I had drap off in a nod, as my head got ruther heavy a-follerin' the 'Postle Paul in his argiments ag'in the fallin' from grace. Because you ought to know by good rights, Br'er Twilley, that widders ain't like tother female winmning; they're a independenter set of people altogether, and a-includin' them that ain't widders in fact, but which thar husbands flings out his threats to that effect, an' which wimming 'll get tired arfter a while of listenin' to sech, continual an' everlastin', an' they'll get independenter than the good Book allows married wimming to be, an' they *is* danger that in the course o' time they'll git so they think they about as soon be widders as not, an' maybe some ruther, an' other have no kimpanion at all, or stand their chances for one that's more to their notion than them they got now. I'm a older man than what you are, Br'er Twilley, some; an' I've had a expeunce of wimming, an' been a-studyin' of 'em ever sence I knowed myself, you may say. Why, sir, ef I was to fling out constant of threats to make a widder of my wife, she'd up and say, arfter a while, ' Well, Mr. Leadbetter, why don't you go 'long an' do it ?' but which I hain't never used them words yit, nor am not a-goin' to. An' so, tharfore, I in your place, I'd go home and make like I done forgot all about my wife pokin' the k'arvin-knife handle-foremost at me, an' I'd go to settin' out them plants and slips, an' which it won't do to put 'em off. I ben at that business myself long before breakfast, an' it ain't through with yit."

At that moment Mrs. Leadbetter, sticking-fork in hand, appeared at the front door.

"Lookee here, Mr. Leadbetter, them plants an' slips— why, howdy, Br'er Twilley ? You've all sot out yourn, I s'pose; got no time to tarry; come on, Mr. Leadbetter, soon as you an' Br'er Twilley through your talks." And away she went.

"Thar, now. See how 'tis, Br'er Twilley ? The creeters is made so, an' a man have to do the best he ken."

"Is he goned ?" asked Mrs. Leadbetter, with a smile, when her husband, a few moments afterwards, joined her.

"Oh yes. Sister Twilley, shore enough, flung him in one

of her parrymoxims. I give him some few gentle cautions, an' you flung in a binder yourself."

"I aimed at it," she replied.

V.

Mr. Twilley returned with slowness, inversely proportioned to the speed with which he had advanced. He took notice all along that the men of the village generally were availing themselves of the gracious season by opportune work in their front yards, and especially their gardens.

"Cabbage an' pertaters is bound to be plenty this year," he soliloquized, "if there's anything in plantin'." On reaching home he paused at the gate, and possibly hoped for an invitation from his wife to enter, as she sat in the piazza. But she was busy with Mrs. Taylor's cap, and did not appear to notice him. He uttered a very loud sigh; then, passing on to a corner of the yard, turned and proceeded to the back lot, through which having passed into the garden, he took off his coat and sorrowfully went to work.

Mr. Leadbetter was gratified by the results of the counsel he had given with various degrees of directness. The paroxysm into which Mr. Twilley had been thrown effected as much of a cure as was possible to human agency in a case so chronic. Henceforth, instead of being resolute to make a widow of his wife, he tried to pay to her every wish a deference that led to the suspicion that he feared that on some exciting occasion she might conclude to make a widow of herself, and painful as was even the thought of doing any sort of domestic work, it was less so than the alternative. His wife, having acquired a just ascendency by heroic employment of her medical skill, held it with a resolution as firm as it was mild. It would have been pitiful, but for being funny, to notice Mr. Twilley's feeble efforts to be—at least to appear—industrious. Fortunately for his wife, though to the regret of the villagers, who without exception had grown to admire and respect her much, she received and accepted from a dry-goods merchant at Augusta an offer to take charge of an annex of millinery which he had made to his store.

"Are you a-intending to proceed along with me, Mr. Twilley?" she asked, in a tone that had grown even more subdued and calm since the establishment of her power.

"Why, the laws of mercy, Sylvy! In course! What else—"

"All right. I only wished to know your desires, your intentions, and your kinclusions. If them are they, I'll take you along with the rest of the furnitoors, what few I've got."

He did not say thanky, ma'am, but he felt it. True to her promise, she hauled him off with the other things. He departed, waving a humbly cheerful good-by to all whom the wagon met.

We heard from the family occasionally. Mrs. Twilley grew more and more in favor with her employer. Her reluctance to part from the practice of her medicinal acquirements was compensated by generous returns for her single occupation. After her husband's discharge of the easy domestic tasks she imposed, she kindly allowed him to go where he pleased, and while thus abroad do what he pleased. True to his traditions, his fondest active service was the carriage of messages among the new brethren. In good time Simanthy married, and married well, and most cordially was her father wont to congratulate himself in every presence (except that of Mrs. Twilley) for the great and successful pains with which he had brought her up.

DR. HINSON'S DEGREE.

"Wounds by wider wounds are healed."—*Hudibras.*

Dr. Hinson had been ordained, after a reasonable license term, to preach, not so much from consideration of special fitness for the exalted calling, as from certain vague apprehensions among the brethren of what might ensue if they heeded not solemn assurances on the part of one of their members that he had received in private unmistakable calls thereto from Heaven. He was not then a doctor, nor did he get his degree either from the reputation of possessing great theological learning or from the faculty of any college of medicine. Yet he was a man of quite pronounced character, bold in the assertion and maintenance of his opinions, and always ready for anybody who expressed a desire to fight him. Though plucky to the last degree, he was not notably vigorous of body nor skilful in combat. It must happen, therefore, sometimes that his adversaries were too much for him. Whenever this was the case, he would cry out in perfect honesty, "Enough!" or "Take him off!" or utter other expressions that indicated his wish for the struggle to be suspended for the present. Yet afterwards, when well rested, he would repair to the field and confidently and defiantly ask for more.

He was a native of the pine region of North Carolina,

and, like all true patriots, was proud of the country that had given him birth. Having settled on the head-waters of the Ogeechee, though he owned a tip-top piece of undulating oak and hickory land, he habitually expressed regrets for the pine levels of his native State, and often he was heard to say that but for an occasional pine-tree (though absurdly short leaf) that grew in his woodland he would return to the banks of Tar River and spend the remnant of his days by the fireside so cheaply warmed and illumed.

After they made him a preacher, his sermons, as well as I can gather from tradition, were not so notable as his prayers. It was in family prayer particularly that he became rather notorious. He never denied being fond of good eating, and whenever he stopped for the night at a brother's house, and the supper was uncommonly nice, he would allude to it in his prayer in thankful phrase that sometimes rose into heartiest encomium on the sister who had provided it. For instance, they used to say of him that, on one occasion when he was tarrying for the night with Brother Daniel Cofer, a small fair man, with a large dark wife, he was exalted to an uncommonly high degree of sweetness, and he intimated to Sister Cofer, on rising from the supper-table, that when bedtime should come, she would hear from him. And sure enough she did. Indeed, Sister Cofer, good, honest woman that she was, said afterwards, in salutary confidence, to a large number of the sisterhood that "Br'er Hinson was a'most too much took up with the supper, and he used not enough words about the conwersion o' sinners, an' 'special' the poor heatherners."

"The fact o' the business is," said Mrs. Cofer, "I were ruthur nonplushed, as the sayin' is, when Br'er Hinson put up his pra'ars an' thanksgivin's specially for the rice and milk we had for supper. In co'se he have considible to say about the fried an' br'iled chicken, the biscuits an' muffins an' hoe-cake, an' the sweet milk, buttermilk, an' clabber, but it 'pear like the rice an' milk were what went more perkindickler to his stomach than any the t'other things; an' he thes' let out on it an' them, an' he ast the good Lord to bless Jincy Cofer all over her, all around her, from the top to the bottom of her, an' that he didn't believe there were a woman livin' could beat her on rice an' milk. An' then he ast the good Lord to bless Jincy Cofer, not only in her goin's out an' her comin's in, not only in her husbon' an' childern, but in her housle an' kitchen furnicher. Did you ever! But it were right funny, solemn as it all were, when he praise Mr. Cofer for havin' choosed me for a wife, an' all I could do, on my very knees, as I were—all I could do to keep from smilin' when he stop in his pra'ar an' say to Mr. Cofer, 'That's right, Dan. Always pick out a big, yaller-skin cow to give good milk.' Did you ever! I were the nigher a-smilin' (which in co'se I know a body oughtn't do right on their knees), because I know sech as that ruther shock Mr. Cofer, who say, to his opinions, they is mighty little religion in it. But I tell him never mind. Br'er Hinson ain't perfec'; but who is perfec'? that's the queschin."

His residence was near the boundary-line of two counties, in both of which dwelt several men who were fond of horse-racing, cock-fighting, and other such sports. At a place known until now as the Battery, very near this line, conflicts of many kinds used to be had. The annals of border warfare have no names more cordially true to tribe and clan than was Dr. Hinson to the men of his ilk. He had been so before he became a preacher. He so continued when he ascended into the pulpit.

"No, no, no!" he would say, often in pious and patriotic fervor, "I ain't o' them kind o' religion that hender people from stannin' up to their own side, right or wrong. I'm for them Bradfids, an' I'm agin them Alsans. I'm a minister o' the Gospil now, an' therefore I can't pit chickens; but I can pray; an' I shall kintinue to pray that Bradfid's chickens 'll put the gaff on them Alsans, every pop, an' my opinions is that my pra'ars has been ansered of'n an' of'n, an' I hain't a doubt they'll be ansered ag'in."

I mention parenthetically that John Kinney, a partisan of the Alsans, used to say, in his tongue-tied phrase,

"We wath alwayth glad when old Hinthon got down on hith kneeth agin us. One fight we had at the Battery, the firth day we had bad luck thomehow, and every chicken we pit got whipped. That night old Hinthon put up one of hith biggith. It were a kind of camp-meetin' pra'ar, or quarterly meetin', or thomethin' on that order of buthneth, and he thanked Godamighty that the Althins have got one good tholid whippin' whith he hoped an' prayed might latht 'em. Thore enough, the very nexth day our chickenth left every one of their'n dead in the pit, and which go to thow me that Godamighty don't ever lithen to seth prayin', nor don't condethend to have nothin' to do with 'em."

Nearest neighbor to Dr. Hinson was Smith Brookins. Smith was from Virginia, somewhere, he did not and cared not to know exactly where; but he was proud of a native country that had reared so many illustrious men. He used to give as an excuse for not having become illustrious himself, that his native State was so far ahead on that line that for one he was willing to wait until others, especially poor old North Carolina, could at least make a start, if without hope of ever being able to catch up. Mr. Brookins either believed, or affected to believe, that the people in North Carolina spent their time mainly in gathering resin, or rawsom, as he called it. Now, the only use he had ever known rawsom put to was chewing, and of that he admitted that from a child he had been fond. He and Dr. Hinson used to have many a discussion upon the relative importance of their native States. "The queschin 'ith me is," he would say, "what in the names o' all creation people wants 'ith so much rawsom. Do they jes' do nothin' but set down all the time, Hinson, and chaw it?"

This question Mr. Hinson had answered a thousand times, more or less, but he kept on answering it until it ceased to be put.

"Smith," he would say, with a solemnity that never tired, "the idee that people done nothin' else on the top o' the ground but gether rawsom, an' that for nothin' else on the good Lord's blessed yearth but chawin', is what I don't hardly believe they is a man in this whole country exception o' you would believe. I ain't a-sayin' anythin' now about the tobarker that North Callina raise, but which it's as good as the very best in old Virginny. Nor I ain't a-goin' to make the slightest illudin to the wheat, an 'the corn, an' the oats, an' the rye, an' the—an' the—no, sir, I won't even call the names of the ten thousand other things that she pejuce. A man like you couldn't 'member 'em if I was to call 'em. An' then agin, a man that don't know that they is other use for rawsom than the jes' a *chawin'* of it, sech a man ain't liable to have any rights to be told any better, in spite o' the thousands an' the millions o' money that is made in the getherin' o' it." Such and similar discussions were often held between these two. It was always remarkable how interesting to each other are men of widely variant experiences. That of the one serves often as a foil to whatever is wanting in the other. Although almost always disputing, these neighbors were good friends. Mr. Brookins often said that he never could understand how it was that he liked as well as anybody a man that had come out of such a rawsom State as North Carolina, and Mr. Hinson, when people would be bragging on old Virginia, would refer to his neighbor, Smith Brookins, as a fair specimen of what that boastful State was wont to produce. It was always interesting to hear the one in efforts to justify himself for having been born in North Carolina, and not less so to listen to the other's apologies for not being more competent to represent in his own career the ancestral glories of Virginia. The volume of understanding lay decidedly with the North Carolina man, and its legitimate influence went along after it. The Virginian was often swayed when he was not conscious of it, but neither had ever so much as dreamed that one would ever become the occasion of the other's attainment of a learned degree.

Mr. Brookins had always been a man of uncommon vigor and activity. He was also industrious and thrifty. If once in a while he became what they used to say "disguised" with one or more over-drinks of whiskey or peach-brandy, he thought it was nobody's business. Nor did Mr. Hinson make this infirmity *his* business, for besides being a liberal man in his opinions of such matters, he would take his own toddy before breakfast or at other convenient times, though it was never said of him that he went too far with it.

As to how Mr. Brookins received the hurt upon one of his legs that afterwards grew so serious, my recollection is that it was never definitely known. *He* always claimed that it came while he was log-rolling in his new ground, the handstick slipping and grazing the skin to a considerable and rather ragged extent. There were those who said they knew better as to the origin, and some went to the extent of hinting that while it may have been true that the injury was received in Mr. Brookins's new ground, it was at night, and when he had gotten there unintentionally while on his way home from a battalion muster. However it came, there the sore was, and there it stayed. After fair trial of the ointments administered by several elderly ladies in the neighborhood who laid claim to skill in such cases, Mr. Brookins called in Dr. Pepper, who said, after working on him for two months without sensible improvement, that the difficulty was to get out the poison that had been put there by old women. One of these being aunt to Mrs. Brookins, the latter's feelings were hurt by the remark, and through her influence Dr. Lancy was sent for. After a three months' treatment, he said for the fiftieth time,

"Smith, the difficulty with this leg of yours is that you let another doctor (I shall mention no names) project with it too far. If this leg had been brought to me six months ago I'd have had you sound as a dollar long ago."

The case was becoming very serious.

"That's the way these doctors will talk," said Mrs. Brookins one day, both distressed and offended. "Dr. Pepper laid the blame on 'old women,' as he call 'em, when he know he were a-meanin' mostly Aunt 'Viny, which she done more for that leg than ever did, an' left it worse off than he found it. Then come Dr. Lancy, and he lay the blame on Dr. Pepper, an' thar it is."

"An' yit," said Mr. Hinson, who happened to be there on a visit, "both them men hails from old Virginny, Smith. I would of supposed that a Virginny doctor would be able to cuore a scratch that a feller got on his leg jest accidental that way. I thought Old Virginny doctors was enough for whatsomever waouns and diseases might happen to the human family of all mankind."

Then the man actually laughed.

Such apparent heartlessness would have offended Mr.

Brookins except for the freedom of his and his visitor's intercourse, and the assurance he felt that there was no want of sympathy. Besides, Mrs. Brookins's mother was a North Carolina woman, who was not only not ashamed, but was proud of her native State. So Mr. Hinson felt himself to be, as he was, perfectly safe in the utterance of these words.

"Well, Hinson," said Mr. Brookins, petulantly, "dadfetch it, what's a feller to do?"

"Can't you ast a queschin 'ithout cussin', Smith, an' 'special' on sech a scrous subjick?"

"I didn't know 'dadfetch it' was cussin'."

"You didn't? Well, sech as that is all cussin', an' it's a sin, an' 'special' it's a sin 'ith them that has the sore leg that a Virginny doctor, two of 'em at that, can't cuore, an' which I tell you now, and I tell Missis Brookins, which is your own blessed wife, that if that leg ain't cuored, an' that in no long time, it'll have to be took off."

"My laws of mercies!" exclaimed Mrs. Brookins; "in the name of goodness, what are we to do?"

"I can cuore it in five minutes arfter I git fixed for it," he answered, with as cool indifference as if he would have said that he could walk to his own home, a mile distant.

"Whyn't you done it, then?" demanded Mr. Brookins.

"You never ast me."

"I didn't know you was a doctor."

"Nor I ain't; but I seen too many o' them kind o' things in North Callina not to know egzact what that leg o' yourn need. People that spends their time much in the woods a getherin' turpentine is liable to jes' sech accidents as yourn every constant, an' they don't have to go to Old Virginny nor send for a doctor from thar to have 'em 'tended to; but they 'tend to 'em theirselves."

"How—name o' goodness!—how, Hinson?"

"That's jes' what I'm not goin' to tell you."

His indifference seemed cooler even than at first.

"Why won't you tell him, Mr. Hinson?" asked the wife, in a tone that showed she was hurt.

"Because, Mrs. Brookins, Smith Brookins's not goin' to 'tend to hisself the way I tell him. Fact, he couldn't."

"Well, couldn't I?"

He reflected a moment and then dubiously answered,

"Well — ah — n - no, ma'am, Missis Brookins, I don't think—I ruther think you couldn't."

"Well, my opinion is," said Mr. Brookins, wishing to be satirical, "that a preacher of the Gospel, ef he have no feelin's in genil, ought to try to have some little feelin's for a man in my fix."

"It ain't a queschin o' feelin's, Smith Brookins. I mayn't have enough o' them to suit you, but that's my lookout. The queschin, as I understand it now, is, Do you want me to cuore that leg o' your'n; an', if so be, will you let me do it in my way?"

"Of course he will, Mr. Hinson. I'll see that he do," said the wife.

"All right; I'll go home an' fix, an' be here in an hour."

"No foolishness, Hinson. This ain't a case for rawsomchawin' ner doin' anythin' else 'ith your old North Callina projeckins."

"Ain't it astonishin', Missis Brookins, the ign'ance o' some people? Why, your own blessed mother can tell Smith Brookins that they is men in North Callina whose mainest business is to gether rawsom, as he call it, that could buy out fifty such men as Smith Brookins an' not miss the money out o' their pocket-book. But that don't hender him from bein' liable to have that leg cuored, which if it ain't done it'll have to be took off, an' then, when his wife take a notion to run away from him, won't it be a sight, him a hoppin' arter to ketch her?"

This joke put all in good-humor. Within the time set Mr. Hinson returned, riding his white mare, Snowy.

"What's that the handle of a-pokin' out o' your pocket, Hinson?" asked Mr. Brookins.

"Never you mind: it's one of my apparatuses. Smith Brookins, what I'm goin' to do 'll hurt for jes' about two minutes and three-quarters and no longer; an' to do this job effecuil, I got to lay you on your back on the work-bench thar by the kitchen, an' then I got to tie your hands and the foot o' your game leg, an' then blindfold you."

"No, sir; no, sir."

"All right; good-mornin' to you both. When the leg is took off, Missis Brookins, I hope, as Smith have no Christian fortichudes, he'll leastway a-try to bear it well as sech a man ken. Good-mornin' to you both."

As he was turning to depart, Mrs. Brookins earnestly besought her husband to submit, as it did seem to be the only chance to save his limb. At length he yielded to her entreaties, after repeated solemn assurance from Mr. Hinson that there was no danger nor very prolonged pain to be incurred from the treatment, and that he should be released almost immediately after its performance. He had to submit to a further requisition that his wife was to remain in the house until called for.

When the patient had been tied, blindfolded, and laid on his back upon the work-bench, the physician, entering the kitchen, dismissed the cook, took from his pocket a small ladle which, after putting a small piece of tallow into it, he set on the burning coals. Returning, he made, with a pan of water, mud from the clay, and began applying it circularly around the wound.

"Gee-er-roos-rooslum! Hinson," said the prostrate man, "that's co-cold as thunder. What in the dickence is you a doin'? I never 'spected to be, that is not quite, in the fix I am now."

"Yes, Smith Brookins," answered Mr. Hinson, rather severely. "I knowed it would feel cool. But my intentions is to try an' take off in about two minutes an' a half some of the aige o' the cold. What I am doin' for the present is makin' around your waounds, bruises, as the Scripter says, an' purtefyin' soreses, is a kind of a wolcano, but which you in your ign'ance would call a doodle-hole. I has no futher remarks to make on that head of my present disco'se."

When the volcano was finished Mr. Hinson returned to the kitchen, took the ladle off the coals, swiftly yet without precipitation returned to the work-bench, and then— But there was wisdom in the advice given by Horace to the young Pisos not to bring everything before the public. I confine myself to reporting a few remarks.

"When I heard the shout," said Dave Towns, a half-mile neighbor, "I says to my wife, 'That's Smith Brookins's woices, an' somethin's gone wrong over thar cert'n shore.'"

Jim Lary, who was yet farther on beyond Little Ogeechee, said, "Upon my heart an' soul, the sound o' Smith Brookins's hollerin'—well, all I can say is, when Mr. Hinson come gallopin' along from thar it seem to me he were what them preachers call death on a white horse. I couldn't but ast him to pause for a few minutes an' norate the awful skene. Coold as a cowcumber he stop and say, 'Jim, the de-ficulty 'ith Smith were his leg, which, as you know, nobody could do nothin' with. Him an' his wife is people I like spite o' Smith's everlastin' pedigices agin things he know nothin' about. But I see that leg o' his'n have to be cuored or took off, an' I knowed the ways the doctor was a-doin' 'ith her, she were obleeged to go. So, accordin' to his request an' his wife's, I took her in hand, an' I burnt her out 'ith hot toller. I told Mrs. Brookins that I has converted the waound on Smith's leg to nothin' on the top o' the ground but a burn; an' that she know for herself that nobody were better than her own blessed Aunt Viny on them. Say you heerd Smith? I ain't a-wonderin'. His woice split the very a'r o' heaven, an' as for his cussin', I dare not try to remunerate them. But Smith Brookins's goin' to love me next to his wife and children; you see if he don't.' "

The prediction was verified, for the cure was complete. The resuscitated invalid, when he next met the man who had cured him, called him "Doctor Hinson," and the title remained with him ever afterwards.

One day Mr. Lary asked of Mr. Brookins, seeing him kicking playfully with his new leg, "It must of ben awful astonishin,' Smith. How did you feel when he were craptin' his hot toller on you? What did you think it were?"

"As for feelin's, Jim, no use a feller tryin' to tell his feelin's when he find hisself an' in the dark a fryin' same as a rasher o' bak'n. My wife say she hope I won't be hilt 'sponsible for all the cussin' I done before Hinson have set on old Snowy an' galloped off. As for what I thought of what he put on me, well, I knowed it were fire, an' for a minute I thought it were also brimstone."

THE MEDIATIONS OF
MR. ARCHIE KITTRELL.

"And thanne with here scharpe speris stronge
They foyneden ech at other."—*The Knightes Tale.*

I.

THE traditions respecting the origin of the name "Hello" of a certain militia district in one of the older counties of Middle Georgia are so ancient and variant that I do not feel myself called upon, at least in this connection, to recite them. My present purpose is to tell of a few persons resident therein at a period many years back, while Josiah Cofield, Esq., presided in the Justice's Court. This magistrate had long considered himself as familiar as any judge need be with principles governing judicial trials. The drift of cases wherein his rulings had been reversed on *certiorari* to the Superior Court had been mainly in the line of exceptions taken to his jurisdiction, about the limits of which he was suspected to be not without the jealousy common to all tribunals not the highest. His temptation to overstep was perhaps enhanced by an enormous fondness for his court costs. It was his habit, therefore, to put upon his docket all cases brought by persons known by him to be responsible for these, without concerning himself about the eventual disposition of the condemnation-money.

I make these observations regarding him preparatory to the introduction of some persons of yet more importance.

Fully a mile above, owner of a considerable body of land, extending as far as the fork where William's and Turkey creeks merge their waters and their names in Long Creek, dwelt Mr. Archie Kittrell, now well spent in years, yet with gratifying remains of strength and activity, bodily and mental. His estate was bounded on the east by Turkey Creek and the Peevys, on the west by William's and the Templins.

It had been fortunate heretofore, for both the Peevys and Templins, that such a man as Archie Kittrell resided between them. In a hill region the number is limited of those who can live persistently, without any hurt to friendly neighborhood, on opposite sides of a creek-line. A benevolent and usually a remarkably calm man was Mr. Kittrell, although it was known that he could become excited on occasion. For very many years he had held not only peaceful but most friendly relations with these neighbors, in spite of the varying channels that the two streams often made before reaching the confluence where the Long began its straightforward, determined course to the Ogeechee. He put his fences sufficiently behind high-water mark, and instead of complaining of infringements upon doubtful riparian soil, he was often known to express placid sympathy when the Templin or the Peevy fence, on occasions of extraordinary rains, would resolve itself into its constituent elements, and every rail go madly rushing in search of more reliable shores. Both Mr. Templin and Mr. Peevy had deceased some years age; but their relicts were women of much energy, and with aid of the counsels of their intermediate friend managed their estates to much advantage.

What separated these ladies yet further than the two

creeks was their difference in religious faith. Three miles north of the fork stood the William's Creek Baptist Church, so named partly from its geographical position, but mainly, as was suggested by one of the deacons at its foundation, because, like Enon of old, there was much water there. One mile south of the fork, on a high land, at the foot of which was a noble spring of water, was the Methodist meeting-house, younger than its rival, and weaker in membership. Its name was Big Spring.

The Templins worshipped at the upper, and the Peevys at the lower house. Both these ladies were pronounced in doctrinal opinions, and therefore neither visited the other often, though each was very familiar at the Kittrells's. If they had been of the same religious faith, they must have been cordial friends. As it was, each must sometimes warm into temporary resentment when one would hear of uncharitable words expressed by the other concerning herself or her meeting-house. It had been observed that such misunderstandings had increased considerably of late, and notably since Miss Priscilla Mattox had been sojourning in the neighborhood.

Whatever worship the Kittrells did was mainly beneath their own vine. Mr. Kittrell, his wife, and his two sons, William and Joseph (always called Buck and Jodie), attended service at both meeting-houses, and though not professors, were as good respecters of religion as the best. Hopes had been indulged, I dare not say how long, by the William's Creek people that Mrs. Kittrell, whose mother in her time was a Baptist, might feel it her duty, before it would be too late, to knock at their door.

"As perfect a patron of a woman as is," Mrs. Templin would often say, "ef she were jest only a Babtis, and which she can't but be obleeged to know it's her juty to foller her own blessed mother that she can have no doubts of her being of now a saint in heaven."

As for Mr. Kittrell, who was at least a score of years older than his wife, it was quite possible that some of the delay in his Church affiliation was due to the thoughtful apprehension that any action in that matter so pronounced on the

JODIE WAS FOND OF VISITING.

part of so great a man might impart to the denomination with which he should connect himself a preponderance that might operate discouragingly upon the other, particularly in the case of his two nearest neighbors. His views and expectations in this behalf, thus far, had not become known to the public, who were wont to speculate that avowed opinions and definite action would depend, if ever to exist at all, upon accidents possible to occur on the borders of the two creeks. The lads—Buck, nearly twenty-one, and Jodie, turned of nineteen—not only went habitually to both meeting-houses, but they were specially fond of visiting at the Templin and Peevy mansions. For this fondness no person ever could have had the face to blame them; no person, I mean, who had seen and known what fine girls were Caroline Templin, aged sixteen, and Sarah Ann Peevy, fifteen years, each only surviving child and heir-presumptive of her mother.

II.

Although nobody ever had any doubt as to the pride that Mr. Kittrell had in his wife, his two sons, and his fine plantation so snug in the fork, yet this pride was never or seldom a matter of distinct public avowal. Not so that he felt in being nigh neighbor to such women as Mrs. Templin and Mrs. Peevy.

"A couple of as fine females and widders as any man mout ever express his desires to go anywheres, makes no defuerence wheres, and locate hisself, and settle hisself, and live neighbor to the said female persons as I've done every sense ary one or both o' their husbands took sick and diseased from this mortual speres. One of 'em's a Babtuis, and the tother a Methudis, and thar they're both as solid as two bricks sot in mortar in two sip'rate chimblies; but nother that ner them henders nary one of 'em from of bein' of two as fine females and widders as this county, nor as to that, this whole State o' Georgy, can pejuce. Ef they wants, and it's thar desires to stand up to thar warous Churches, and they feels it thar juty to argy for 'em, whose bisuiness is it to hender

"AND I'M A-NAMIN' O' NO NAMES."

'em? and speshual them that takes it on theirselves (and I'm a-namin' o' no names) to go about a-repeatin' of what one have said about the tother, and her sanctufication and her fallin' from grace, and what the tother say in respects of her finual pesseveunce o' the saints, and her dippin' or her pourin' o' water, mo' or less? Ef people 'd keep thar mouth shet about them two fine wimming (and 'member, I'm a-namin' o' no names), they'd be as friendly 'ith one 'nother as they both are and is 'ith my wife; and anyhow, I say it open and above board, I knows not ner I don't know the equils o' them nor nary one of 'em. And, as for Calline Templing and Sarann Peevy, ef I wer'n't a ole man as I am, an' already got my quimpanion, my opinions o' them childern is, I wouldn't posuitive, I wouldn't know how ner when ner which to forbar."

Benevolent, calm man as was Mr. Kittrell, he had withal an eye ever watchful for the interests of his family. That eye, for many years, had been growing more and more watchful until now, when he was sure in his mind that the time had come for him and his boys to move towards the consummation of a project that was the very nearest to his heart. From time to time he had sounded Buck and Jodie together and apart. He was delighted with the exquisite modesty and slyness with which he had discovered to them his own plans, and the facility which they, dutiful, splendid boys as they were, suffered themselves to be put forward by himself. But he knew that they were very young, and somehow both, especially Jodie, had inherited rather more of their mother's sentiment and artlessness than he considered quite well for perfectly successful careers, in what he would have styled "in a bisuiness pint of view," and that his own aged and wise head must take the lead. He always talked freely with his wife, who was a woman of few words, and whom he well knew to have been ever thankful for having married, when a poor girl, a man of his property and intelligence, and therefore was a most faithful recipient of his confidences.

"I jes' tell you, Jincy, what the fact o' the bisuiness is. The good Lord never flung these three plantations in the siticooation they are, and is and has been every sense I've knowed 'em, and a-diwidued out the childern that's now are of a-waitin' to be thar ars and egzekitors, so to speak o' the case at the present bare, 'ithout he'd of had some meanin' of His idees along of all up an' down, in an' out, along both o' the banks o' them crooked an' oncertain meanduerin creeks. For I hain't the littlest idee myself but what He have freckwent got tired o' hearin' o' the everulastin' fussin's o' people that has creek-lines both betwix' an' between, and no yeend of 'sputin' about water-gaps, and stock a-breakin' in bottom fields, and which, tweren't I were a peasuable man, I mout of been cats and dogs with both them wimming; and they ain't no doubt about it in my mind but what these three plantations oughtn' to be—finally, I mean—they oughtn't to be—but two, with the lines a-tuck off'n them creeks and run into one line high and dry plump through the middle o' this one, and Buck, him a-havin' o' the Turkey Creek side, and Jodie, him the Williamses, when *in* co'se my head and yourn git cold, and the famblies, both they and them and Buck and Jodie, a-nunited and jinded together in sich a jint and—well, I would not say compactuous way, that nobody nor nothin' exceptions o' death *er* debt could never sip'rate 'en no mo' ner never henceforrards. And it's perfec' plain to my mind —for I've been a-pickin' all of around of both o' them boys, and it's perfec' plain to my mind that they both has and have the same priminary idees, only they're nary one o' the pushin' kind o' boys, I would of some of ruther of saw, and in which they don't take arfter the Kittrells quite as much as I should desires, and mo' arfter the Kitchenses; not that, as you monstrous well knows, my dear honey, that my wife were a Kitchens, and no man never got a better, but which a-not-'ithunderstandin' them boys is the obeduentest and splendidenest boys in this county, and them wimming and them gals is obleeged to know the same, only it's a marter that need pushin', because they're all grownded, at leastways in size, and it's a marter that it ain't to be kep' a-puttin' off."

Mrs. Kittrell listened with the usual profound deference to her husband, and ventured only a remark that they were all very young, and that, as for her part, her ideas had always been that marriages were made in heaven.

Mr. Kittrell smiled benevolently at suggestions that he knew were not intended to be pressed, and revolved how he was to begin. At supper that night he grew more assured than ever when Buck had so much to say in special praise of the Turkey Creek side. Jodie said but little about either of the girls. But Mr. Kittrell knew the peculiar modesty of Jodie. Besides, intending himself to lead in the important enterprise, he did not know but what he rather preferred not to be embarrassed by too great a multitude of counsel, even in his own family.

"But, my dear," said Mrs. Kittrell, when Buck and Jodie had retired, "hadn't we better let them boys manage for theirselves? Because I'm not shore—"

"My dear Jincy," interrupted Mr. Kittrell, not impatiently, but with the decisiveness of tone which a great man employs when he is talking with an inferior being. "WE— yes; *we*. *You'll* have to keep still as a mouse, and lay low. This here case take a man o' expeunce and observation, and it won't do to be meddled with. You don't mean to insinooate that them boys ain't speshual fond o' them gals, Jincy?"

"Oh no; but I ain't adzactly made up in my mind as to which—"

"'Nough said," Mr. Kittrell again interrupted, waving his hand. "Stick a pin right thar, and keep her stuck; lay low and wait and see what a man o' expeunce and obser-wation can do."

It would not be possible to express the kind condescension with which these words were uttered. The consciousness of being one of the greatest of mankind was not able to make Mr. Archie Kittrell forget what was due to the mother of his children.

III.

On the following day Mr. Kittrell rode extensively over his domain. He had been heard often to say that of the thinking he had done—and he might go far enough to say that, in his opinion, his friends and neighbors would bear him out in claiming to have done a right smart of thinking in his day and generation—the biggest part had been done on horseback. On this day, therefore, he made what he would have styled a perusual of his whole plantation, after which he crossed both creeks consecutively on visits to his nearest neighbors.

"And how is Missuis Templing this fine mornin' like? Busy, I see; busy as a bee, if she'll take the rhyme in time, though I don't but sildom make 'em, at leastways not intentual. And whar's Calline? Gone to see Sarann, eh? All right, bless her heart. Look so well, neighbors' children a-wisitin, when they too busy and too much occuepied to wisit tharselves."

Mrs. Templin, now about fifty years of age, stout and comely, was noted for good house-keeping and hospitality. If she was somewhat aggressive in the matter of her religious faith, it was, as she often candidly contended, from no reason on the good Lord's blessed earth, but because she pitied the ign'ance and predigice of people who, if they ever took the Bible into their hands, it seemed like they could never learn where to open and how to read it. She had been heard often to admit that but for Mrs. Peevy's ig-n'ance, but 'specially her predigice, she would be a great deal better person than herself was or ever hoped to be. As for the Kittrells, she believed in her heart that their becoming Baptists was only a question of time, when, as she was wont to express it, they could see their way clear to mansions in the skies.

"SOFT-HEARTED WOMAN AS MRS. TEMPLIN WAS."

I may not delay to repeat all the conversation of the occasion of the visit. What dwelling Mr. Kittrell made longest was when he spoke of his own great age, now sixty-eight, and a-going on to sixty-nine, and the provision a man at his time of life might naturally be expected to wish to make for his children. There is a pathos which parents are gifted withal when speaking fondly of those dearest to them that sensibly affects persons even less responsive than Mrs. Templin. She felt for her handkerchief more than once, and not finding it, tenderly drew up a corner of her apron.

"Yes, yes," continued the father. "I'm a gittin' of what ef a body moutn't call old, they'd go as fur as to call at leastways aijuable, and it 'pears like that as I'm the onlest father them boys has got—"

Soft-hearted woman as Mrs. Templin was, her apron could not but do its becoming service at this tender pause.

"Now, Jodie," Mr. Kittrell resumed, when he felt that he had partially recovered his strength, "as for Jodie, it seem like that boy—boy I calls him, but *he* feel like he's a man, Jodie do; and which it weren't no longer'n last Sadday, I see him with my own eyes fling down Buck in a wrastle, and Buck say Jodie's the onlest man in the county, white or black, that can put his back to the ground—now, Jodie, I spishuons, he have a likin' for this here side o' the plantation, and I have notussed that he 'pearantly some ruther go to William's Creek than Big Spring, while, I ain't shore in my mind, but my spishuons of Buck is and are of his bein' of a Turkey Creek man, and possuable a Big Springer. Now, when Jodie want to settle hisself, and a nut with of understandin', Jodie is a silence an' a by no means of a pushin' of a b-b—but I s'posen I has *got* to call him a young man now, sence he's the onlest man any whars about that can put Buck Kittrell's back to the ground, and has the idees of a man in the bargain—my opinions is, Jodie is arfter a settlement o' some kind; and I'll have to lay off a toler'ble siz'able piece o' the plantation next to and a-jinden of you an' Calline, an' you an' Jodie an' Calline 'll have to settle it betwixt you three the same as me an' you has an' have done about gates an' water-gaps. An' a-speakin' o' Calline, I do think, upon my soul, I never see a daughter mo' like a mother in every respects, though I were never a person that in the payin' o' compumnents to female wimming, and speshual them that kyars thar age like some I've knowed, to actilly name names. And, *as* for Jodie—Jodie Kittrell I'm a-talkin' about now—well, Jincy say, and she's a relijuouser person 'n what I am, she give it as her 'pinuons that marriages is made in heaven; and ef so be it, I can't but hope the good Lord won't send Jodie, who, 'twa'n't for me he'd be a orphing, too fur and too illconwenant from home for his quimpanions."

Then he cast a brief melancholy look towards the far distance adown Long Creek. But it was too forlorn for a father so fond and aged, so he withdrew his eyes, and fixed them, with soft appealing, upon Mrs. Templin.

"And I don't think," she said to her daughter that night, on her return from the Peevys', "nor neither do I believe, that I ever see a person more 'fectionate as a parrent, and more fittin', ef he jest only see his way cle'r, to give up and give in a expeunce and march straight into Rock-hole pool; and what he said, Caline, of me an' you of bein' of adzackly alike—well, my ap'on—for I had drap' my hankercher somewhars—but my ap'on were positive wet. And it's astonishin' that of two brothers Jodie Kittrell, and him the youngest, would be so much more knowin' what were his juty in the warous Churches it were his juty to stand up to ef not to jind imegiant out an' out; and I wouldn't desires to hear more dilicater langwidges than that same man have insiniwated about the settlin' o' Jodie on this side o' his plantation."

Caroline, tall, blooming, merry-eyed, smiled, well-pleased at the report, and made no further reply than that, in her opinion, a finer young man in the whole State of Georgia was not to be found than Jodie Kittrell.

From Mrs. Templin's Mr. Kittrell rode by the nearest way

straight on to Mrs. Peevy's, and one who had witnessed the gayety of his recent salutation might have been surprised at the solemnity with which he greeted his neighbor to the left. Of about the same age as Mrs. Templin, though shorter and thinner, she was more reticent and serious, and showed more of the wear of time. Mr. Kittrell's voice had a most respectful and kind tremor when he said how thankful he was to see her looking so remockable well. In answer to her inquiry about himself and his family, he answered, after a brief, thoughtful pause,

"All of us is in middlin' fa'r health, Missuis Peevy, thank the good Lord, exceptions of Buck."

"Buck?" quickly asked Mrs. Peevy. "Why, I see him and Jody both a-Sunday, and I never see him a-lookin' better or healthier. What ail Buck?"

"Not in his body, Missuis Peevy," answered the old man, with moderate gratitude; "not in his body, I don't mean. In Buck's body, and I mout say in all his warous limbs, Buck Kittr'l's sound as a roach, strong as a mule, active as a cat, an' industrous as they genuilly makes 'em. It's the boy's mind that's a-makin' o' me oneasy."

"Buck's *mind*, Mr. Kittr'l?" she asked, in candid anxiety, for she liked both the boys well. "Why, what upon the yearth—"

"Yes, madam, his mind. You see, Buck have got now to whar he's a-goin' on, and that monstuous pow'ful rapid, to his one-an'-twenty, and he know it; an' when an' at which time he can wote, an' be a man besides, an' which, though Buck hain't told me so in them many words, yit I consate that Buck want to settle hisself; and he, a-bein' o' my oldest son, and a studdy, and of afectuonate natur', a parrent, speshual when he know hisself on the vargin o' the grave, mout natchel be anxuous about what perwision to make for him who ain't one o' them sort that'll up an' out 'ith what he want, but'll take what his parrent father 'lows him and never cherrip. For my desires is to settle them boys, or leastways Buck, before my head git cold, and not to be a-leadin' 'em to the temptations o' wantin' gone the only father they've got, and that before his time come to go."

Mr. Kittrell paused, took out his white square-spotted red silk handkerchief, and mildly blew his nose. Mrs. Peevy, making no reply, he continued:

"This here side o' my plantation that lays on Turkey Creek and perpuendickler betwix' me and them that I've said it freekuent, open an' above bode, nobody oughtn't to never desires to have a better neighbor, and which, ef I weren't a-settin' in thar very pe-azer at this minute, I should name thar names, and which some people say this the best side o' my plantation, and mout natchel expect for me to lay it off to my oldest son, and which they ain't no doubts on my mind that Buck have a sly leanin' to-wards this side, and possuable may be mout be to cross the creek and go as fur as Big Spring, which— But bless my soul! whar's Sarann? I don't know how I could have been here this long 'ithout a-askin' for that lovely child, which my wife declare she's the very picter of her mother in all an' every p'ints of view."

"Sarann and Calline rid over to Mr. Ivy's this evenin'," answered Mrs. Peevy.

"Umph—humph! Love to see young people a-goin' a-wisitin' when it's done in reason. As for Buck, 'pears like he never here lately seems to keer about a-wisitin' no great deals, exceptions he's evident a Turkey Creeker thoout its muanderin's, and the child's mind seem to be of a-oc-cuepied here lately. I hope it'll all come right, and I'm a-studdlin' about him a-constant, and a-constant a-askin' myself in pow'ful langwidges, what do Buck Kittr'll mean by his constant a-muanderin' up and down Turkey Creek on both sides of her and to-wards Big Spring? And ef I know myself, and it 'pears like a man o' my age ought to know hisself, I wants and desires to do a parrent's part, and speshual along 'ith them that's the oldest, a-goin' on rapid to thar one-and-twenty, and a-lookin' forrards 'ith the serous and solemn p'ints of view that boy been here lately a-evident a-takin' o' matters an' things in gener'l and speshual o' hisself. And you say the gals rid to Joel Ivy's?"

"Yes, sir. Caline said she heerd Prissy Mattix's feelins—"

"She thar?" asked Mr. Kittrell, quickly.

"Yes, sir; a-doin' o' some weavin' for Missis Ivy; and Caline was afeard, she said, that Prissy's feelins was hurted by her mother a-givin' the weavin' of her jeans and stripes to Sophy Hill; and so she and Sarann rid over jes' natchel, and to ast to see Prissy well as Missis Norris."

"Umph—humph!" Mr. Kittrell prolonged the exclamation, and was ruminating what remark he should make about Miss Mattox, whom he both disliked and feared, when the two girls came cantering up to the gate. Somehow Mr. Kittrell felt a little embarrassed at meeting them together; yet he shook hands heartily with both, as alighting from their horses they came running in. Sarann, somewhat *petite*, but as rounded, as well-developed, and as pretty as Caroline, was not quite so demonstrative, though in her own home, as the latter. Yet she said with simple candor that she was glad to see Mr. Kittrell.

"Now, Godamighty bless both of you, your souls and your bodies," he said, gallantly. Somehow he could not see his way clear as to what to say to each in the presence of the other; and so, after a few general observations, he took

"SOMEHOW MR. KITTRELL FELT A LITTLE EMBARRASSED AT MEETING THEM TOGETHER."

his leave. On the way home he soliloquized much. One of the subjects of this interior conversation may be guessed from an audible remark that he made to his horse, while the latter was drinking at the ford of Turkey Creek.

"Selom," said he, pointing and slowly shaking his finger at the beast's head, "ef any flaw is to come to this bisuiness, you hear me, it'll be flung in by old Priss Mattix."

He looked quickly all around to see if possibly this unintentional exclamation had been overheard; then, tightening the reins, he urged Selim on. Reaching home, he informed his wife of the events of his visits, and added,

"My opinions is, Jincy, and my believes is, that at the Templings' the iron are hot, and at the Peevys', ef not hot, it's of a-beginnin' to git warm. Ef only ole Priss Mattix will keep her everulastin' mouth shet, it'll go through sleek as a bean, or a ingun, which of the two you mind to choosen. But, to save my life, I can't but be afeard o' that ole creeter."

He said as much to Buck and Jodie. The younger looked at his brother with a face partly gay and partly serious. Buck received the news with hearty satisfaction, saying boldly that in his opinion a finer girl than Sarann Peevy the State of Georgia never produced, but that the sooner the name *Peevy* was changed to Kittrell, a thing he was glad to hope was possible in time, the better it would be for— Here Buck and Jodie both blushed somewhat; for, great, stalwart, fine, glorious fellows as they were, they were modest and gentle, and this was the main reason why their father felt it to be his duty to take the lead and urge them to follow in this most delicate pursuit.

"You two keep cle'r o' ole Priss ef you can," said Mr. Kittrell, in conclusion; "or ef you meet up along 'ith her, be monst'ous perlite. 'Twa'n't for hurtin' o' Sophy Hill's feelin's, I'd git her to weave my jeans. And you can't be too peticualar in keepin' both your bisuiness a secret, and speshual from her."

IV.

Miss Priscilla Mattox, who had come up from one of the wire-grass counties below—I believe it was never precisely known which—had been making temporary sojourns the while with various families in the county, for whom she had been doing jobs at weaving. Tall, thin, wiry, and of extremely uncertain age, she had gotten the reputation among many of being as swift with her tongue as with the shuttle. She might have been the equal, even the superior, of Miss Sophy Hill in counterpanes; but in jeans and stripes Mrs. Templin, at least, who had tried both, preferred the latter, and at this very time Miss Hill was engaged at her house on a job in this special department. The preference hurt Miss Mattox's feelings, as she frankly confessed, and the more because she felt that she knew Mrs. Templin had shown her partiality for Miss Hill mainly because of herself being poor and—as she expressed it—a furriner.

Miss Mattox had not yet connected herself with either William's Creek or Big Spring; but if Mrs. Templin and Mrs. Peevy had been put upon their oaths, each would have been compelled to say that she had thought she had had reason to expect that Miss Mattox, at no very distant day, would feel it her duty not longer to delay proceeding to the place where she was obliged to know she belonged. Indeed, most lately, ever since the disappointment in the matter of the jeans and stripes, Mrs. Peevy particularly must have been rather pronounced in such opinion, even upon the witness-stand.

Now, it so happened that Mr. Kittrell, in pursuance of the

double project so near his heart, had been engaged for some time, as preliminary to and believed by himself likely to assist and expedite its consummation, in making two small clearings on the high ground in the woods on either side of his mansion, and had blazed the trees on what seemed to be intended as an avenue to lead from each of the clearings, one to the ford of William's Creek, the other to that of Turkey. Such action was obliged to be talked about, and Mr. Kittrell well knew it. So he counselled his wife, whom he knew to be entirely artless, rather too artless indeed, to keep herself at home for a while, and refer all inquirers to himself. He was conscious of being too shrewd a man to be caught divulging important intentions relating to his own business. Therefore he smiled inwardly when away, and laughed broadly when in the bosom of his family, at the one answer he had given to all inquiries—that he was clearing places to set some traps. For, indeed, everybody had to complain of the ravages made by crows and blackbirds on the newly planted low-ground corn.

It was one of those things that could never be satisfactorily accounted for how the suspicion came to the mind of Miss Priscilla Mattox, a few weeks after Mr. Kittrell's visits to his neighbors, that Buck Kittrell had dropped Saraun Peevy, to whom lately he had been paying marked attention, and was now doing his utmost to supplant his brother Jodie in the regard of Caroline Templin. Miss Sophy Hill, indeed, had admitted that she had suspected of late that Caroline had seemed to her rather more fond of Buck's than Jodie's closest society. But the relations between the two distinguished weavers were well known to be far from cordial. Besides, Miss Hill declared upon her honor that she had not so much as spoken to Miss Mattox since the eventful change in the relation of the latter to the Templins; and, moreover, that she had communicated her own suspicions only to three or four, or, at least, to not more than from five to six of her lady acquaintances, and even then in the strictest confidence. However, the suspicion had gotten into the mind of Miss Mattox, and she resolved to hunt for its foundation. The result of her search may be surmised from the report Mr. Kittrell made to Buck one evening of an accidental visit he had made to one of his neighbors.

"I stopped at Jeemes Lazenberry's on my way from town, and I'm sorry I done it, and I wouldn't of done it ef I'd of knew that ole Priss Mattix were thar, and which I didn't know it untwill I were plump in the pe-azer. The ole creeter, soon as I come 'nigh an' in an' about, at me she did about them clerruins; and when I ans'ered as I ans'ered everybody else to thar satersfactuon, blame ef she didn't show plain as that crooked ole nose on her face, that she didn't believe nary singuil one, ner nary blessuid word; and when she 'lowed she had beerd that you was a-courtin' o' Calline Templing, I couldn't, not to save my life, I couldn't keep from bein' of a little confuseded in my mind, though I don't think she see it; for I tuck out my hankercher and blowed my nose tremenjuous; and I told her that, pine-blank, it weren't so. I were thankful she were on the back track; but I tell you, now, you boys better hurry up, for that ole nose of hern, to my opinion, have a scent same as a hound; and when she see Buck's track to-wards Missnis Templing's of gittin' of cold, you'll hear her a-yelpin' back across Turkey Creek, and have him an' Sarann treed same as a possum in a simmon."

Buck laughed heartily at his father's report, and assured him that he had no apprehension of harm of any sort from Miss Mattox.

On the next day Miss Mattox, having gotten from Mrs.

Lazenberry's a brief release, hastened over to Mrs. Peevy's, and reported to her the conversation she had held with Mr. Kittrell the day before, and his confusion when she told him that everybody knew that Buck Kittrell was courting Caroline Templin, and almost knew he was engaged to her. Mrs. Peevy was acutely pained at this news. She hoped, vainly indeed, that Miss Mattox did not observe her emotion.

"Why, lawsy me, didn't you know that, Missis Peevy?"

"I did not," answered Mrs. Peevy, faintly.

"It's so, shore as you're settin' in that cheer. And I can tell ye how it come about to my 'pinions; and my 'pinions, Missis Peevy, is things that gen'ally knows what they're about. Polly Templin's at the bottom o' all the business. Now, I ain't a person that meddles with other people's business, a-not'ithunderstandin' she have tuck from me the weavin' o' her stripes and jeans; but she's at the bottom of it, and when she heerd, as everybody else did, that Buck Kittr'll were a-freekwent crossin' o' Turkey Creek, a-goin' to Big Spring, and to another place, and which it is too dilicate for me to forb'ar where that other place are, and she went for him, and she sot that Calline arfter him—"

"Stop right thar, Prissy," interrupted Mrs. Peevy. "I can't think Calline 'd o' done anything that ain't modest."

"Well," said Miss Mattox, shrugging her shoulders, "drap her out o' the case; but her mammy have been a-pessecutin' o' that boy, and tryin' to clinch the nail on him, and as shore's you're born'd she's got him; and they'll all do of their level best to make a bachelder out o' Jodie, and which he's jes' that kind o' good-natur'd feller as'll let 'em do it, an' everybody been a-notisin' how low-sperrited Jodie is, an' him and Buck scacely speaks."

"Well," said Mrs. Peevy, in a low, constrained voice,

"I'm shore I don't know that it's any business o' mine." Yet a tear was in her eye.

"May be not," replied Miss Mattox; "but I jest natchel hates to see people a-meddlin' 'ith other people's business, and I used to try my level best to keep Polly Templin from runnin' on in the scand'lous way about some people that she know are her betters, a-believin' in sancterfercation, and fallin' from grace, and how she said that she knowed of things about them people that—well, she jest out and said that it were perfec ridicklous when Malviny Peevy sot herself up for one o' them saints that's been dead every sence the 'Pistles o' the 'Postle Paul."

"Did she say them words, Prissy Mattix?" asked Mrs. Peevy, panting.

"To the best o' my ricollections, Missis Peevy, them was not only her words, but her wery langwidges. But, oh, my dear Missis Peevy! if I was in your place, I'd let Polly Templin go, and I should desires, by no manner o' means, for my name to be named. Because, as everybody know, I'm a orphin person, and has to work for my livin', and tharfo' and wharfo' I ain't o' them that 'd wish to make innimies."

Mrs. Peevy rose and walked up and down the room for a minute or two, then stopped and quietly asked Miss Mattox if she would stay to dinner. But, bless her heart, Miss Mattox had left the shickle in the loom and was promised to return. When she was gone, Mrs. Peevy ruminated the livelong day. But a short time before the arrival of Miss Mattox, Sarann had gone to Mrs. Templin's to spend the day. The mother resisted the first impulse to send for her. Sarann returned in the evening, and the innocent heartiness with which she spoke both of Caroline and Mrs. Templin touched her mother's heart so sensibly that she had never before realized so fully how dearly loved was her only child. That night, after Sarann had gone to bed, she sat up far beyond the usual time. When she had risen at last to retire, she went softly into her daughter's

"'THEM WAS NOT ONLY HER WORDS, BUT HER WERY LANGWIDGES.'"

chamber, a small shed-room next her own, and shading the candle, looked upon the face of the sleeper, while tears ran down her cheeks. After gazing upon her several moments, she leaned over and softly kissed her forehead. Sarann momentarily smiled, and then gently sighed. The mother went silently back, then, throwing herself upon her knees by her own bed, wept sorely.

The next morning, after breakfast, she said to Sarann,

"I'm goin' to Hello on a little bit o' business, precious; I sha'n't be gone long. Give out what you ruther have for dinner. I hain't much appetite to-day."

V.

Take it all in all, the experience of Mr. Kittrell during the greater part of this day was the most excited and painful in his recollection. "Because," as he would sometimes remark when recurring to it, "I'm a man that never likes to git mad, and it's because when I does, ef it's ragin', viguous mad, they is danger o' my hurtin' somebody or somethin', apowiduin' they don't git out o' my way."

It was about ten o'clock. Buck was out overseeing the plough and Jodie the hoe hands. Mr. Kittrell, having returned from a meditative ride over both fields, was sitting in his piazza, indulging the pleasing, anxious pains of incubation over his plans, with an occasional inward affectionate chiding of his boys for not being more pushing each in his own most fond endeavor, when he saw a negro riding a mule which he urged with kicks and a hickory on the road that led from Mrs. Templin's. It proved to be her man Si.

"Marse Archie," said Si, "mist'ess say come dar quick's your hoss can fetch you."

"My good-ness grasuous, Si, what *can* be the matter?"

"Don't know, marster. Marse Jim Hutchin' fotch a paper which mist'ess say have ruin' her. *Never* see mist'ess so 'flicted, not even when marster died and leff her."

"Ride on back and tell her I'm a-comin', and that amejuant."

"What can the matter be, honey?" asked Mrs. Kittrell, in great anxiety.

"Don't ast me, Jincy," answered her husband, almost angrily, painfully humiliated by not being able to answer the question of one so far his inferior. "I knoweth not, ner neither doth I know."

While his horse was being brought out, he walked up and down the piazza, muttering to himself. His wife, knowing what a desperate man he was capable of becoming, was appalled at overhearing him say,

"No, no; the techhole's stopped up and the cock's broke, and it hain't even a ramrod. 'Twouldn't be no manner o' use." He looked as if he could have wept from disappointment.

"My dear honey, what *are* you a-talkin' about?" exclaimed Mrs. Kittrell, pale with horror.

"My pischuel, 'oman, my PISCHUEL!"

"My Lord!" she cried, throwing up both arms and bowing her head.

Now, Mr. Kittrell had not only great affection but much considerateness for his wife.

"Oh, Jincy, if you don't want me, I sha'n't take her. Tell Buck; no, tell Jodie; no, tell nary one of 'em to do nary blessed thing ontell I find out what's turned up all cruation, and can then tell what can be done and what can be did."

"Be calm, my precious husband, be c-ca-alm-alm!"

"I'll try to be calm, Jincy," he answered, in sepulchral tone.

"When I got thar," said Mr. Kittrell, later in the day, "thar were Missuis Templing, red as a beet, hot as a piece o' i'on jes' out'n the bath, and a-holdin' in her tremblnin' hands a piece o' paper. Calline, she were rid over to Harrell's stow, and conshuequently she weren't thar. The minute I lay my eyes on the back o' the writin', I see it were Joe Cofield, and I says to myself, ' High, name o' goodness, high!' for I knowed that 'oman were afeard o' debt as she were o' the grave; and I did not supposinged she owed nary dollar ner nary cent to nobody, let alone of Missuis Peevy. But, lo and behold, Missuis Peevy have sued her for thirty dollars for *scandle;* and not only so, but Jim Hutchins, the constuable, he had to tell her that the plantuff 'd of fotch for a hundred, exceptions that Joe Cofield told her she couldn't sue in his cote for but thirty dollars, 'ithout she'd diwide up the words and fetch on three of 'em for thirty and one for ten, but that Missuis Peevy wouldn't diwide the words, because she were onnly arfter keepin' Missuis Templing's mouth shet. Befo' I have sot down in a blessed cheer, I says to her, 'Missuis Templing,' says I, 'to my opinions, it's Priss Mattix. But, how-be-ever, Joe Cofield ought to be 'shamed o' hisself for fetchin' of a case that he know, well as I know, belong not to his little ole cote. But that's jest Joe Cofield. When he's shore o' his cost, he'll put on his everulastin' docket whomsoever 'll ask him. Why, didn't he let Bias Buggamy sue a stray stump-tail yearlin' for breakin' in his field; and didn't Bias call for bail, and stan' bail for the said yearlin' and take possession of him? And didn't he git a jedgment, and a exercution; and didn't Jim Hutchins level on and put up and sell the said yearlin' in Bias Buggamy's cuppin'? And didn't Bias Buggamy buy him in for the cost, and kill him, and skin him, and eat him? *The* good a'mighty! Why, I tell you, madam,' says I, ' anybody that he know good for cost, he'd let 'em fetch suit in his cote agin the moon for spilin' a string o' fish er a pot o' soap. And as for Priss Mattix — but she's a female person and —' "

"Ef her everdence is Prissy Mattix," said Mrs. Templin, suddenly, "she have told me worse things of Malviny Peevy's a-sayin' agin me than she have sued me for sayin' agin her."

"Thar it is now, thar it is," said Mr. Kittrell, his eyes sparkling with gratification.

"Didn't she tell me that Malviny Peevy called me the 'Postle Paul, and made game o' me, and say nobody but me could of p'inted his 'Pistle to the Romans?'"

"Ah, ha! umph, humph! ah, ha! and it were to keep you from takin' from her the weavin' o' your stripes and jeans, and she sot Missuis Peevy agin you because you did. Now, don't you know, Missuis Templing, that Priss Mattix know, ef she know anything, that Missuis Peevy know you ain't no 'Postle Paul, or couldn't be, a-bein' of a female, and that the whole of it is her inwentions?"

Other conferences the friends had which, being confidential, I leave to be inferred rather than mentioned in detail.

In less than an hour after Mr. Kittrell's departure, Mrs. Templin was at Hello District Court. Calling for the docket, she read,

> Missis Malviny Peevy
> vs.
> Missis Polly Templin. } Debt for scandle.

She left for home immediately after the justice had made underneath the following entry,

> Missis Polly Templin
> vs.
> Missis Malviny Peevy. } Debt for mene an' oudacious insiniwations.

"Jincy," said Mr. Kittrell, after giving his wife a hurried account of the suit of Mrs. Peevy, without mention of the cross-action, "I must go to town on a little bisuiness, and sha'n't be back tell late this evenin'."

12

And he rode off straightway. It was the first time that Mr. Kittrell had ever run away from the prospect of being called upon to assist a neighbor. This is what he did; for he had had little doubt but that Mrs. Peevy would send for

"MISSIS POLLY TEMPLIN *vs.* MISSIS MALVINY PEEVY. DEBT FOR MENE AN' OUDACIOUS INSINIWATIONS."

him when the summons should be carried to her, and he could not see how, at least yet, he was to deport himself towards her after the counsel he had given, or at least hinted, to her adversary. Intent upon bringing about peace, he knew, at the same time, that his influence with Mrs. Peevy, because of her more serious, determined character, was less than with Mrs. Templin; so he deemed it the part of prudence to get out of the way for a brief time.

"I were never a person that were usened to dodgin', but

I had it to do, and I done it. I wanted to see how the hoarhound wer' a-workin' all around, and then I wanted to cool off a little bit afore I see Joe Cofield. Po' ole Priss wer' a female; I knowed that, and she wer' beyant me; but when I thought about Joe Cofield, I tell you I were oneasy fer him. But I promised Jincy to be cool and calm as possuble, and so I concluded to let things lay for that day."

It was supper-time when he returned. The boys had just returned from some visits they had made in the afternoon. Both seemed concerned, notwithstanding an occasional smile on Buck's face which would immediately disappear. The mother had been full of anxiety all day, in spite of the gratitude she felt that her husband had not taken his pistol. Not a word was said for some time after they had sat at the table. Suddenly, with impatience, Mr. Kittrell cried out,

"Ef anybody know anything, can't they tell it? Is it got so that people's own famblies can't talk to 'em? Is everybody done gone and got mad and distracted? Have Missuis Peevy sent words to me?"

"No, sir. You know, pa," said Buck, with great respect, "that Mrs. Peevy have sued Mrs. Templin."

"I should some ruther supposing I did, havin' saw the summons that Joe Cofield sent her."

"Well, now Mrs. Templin have sued Mrs. Peevy."

"Who said so?" asked Mr. Kittrell, firmly, yet casting down his eyes the while.

"Mrs. Templin told me this evenin', and Mrs. Peevy told Jodie."

"Missuis Templing told who?"

"Me."

"Missuis Peevy told who?"

"Jodie."

Mr. Kittrell looked dazedly at one and another of his family.

"Can anybody tell me how come them boys at them houses in that kind o' style, and in skenes like the present?"

"We both went on business, pa."

"Bisuiness!" and Mr. Kittrell opened his eyes and his mouth.

"Yes, sir. Pa, I and Jodie have done wrong; that is, I have—that is, me and Calline—and we overpersuaded Jodie and Sarann, which they didn't want to do it, but we overpersuaded 'em."

"Buck Kittr'll," said his father, "for ef my 'membuance an' my riculection ain't clean gone, that were your name, or at leastways it usened to be, what you mean by you and Calline, and by Jodie and Sarann?"

"I mean, pa, that I went to ask Mrs. Templin for Calline, and Jodie went to ask Mrs. Peevy for Sarann."

Mr. Kittrell gazed fixedly at Buck for several moments, then at Jodie, then at his wife. Then looking up towards the ceiling, he combed with his fingers his hair from the left side of his head to the right, then from the right to the left. Afterwards lowering his head, he seemed to be carefully endeavoring to make an accurate parting in the middle. Then he said, in a mournful voice,

"Ef my fambly Bible don't tell no lies, and she were the fambly Bible of my parrents that's dead and goned, and she have never been caught in nary one that I've ever knewed of ner heerd of, I'm of sixty-eight year old the tent o' March, and which I've freekwent heerd my father and my mother also an' likewise say it were the time o' the last plantin' o' corn, and by good rights, if I live ontell the next tent o' March, I shall be to my sixty-nine; and in my time

I've saw of swappin', and heerd of swappin', and done some of swappin' myself. Buck Kittrell," he suddenly demanded fiercely, " is you a-foolin' o' me? and ef you ain't, when did you and Jodie swap, and how come you to swap? *The* good a'mighty !"

"We are not foolin' you now, pa, but we have been. When we found that you made the mistake of my bein' for Sarann, and Jodie for Calline, as you sort o' fixed it in your mind, I and Calline thought we'd play a little joke on all of you, and we overpersuaded Jodie and Sarann to jine in it. We didn't mean to keep it up but a fortni't more, when poor Miss Prissy, she come in yistiday and spil't the joke by tellin' o' Missis Peevy that Calline and me was engaged, when you know you'd hinted to Missis Peevy that I wanted Sarann, and poor Miss Prissy told her a whole lot of stuff besides about the Templins, which all hurt Missis Peevy's feelin's so much that she give way to 'em, and is now sorry for it. Miss Prissy—you see how it is, pa—she spil't the joke."

"Yes, she'd spile a pan o' milk jes' from the cow by lookin' at it, and, quicker'n vinegar, turn it to clabber."

"I'm sorry for it all, pa," said Buck, humbly, "and I beg your pardon; but it's me and not Jodie that's to blame for it!"

"No, pa—no, sir," remonstrated Jodie. "If Buck's to be blamed, I want my share. He went in seein' the fun of it, and I went in not seein' it. I think I'm even more to blame than Buck. But, pa, I know you would rather we'd both marry them we love best."

Tears came pouring from the father's eyes. "Jincy," he said, softly, "didn't you say weddin's was made in heb'n? I think you did, and now I know it's so, an' I 'knowledge I were mistaken to deny it."

He rose, walked to a corner of the room, leaned his head against the wall, and wept for several moments in his limitless joy. Then he turned, beckoned them to come to him, and sobbed first upon Buck's shoulder, then Jodie's, then his wife's.

"Ef anybody," he said, when he had strength to speak— "ef anybody 'd a-told me to-day that I'd of felt as good as I do now, and at the present time, both afore and before of my goin' to bed, I should of told 'em they was a liar. Yes, yes— But hello thar! did them wimming give thar consents, and thar permissions, and thar—"

"Oh, yes."

"*The* Lord of mighty! what *did* they think of me?—but let that all go. Yes, it wer' a powerful good joke. Them's allays good jokes, my boys, that eends well. 'Member that. Allays let your jokes be them that's to eend well. I don't blame Jodie and Sarann for not seein' the fun, because they're young, and bless old Jodie's heart for not of wantin' his brother to have all the blame. It's like the Kittr'lls has been from everlastin' and for evermore. And now, to-morrow mornin' yearly—but, ef you'll believe me, Jincy, the anexities I've been through this blessed day has made me that sleepy that I got to go to bed."

He went straightway to his room, and five minutes after they heard as hearty snoring as the most affectionate of wives and children could have desired. Mrs. Kittrell gently chided her sons, especially Buck, for the untimely jest. Buck was the more penitent because of the deep regret which Mrs. Peevy felt for having brought the action against Mrs. Templin. The fact was that neither of the mothers, each restrained by natural delicacy and self-respect, had inquired of her daughter respecting her relations with the lads; and though both had possibly dreamed of alliance

"IT'S LIKE THE KITTRILLS HAS BEEN FROM EVERLASTIN' AND FOR EVERMORE".

with the Kittrells, they would have been among the last so to admit, even to their own daughters, until knowing that decisive movements had been made by their suitors. Oh, how Mrs. Peevy that night did wish that she had never laid eyes upon Miss Priscilla Mattox!

"Your pa's the man to settle it, Jodie," she had said to the latter that evening. "Tell him to please see Squire Cofield, and see what the damages is for stoppin' o' the case. I sha'n't git no sleep, that is, no healthy sleep, until it are stopped; and I do think I ought to pay Polly Templin her thirty dollars, though Prissy Mattix know I never used them words, nor neither do I believe now that Polly Templin used hern."

VI.

Mr. Kittrell rose next morning, his countenance exhibiting extreme satisfaction, with brief intervals of vast indignation. When a great man has become exasperated with anger, it is not to be expected that he should at once subside, even when what originated it has been found to be without adequate foundation, or the foundation has been removed. If Mr. Kittrell had thought to employ a figure of speech about his own condition of mind that morning, it is not impossible that he might have compared himself with the lion who, while conscious of the full security of the objects of his care, however young or however frail, yet deems it not improper sometimes to go forth and roar in hearing of the insignificant beasts that had dared to molest their hitherto tranquil existence. So, before saying another word to anybody, he ordered his horse and urged the breakfast to be hurried.

"Pa," said Jodie, "Mrs. Peevy asked me to tell you to please see Mr. Cofield for her."

Mr. Kittrell smiled compassionately, and gave only answer,

"Like I weren't goin' to do that, and that amejuant."

On arriving at Hello, and hitching his horse at the rack, he walked with solemn firmness to the court-room, a small unceiled and otherwise airy house, situate on a corner of the justice's lot.

"Do, Mr. Kittrell?" said the magistrate and his constable simultaneously.

"Do, your honor? do, Mr. Hutchins?" answered the comer in a voice that neither of the officials remembered to have ever heard from him before. "My bisuiness here, your honor, may it please the cote, is to fetch several suits, and ef it's the same to you, and you will be so kind and so conduescendin' as to lend me your pen, I would wish and desires to enter 'em up myself, as some of 'em's dilicate cases, and would wish and my desires 'd be that they're dictatued right."

"Cert'nly," answered the squire with alacrity, handing him a pen. Knowing that Mr. Kittrell had a good deal of money out, he attributed his manner to his well-known aversion to press any of his debtors. So, as Mr. Kittrell, deeply sighing, began to write, he thought he would offer a word of consolation.

"People, Mr. Kittrell, has to know that people they owes money to has to sue sometimes, and them that has it to do, hate it as they mout, ought to try to git riconciled to it."

Mr. Kittrell looked up at the squire solemnly for a moment, then continued to write, and write, and write.

"Monst'ous good man," whispered Mr. Hutchins; "wonder he don't call us Jim and Joe, jes' dry so, like he allays do."

At length Mr. Kittrell rose, and thanking his honor and Mr. Hutchins for their kindness, walked slowly to his horse, and, preparatory to mounting, looked at the stirrup-leathers, throat-latch, and martingale. In this while the officials were reading over the entries, holding the docket alternately close to their eyes and at arm's-length, until, at last, they dropped it upon the table and looked at each other with dismay. There were suits of Archibald Kittrell against Turkey Creek and William's Creek for "breakin' inter his bottom cornfields corntrary to law." One was the State of Georgia "against warous persons, o' warous sections not yit quite found out who they is and air, for tattlin' and raisin' fusses betwixt warous females and widders, in warous neighborhoods in the county and State aforesaid." Then there were an action and cross-action between Turkey and William's Creeks each against other for "crossing one 'nother's banks onbenownst an' onlawful." The list wound up with

The State of Georgia *vs.* Josiah Cofield and James Hutchins.	J'intly and severially for misdemeniors of warous kind.

"*Mister* Kittr'll," said the squire, rushing out as the former had just mounted his horse, "I don't understand them cases, and 'special' them that's agin them two creeks and agin me and Jim."

"Why, w'at the matter 'ith the creeks, Joe Cofield?"

"I don't see," said Joe, in candid remonstrance, "how we're to send summonses to them peop—to them—creeters."

"Didn't you send one to that stray stump-tail yearlin' what broke in Bias Buggamy's field?"

"Yes, sir, but Bias 'knowledge service."

"Well, sir," answered Mr. Kittrell, growing louder and more loud, "can't I, or can't Missuis Peevy, or can't Missuis

Templing 'knowledge service for them creeks, as we all three of us is linded and bounded by 'em? And as for the case agin you and Jim Hutchins, I supposuing that the State o' Georgy ought to know how to take keer o' *her* cases, both them everywhar else and them at the present bare."

Then, lifting high his arm, and standing heavily upon the stirrups, Mr. Kittrell roared in a way that—well, both his auditors declared upon honor afterwards that "if anybody had of told them that the ole man Kittr'll could of got mad as he were then, they should have been obleeged to call 'em a liar."

"I got no *time*," said Mr. Kittrell, foaming at the mouth, "to tarry along o' you and Jim Hutchins about the p'ints o' law in your little ole cote o' suin' o' creeks and stumptail yearlin's. They can be 'tended to on *sossorarers* to the s'perior cote. You two men, both o' you, knows that ef I'm a man of not many words as some, I allays *means* 'em when I says 'em; and sence this Hello deestric' is open, 'pears like, for all kind o' suin', man *an*' beast, maled *an*' femaled, widders *an*' widders—mark what I say, *widders an*' *widders*—I ain't goin' to stop tell I find out who started this bisuiness, not ef I has to sue the nuniversual *world*. And as for your *witnesses*—but go 'long, Selom. If I stay here, I mout git to cussin'. Go on, Selom, and less leave this awful place."

Selim dashed off in a canter, as if eager, equally with his master, to turn his back upon the scene.

"The fact of the whole bisuiness were," said the old man, in telling it, "I were that mad that I daresn't begin on Joe Cofield and Jim Hutchins ontell I got on top o' Selom ready to leave 'em. For I didn't want to skeer the po' creeters out'n thar very hides; but even the gentuil cautions I let out on 'em come a-nigh of doin' of it, an', as I knewed it would, scattered thar perseduances to the four cornders of the yearth."

Jim Hutchins used to give a brief account of his first actions after Mr. Kittrell's departure.

"Joe said I better go amejiant to Jim Lazenberry's and see ole Miss Priss. I found her in the weavin'-room, and she hilt her shickle ready to put her through the warp. I told her how Missis Peevy have sued Missis Templing, and how Missus Templing have sued back on to Missis Peevy, and both a-countin' on her for everdence. That made her turn pale. Then I up, I did, and told her of the ole man Kittr'll a-fetchin' suit agin me and Joe, and agin both the creeks, and them agin one 'nother, and the way he talk, I were a-spectin' he'd begin soon on the two meetin'-houses; and, the fact were, they warn't no tellin' whar the ole man would stop, he were that mad about Missis Templing and Missis Peevy of bein' of onuseless put agin one 'nother by onknown people; and I wouldn't be s'prised ef he didn't stop ontell he had fotch suit agin every man, 'oman, and child, black and white, in the neighborhood, and the 'Geechee River to boot. The ole lady dropped her shickle, she did, she slid off the loom-bench, gethered her things in a hankercher, and scooted. Whar she halted and put up at I never knowed."

If Mr. Kittrell became a little "disguised" at the infare, from apple-jack, as he rather admitted afterwards, it was the first and only time in his married life, and was due to a fond intention to set his boys, at the outset of their adult careers, an example of "giving and taking," by imbibing toddy out of what he named Buck's bar'l (that had been distilled at the latter's birth), to Buck and Calline, and another to Jodie and Sarann, and afterwards reversing from Jodie's bar'l. "I were arfter settin' a egzampuil, an' the mixin' o' defferut sperrits, I'm afeard, made me k'yar the thing a leetle too fur." He ever was fond to speak at length of the profound wisdom evinced by himself in the reconciliation of the Templins and Peevys, and its just reward, the obtainment of Calline and Sarann for his daughters-in-law.

"Hadn't been for me, them wimming ud of been cats-an'-dogs now an' for evermore; and, as for Calline and Sarann, they'd a-been scattered to Dan *and* Basherby."

Calline having made a Baptist of Buck, and Sarann a Methodist of Jodie, Mr. Kittrell knew that it would never do to ruin, or at least discourage and perhaps demoralize, Big Spring or William's Creek, by throwing the weight of his mighty influence upon its rival; so he continued to maintain with calm firmness the balance of power.

"Yes, yes, yes," he would often say blandly, yet with decision—"oh, yes. It's your Babtuis, and your Methudis, and it's your sprinkuling, and your pedestruinashing, and it's all right; but my moto is — you all better 'member them words, and not forgit 'em—my moto is—egzampuil."

THE RIVALRIES OF
MR. TOBY GILLAM.

"His rolling eyes did never rest in place,
But walked each where for fear of his mischance."
Faerie Queene.

I.

FOR quite a time anterior to the events I propose to narrate, Mr. Toby Gillam had been the leading coffin-maker in the neighborhood, priding in his art and charging for it. For jobs done for the dead, I often have observed that not only artisans, but workers of all grades, grave-diggers, physicians, lawyers—I do not know who all—generally claim what by a sort of ironical grim antithesis they call a living compensation, which is higher than that exacted for those done on other occasions. Perhaps these industrious persons deem it advisable to make the best possible out of last opportunities. Perhaps they imagine themselves to be aiming for what will console, as far as such a thing can be made adequate, for the loss of friends and neighbors. Anyhow, Toby Gillam was not the man to turn aside from all precedents, and have his feelings wrought upon by the saddest of all work, for nothing, and he as good as said so many and many a time. Resoluteness in this behalf, and possibly habitude, had served in time to let him appear placid, if not with some little grain of cheerfulness, when engaged in what he had learned to do so well.

This was all before the Griggses moved in, settling within a mile of where the Gillams had dwelt always.

Now when it was ascertained that Mr. Griggs (Harmon Griggs was his name in full), though mainly a farmer, had often made coffins, and would take jobs of the kind yet if pressed, Mr. Gillam's mind was disturbed; and when, not long afterwards, old Mr. Pucket died, on whom he thought he could count with entire security, and the new-comer was employed to put the old man away, Mr. Gillam was outspoken. Yet what he hated the most about it, he said, was that the whole thing was such a piece of botch-work. In time the question arose, who was the better workman? The most thoughtful and fair-minded among the neighbors, though never very pronounced anyway, yet, if compelled, would probably have rated them about even in jobs of the kind for adults, and in those for children, especially in poplar, given Mr. Gillam some advantage. As for him, he never went, as well as I remember, to the length of saying that rather than be put into one of Harmon Griggs's *boxes*, he would prefer never being buried at all, but he nearly intimated as much; and as for Harmon's charges, why, a man that did half work, he contended, must expect to get half pay. Harmon's opinions on the subject nobody knew, for he was a quiet, reticent sort of person, neighborly, accommodating, and everybody in the community except Mr. Gillam grew to like him. Even Mrs. Gillam and her two daughters—Jane, twenty, and Susan, fifteen—had been heard often to say that the Griggses, the whole of them, were as good neighbors as they should ever wish to live by.

Mr. Griggs had been a widower some two or three years. His children were Morgan, now eighteen, and little Betsy, born a week before her mother's death. His house since that event had been kept by his sister Mandy, who was about twenty-one.

"A MAN THAT DID HALF WORK, HE CONTENDED, MUST EXPECT TO GET HALF PAY."

Both men had good farms and a few negroes, Mr. Griggs rather more of these than Mr. Gillam. He was tall, dark, deliberate in his conversation and carriage. Mr. Gillam, rather under middle height, of reddish hair and complexion, was restless, nervous, suspicious. People used to say that he would have practised despotism at home if his wife, who was some larger than he, had allowed it. Mr. Griggs, who in his family was quite a gentle, indulgent man, had always shown the disposition to be as friendly with the Gillams as with the rest of the neighbors. Indeed, if anything, he was specially so to them in all neighborly offices. "No, sir—no, *sir*," he would say, with moderate emphasis, in answer to certain remarks that came to his ears sometimes, "it's *not* because o' Jane Gillam, a-not'ithunderstandin' to my opinions she's a oncommon fine young 'oman; yit I'd feel like bein' jest as obleegin' to Mr. Gillam ef he didn't have no daughter Jane; fer I'm a man, and if I know myself I've allays ben a man, that would wish to live an' let live."

I declare I don't remember what kind of sickness it was that carried off little Betsy a year or so after the settlement there. But Jane Gillam, and Susan too, young as she was, rendered as willing, constant, efficient service as if the child had been their own dear sister. But what touched the heart of Mr. Gillam, temporarily at least, was what Mr. Griggs said to him when, in pursuance of a request sent through Morgan for him to please come over there, he did so promptly.

"Mr. Gillam, I not only hain't the heart to do it myself, but also them lovely poplar coffins you makes fer childern is better work 'n I can do. Won't you make one to put poor little Betsy away in?"

Mr. Gillam acknowledged to several persons that he could have cried when he heard these words. After that the good feeling that had already been among the ladies of the two families included, to a degree, the men. A little more visiting began, most marked, and naturally, on the part of Mr.

Griggs, who being, as he was wont to style himself, nobody of any description but a poor lone widower with just one child, and him about a man, or at least thinking himself a man, would ride or walk over, and sit and chat with resignation, and sometimes, it might be, with a bit of cheerfulness. During such visits, and when the ladies would visit at his own house, he was always decorous, especially towards Jane. If he ever had a heart for remarks that were at all playful, these for the most part were addressed to Mrs. Gillam or Susan, or both.

"The ijee! Harm Griggs ole enough to be Jane's father, Missis Rainwater!" Mr. Gillam said one day to a neighbor.

"He ain't. An' sposen he is: what man-person stands on age in sech cases?"

"Well, now, Missis Rainwater, it 'pen' on circum'ances. Ef Harm Griggs is to keep on—"

"Stop right thar, Mr. Gillam—stop right thar. Jane Gillam is a grown 'oman, an' if she an' Mr. Griggs make it out betwix' theirselves, why, it ain't worth your whiles to try to hender 'em."

Mr. Gillam ruminated over these remarks. Now that the season of bilious-fever was coming on, he was conscious that the friendly feelings which he had been indulging towards his rival were beginning to subside with the lapse of the last of the summer months, and he was not certain in his mind how he ought to regard the hints of Mrs. Rainwater. Little had he foreseen that his own wife was to be the first victim to the autumnal malady. It is not strange how kindly services on such occasions subdue envyings and jealousies. Day and night had Mandy Griggs tended that bedside, and her brother and Morgan had done all that was possible, and showed every disposition to do more. Nobody was surprised that Harmon Griggs was to make the coffin, and some tears stood in the eyes of the latest bereaved at these words:

"In co'se I make it, Mr. Gillam, an' I'll do my best to do jestice to the—to the 'quirements of—of as fine a 'oman, to my jedgments, as this or any other country—in fac', I feel tow'ds Missis Gillam like she were—why, law, Mr. Gillam,

HARMON GRIGGS'S.

I couldn't agzactly tell how I did, an' how yit I *do*, feel tow'ds Missis Gillam. An' as it's the last coffin I ever expects to make, an' as it's for one who were to me what Missis Gillam were, I'll do as well as I know how, an' my feelin's 'll be hurted ef anybody offers to pay me one single cent for it."

Mr. Gillam knew that he would be a brute not to be affected by such words, and as he wrung Mr. Griggs's hand the tears actually dropped from his eyes.

If ever a man faithfully tried his hand at his art, it was done then. The most intimate friend and zealous partisan that Mr. Gillam ever had could hardly have said, with his hand on the Book, that he could double it in every particular.

"Look like to me," said old Mr. Pate, "that Harmon were never goin' to git done san'paperin' his planks, an' I don't 'member as *uver* I see a man that tuck the time Harmon tuck in the mixin' o' his lam'black an' his sperrits o' turkintime."

"What tuck me the moest," said Mrs. Pate, "were the turn he give ter them elbows. They was jes' lovely; an' when they laid poor dear Polly Gillam in, it seem to me, 'pear like, that they wa'n't no deffunce more'n she'd 'a' been a-layin in her own blessed bed."

II.

Equidistant from the two families, near a country road that crossed about midway the public on which the two families resided, dwelt the Rainwaters. But for her emphatic remonstrances against such a figure, Mrs. Rainwater might have been taken for forty, or a little on the rise. Her husband had deceased four or five years before, leaving a right snug little property to her and their only son Ben, who was about the same age as Morgan Griggs—perhaps a year older.

Ben always became indignant whenever the possibility of his mother's marrying again was mentioned in his hearing —too much so, she thought.

"Benny," she said to him more than once, "don't you bother your head and fret about my gitting of married again. I've got no idees on top o' that subjec', an' don't expect to have 'em, *onlest* my mind change. But that'll be *my* business, an' nobody else's. It'll come to a nice pass when a body's own an' onlest son have to tell his own mother what she must do an' what she mustn't. Look like *you*, when to my knowledge your wisdom-tooth's a-hurtin' you now a-tryin' to push through your gums, is a-thinkin' about settlin' o' *yourself* 'ithout a-consultin' o' me, an' by good rights you might let me 'tend to *my* business, if I ever git any o' that kind *to* 'tend to."

Ben pondered such words at his leisure. Nobody that knew Susan Gillam ever blamed him for thinking a great deal of her, for though not as handsome as Jane, yet she was plump, taller, fairer, and kept up a steady improvement as she grew on, in the matter of the various qualities of person and deportment and character that the unmarried, whether those who have or those who have not quite cut their eye-teeth, like to see in a girl.

If Morgan Griggs had not been so intimate and dear a friend of Ben's, it was thought that he might have run against him in that race. But Morgan was an honorable boy, or young man, as, in spite of the absence of all rivalry with Ben, he perhaps would have preferred to be called, and Ben was without the shadow of jealousy towards him.

The very best feeling had always been between the Rainwaters and both the other families. Ben confided all his secrets to Morgan whom he loved like a brother, and they would sometimes laugh together at the idea of Mrs. Rainwater or anybody else supposing that they were not men, and did not know how to take care of themselves. If Morgan ever revealed to his father and aunt any of such confidence, it was not done in a way that would hurt. Instead of that, they, especially Mandy, seemed to take an interest in Ben's hopes and ambitions. Indeed, Mandy Griggs, though not as handsome as some, was one of the very nicest young women every way in that whole country. If she had not married, it had not been for want of opportunities. Her devotion to her brother and his family was ardent, and possibly that had been the reason for apparent indifference on the subject of beaux.

We have seen that Mr. Gillam had received Mrs. Rainwater's allusion to some special liking on the part of Mr. Griggs for Jane with a sort of contingent resentment. This had about gone out of his mind since the utterance of the words of Mr. Griggs on the occasion of the melancholy service which he had lately rendered in a manner so eminently conciliatory, and in a few weeks it had been succeeded by a cordiality that in a man like Mr. Gillam might be called extreme. His daughter Jane, if not the first, was among them, to observe this change, and to divine its most controlling cause.

"Pa," she said to him one day, "it seems to me that people, when their wives haven't been dead but just three months, that they ought to try to be decent. Ma's children haven't forgot her if other people have."

"Now lookee here, Jane. I 'members your ma, an' I misses her more'n you an' Susan do. But your ma's dead an' goned, an' she's goned to heb'n, an' even if a body was to want to fetch her back, you know well as I do that they couldn't."

"The question ain't for bringing ma back, pa; it's for trying to bring another woman here to take her place, and that before— Look at Mr. Griggs, pa. See how long his wife's been dead, and him single yet."

"And what's the reason? It's only because Missis Rainwater wouldn't have him—"

"I haven't an idee that Mr. Griggs ever asked her," Jane interrupted, with what to her father seemed considerable feeling.

"Umph, humph!" he said, rather pleased at the sight. "Then I suppose, because Harm Griggs, havin' nobody to powide for exceptin' o' them that's able to powide for theirselves, an' havin' of a sister to take keer o' his housell affairs, may take his time, an' wait tell the pullets is got grown, an' I'm to roam aroun' like a ole rooster in a flock all by myself, ner nother look ner nother—"

"Law, pa! *such* talk from a man that's just been made a widower, and as old as you are in the bargain!"

"Old as I am! I'm as young a man as Harm Griggs, er nigh an' about."

"That you ain't. I heard him tell ma, not long before she died, that he was thirty-seven, and would be thirty-eight his next birthday, while you know, and your face and head shows, you're over forty-five."

"What a man, an' 'special' what a marryin' man, says 'bout his age ain't allays the Bible truth; I've allays knowed that from a plenty o' expeunce. An' as fer waitin' like him, maybe ef my wife had of died when I were younger—"

"Ah, pa, you'd have done just as you are trying to do now. I say *trying*, for that's all you'll do in what you've first got on your mind. That is, that's my opinion."

"Maybe so, madam, maybe so. But they ain't jes' one lone fish in the sea. You think, Jane Gillam, because you an' Harm Griggs has settled everything betwix' you two, that—that—"

He did not finish the sentence. She looked at him with a look that indicated grief, ridicule, and compassion; then turned away.

He had always been a man that acted promptly upon his

convictions and the purposes that he had formed in his mind. Doubtless his action was now accelerated somewhat by Jane's interference, in his opinion wholly unwarrantable. A day or two after this brief conversation, happening to meet Mr. Griggs in the road, he said, after multitudes of preliminary words, " Harmon, ain't it cur'ous how deaths in famblies does fetch a man down, an' fetch him up also likeways, in his feelin's? I declar' the makin' o' that coffin fer your little Betsy, an' your of makin' o' that *lovely* coffin fer my po' wife—an' which I know the same as ef I were thar myself this very minute that she's in mansions in the sky —them coffins has somehow—them same blessed coffins, Harmon Griggs, they jes' natchel makes me feel like me an' you was jes' jinded together, an' bounded together, an' multi*plided* together, like, you may say—like brothers, Harmon."

The habitual paucity of Mr. Griggs's words, contrasted with his own, had led Mr. Gillam to regard his understanding of comparatively limited volume. Yet now, since he had announced his retirement from the coffin-making field, and especially as he had Mandy for a sister, he thought him of sufficient consideration to be treated with concerning certain items of merchandise that each considered valuable.

After some little delay to this last remark, Mr. Griggs answered, " Yes, sir, Mr. Gillam " (he always addressed him with *Mister*), " I done my levellest best on that coffin. Because Missis Gillam somehow allays felt to me like, I may say—like a mother."

Mr. Gillam winced at this alteration of his idea of their relationship, but answered, " She were a older person 'n me, I s'pose you knowed, Harmon."

" So I—so I've heerd you say, Mr. Gillam."

Mr. Gillam excused the use of the word " mother " in that

connection, knowing, of course, that Harmon was thinking mainly of Jane.

"I do think, 'pon my soul, Harmon," said he, changing the subject, "I've often 'mired how your sister Mandy, fine a young 'oman as she is, could jes' fling down ev'rything, an' go an' take charges o' her brother's dimestic business ontwell he got ready to settle hisself ag'in, an'—in fac', Harmon, you've stood a-bein' of a wid'wer longer'n I could, an' in which events, reason'ble to s'pose, Mandy might see, by good rights, that she well change her kinditions—ahem!— *fer* when once a female 'oman have k'yard the smoke-'ouse keys, she ain't goin' to be riconciled to be 'ithout smoke-'ouse keys o' some kind."

"Mandy, Mr. Gillam, have been a mighty good sister to me, an' a mother to my childern, you may say, an' ef she ever make up her mind to change her kinditions, *she* know I ain't goin' to be ag'in it, an' *I* know that ef I were, make no deffernce; for Mandy's a woman o' her own head, Mandy is."

In the course of the conversation Mr. Gillam raised and dwelt at some length upon the great subjects of barter and exchange, without special naming of any one commodity. He coursed around and about, and ended by saying: "My ijees is, Harmon Griggs, that when a couple o' men has a couple o'—well, you may call' em a couple o' *goods*, for the present argament o' the time bein', an' one 'll suit one, an' t'other t'other, an' both feels like they ruther give an' take, take an' give, than to hol' on jes' so to what they got, which ain't adzackly the article both of 'em need *fer* the present time bein', an' no multiplyin' o' words about boot, an' the askin' o' boot, an' the payin' o' boot, why, now, sir, thar's what I call doin' o' business in a straight-up-an'-down, pleasant, an', you may say, satisfactuous way—ahem!"

Mr. Griggs, with his comparatively inferior understanding, could only answer to this profound discourse: "Of co'se, Mr. Gillam, I suppose you're about right. I were never a man as studied politics, that is, to no great extents' except a-wotin' for them I knows the best an' likes the best; but I s'pect you're right."

That night in his family Mr. Gillam, in spite of any mental reservations regarding Mr. Griggs's intellectual vigor, spoke in more cordial terms of him than any that he had ever employed before; so much so that not only Jane, but even Susan, was gratified.

III.

Mr. Gillam did not make the visit contemplated by him on the very next day, for I must do him the justice to say that he had waited full three months before ordering from Mr. Jordan, the tailor, a full new suit, out and out. This was received on the evening of the day after that on which the late conversation with Mr. Griggs took place. The latter gentleman had been wearing *his* new suit for some time, not only on Sundays, but occasionally week-days. On the next morning the two met each other at the cross-roads, and both smiled, Mr. Gillam audibly, before and after their salutations. They had exchanged only a few words when who should come up but Mrs. Rainwater on her riding-horse, dressed in her best frock.

"Well, well," said the lady, "when *did* we three expect to meet at the cross-roads before, as the Bible says—I believe it's the Bible—and all three got on our best, same as if it was of a Sunday like, and us on the way to meetin'! I were on my way to your house, Mr. Gillam, to see the girls, poor childern. You goin' to town, I see. All right.

I can have better time with Jane and Susan. Where *you* goin', Mr. Griggs?"

"I—I were jest a-ridin' pe-rusin' about, Missis Rainwater. As you goin' to Mr. Gillam's, an' ef you can't do no better, I'll ga-lant you that fur."

"All right. Mornin', Mr. Gillam."

Without further speech she rode on, joined by Mr. Griggs. Mr. Gillam looked at her for a moment or so before resuming his journey. She was a handsome woman, and had never appeared to better advantage, he thought, during all her widowhood.

"Marryin' female person, cert'n," he soliloquized, and rode on.

Voluble of speech as he was in general, somehow the words which he would employ in hinting to Miss Griggs his intentions were unsatisfactory at the start. Morgan, upon his arrival, of course, after the most polite salutation, vanished, and left the field clear; for Morgan, young as he was, knew what that suit of clothes meant. Mandy (none but the youngest persons in those times said *miss* to girls)—Mandy, though no doubt at least as observant as Morgan, received the visitor in her working-dress and apron, looked calmly at him, talked calmly with him, asked calmly about the girls, and spoke calmly about the state of the weather. This calmness embarrassed Mr. Gillam. He had hoped to see some impartation of the warmth he felt in his own being. For he had thought that unless such appearance was vouchsafed he would merely feel his way along, and not make at once a positive committal. A shrewd man like him could not fail to understand that other possible matrimonial prospects might be hurt by a flat rejection of his first essay on that line. He discoursed at length on the married estate, its superiority to the single in all points which the imagination of man could possibly conceive. Then he indulged in expressions of unlimited wonder how a person, a widower like Harmon Griggs, about whom he had asked of himself the question over and over again, especially of late, how such a man could have remained a widower so long, with the world before him. After such and other extended preliminary remarks, he said that another question, more important and interesting still, had been on his mind lately, and that was what various young women—he need not say that Mandy knew what particular young woman he intended by the question, and the question was what they, or, as the case might be, what she, would do when widowers had concluded to wait no longer, and then another woman might come in, and, to make the matter short, ask them that had been keeping house for their brothers for the smoke-house keys.

"If you mean *me*, Mr. Gillam," answered Mandy, simply, "I should give them up at once, of course."

"Then what?"

"Wait for what Providence sends to me."

"An' supposin'— You b'lieve weddin's is made in heb'n, Mandy?"

"I've not a doubt about that, Mr. Gillam."

"Well, then, is your mind predijiced fer an' to-wards—ahem!—I may say any man-person in any—so to speak—wocations o' life?"

The very voice of Mr. Gillam, let alone his words, was artful.

"I couldn't say, Mr. Gillam — now," answered Mandy, calmly as before, and unblushing. "As to that," she continued, after a pause, "of course a woman would have to think, and think a long time, before making up her mind."

"Too cool, too cool to try to push, yet awhile," thought

Mr. Gillam. "Harm Griggs got to help in this case; ef he don't—"

He rose, and in a distant way said that he might make another call there in a few days.

"'YOU B'LIEVE WEDDIN'S IS MADE IN HED'N, MANDY?'"

After supper that night, Mr. Gillam, having sent out of the room Susan, as being too young to understand and appreciate the circumstances, had a talk with Jane.

"Law, pa," said Jane, sadly and reproachfully, yet smiling somewhat, "when you was primping so, I thought all the time it was for Mrs. Rainwater, and lo and behold it's Mandy!" Then Jane laughed out.

"Don't see anything to laugh about," said her father, looking alternately at her and the finely dressed image he saw in the mirror that hung on the wall.

"Pa, the i-*dea!* Mandy's young enough for your own daughter."

"And ain't *you* young enough for Harm Griggs's daughter?"

"Not quite. But I don't see what that has to do with you and Mandy."

"Well, I'll show Harm Griggs what it's got to do with me an' her. He comin' here hangin' round you, an' kickin' up his heels like a yearlin' boy, an' *me* have to set in the chimbly-cornder an'— Harm Griggs will find out which side his bread's buttered."

"Pa, I don't know what all you're talking about."

"You set thar an' tell me Harm Griggs ain't arfter you, an' a-gainin' on you rapid?"

Jane hesitated before answering. She thought that it might not be best for her to be outspoken regarding her relations to the Griggses, but she felt it her duty to warn him against attempting to win Mandy, and she did so. Then she said, "Pa, Mr. Griggs never courted me, and I've not the slightest idea— Law, pa," she added, almost petulantly, "can't you see that Mr. Griggs, if he's courting anybody, it's Mrs. Rainwater he's a-courting? and which a body would suppose would be a heap more suitable than to be courting such as me."

But Jane Gillam did not look as if she was telling the whole truth about matters that she saw were beginning to grow complicated. Her father, mobile as he was, and knowing how candid she had been always, did not suspect her, and in spite of his exalted estimate of his own value he became convinced that further pursuit of Mandy would be useless.

"Well," he said, "ef it don't beat the everlastin' creations of a ontimely an' gainsayin' world. Never you mind, Harm Griggs! That widder—why, didn't she tell me with her own mouth that Harm Griggs were arfter you? My bloods and thunders! *Somebody* better stand from under, for if they don't mind, somethin', an' somethin' that's heavy, is a-gwine to drap."

Then he went off to bed, but not to rest for a long time. The jealousy that he had felt from the first coming of Harmon Griggs into the neighborhood again seized upon his mind and racked it. If the whole truth could be known, it is probable that his first hostility to the thought of Harmon's marriage with Jane, and afterwards his notion towards Mandy, were prompted in some degree by the pain he felt in contemplating the case of Harmon having a younger wife than he had. He was obliged to know that a match between Harmon and Jane would not have been far disproportionate, and it stung him deeply now to feel how he had miscalculated in that behalf. Then to think of Mrs. Rainwater, who had only lately been so prim and dressy, so cheery and nice and wholesome—to think of her and that plantation, with all that white-oak timber and bottom-land, falling to Harmon Griggs, and him and his children left out in the cold; nay, in all human probability, that same Harmon Griggs proving to have lied about his intentions of quitting the making of coffins, and resuming that business with the enhanced reputation gained from the work he was allowed to do in the case of his, Toby Gillam's, own wife. "Oh, my goodness of gracious! laws of mercies!" Mr. Gillam had to exclaim many times during that night, both when awake and when he slept. The next morning he had no sooner gotten his breakfast than he was on his horse pacing over to Mrs. Rainwater's.

IV.

Her father had been gone but a short time, when Jane, taking a horse from one of the hands who was ploughing in a field near the house, and sending him to the hoe, rode down the road to Mr. Griggs's. She had advanced but a brief distance on her way when she met Mr. Griggs, going, as he said, to the saw-mill. After some conversation, more or less confidential, they parted. Checking her horse a moment thereafter, she called to him, and said, "Mr. Griggs, if it won't be too much trouble, I wish you'd ride up to the house and tell Susan that the smoke-house key is behind the glass drawer on my bureau. I forgot to tell the child about it when I left."

"Cert'nly, Jane, cert'nly."

Even if Mr. Griggs had had no motive in obliging Jane Gillam, he was naturally as accommodating a man, I suppose, as you ever saw. When he had reached the gate, he went so far as to dismount, go into the piazza, and seeing that Susan looked rather lonesome there by herself, not doubting that she, too, was somewhat disturbed by her father's conduct, took a seat and chatted as cheeringly as he knew how for probably an hour; then went on about his business.

"Oh, Mandy, I'm in *such* a flurry about pa!"

In the midst of a talk between the girls, in which Mandy tried to console Jane for her anxiety, Morgan came in, and he lent what service he could render to this kind intent. But Mandy and Morgan, after Jane had left, admitted that Mr. Gillam, in the present condition of his mind, was apt to give trouble all around, and they felt some anxiety, which in Jane's presence they had tried not to seem to indulge. The fact is, there is never any telling how many people may be made anxious by the wayward conduct of such a man as Toby Gillam, especially when lately made a widower.

"You think," said Mr. Griggs, when he had returned home, " that as I rid by Mr. Gillam's a-comin' back home, an' howdyed to him as he sot in his peazer, he never peached a single word, ner never not even nodded his head?"

Yet in this and further speech about the slight he was very calm, and he cautioned his family to be prudent in what they did and said about Mr. Gillam, who, he hoped, would come around right in good time.

Matters were bound to become more complicated and productive of anxiety, considering what kind of reception Mr. Gillam had in his morning's visit. There happened to be at Mrs. Rainwater's her cousin, Miss Cynthy Spears, who, a few days before, had come for a visit of indefinite duration. Plain, slender both in figure and pecuniary or other worldly property, and we'll say from thirty to thirty-seven, Mrs. Rainwater thought much of her for the many excellent traits she possessed, and had sent for her, away down on Buffalo Creek, to come and stay with her as long as she felt like it. Mandy, Jane, and Susan had called upon her, of course, and all said that in their opinion Miss Spears was a good, fine woman. I will let Mr. Gillam tell a few incidents of his call. He addressed himself specially to his youngest.

"Susan, the fact o' the business is, I want you to tell Ben Rainwater that my wishes is he shall keep his k'yarcass away from this house."

All that Susan, stupefied as she was with astonishment, could say, was, " What in the world for, pa?"

"Because I 'tends to show them Griggses *an'* Rainwaters that I'm not the man I'm tuck fer, to be runned over an' trompled on like I had no feelins, no more—no more'n a stump."

"Pa," said Susan, when she could recover her mind, "somebody has gone and hurt your feelings, and I'm just as certain of it as if I'd been there and heard 'em; but I do hope in my heart that it wasn't poor Benny."

"Poor Benny! No, indeed! *He'd* know better what were good for *him*. But you hit the nail on the head. I don't know as you an' Jane know whar I've ben. But I ben to Missis Rainwater's, whar I 'lowed to have a little talk—a civil talk—along 'ith her about one thing an' another. An' you think she didn't set thar an' run up Harm Griggs to the very sky o' heb'n, to that ole maid cousin o' hern, an' prove by me, dad fetch it, every blessed word she said? an' with all the lookin' *an'* coughin' at ole Miss Speeries, or whatsomever her name is, I couldn't git her out o' the room? an' Missis Rainwater had no more politeness than to not let her go, as that ole thing wunst, when I starr'd at her pine blang, riz an' look like she wanted to git away? an' mebbe tired o' hearin' a man so hilt up, an' kep' up, an' proved to *be* up, by gracious, by another man that's his *innimy?*"

His face, naturally reddish, was now near the color of blood.

"Pa," said Susan, as mildly as she could, "I thought you had come to like Mr. Griggs after he got you to make little Betsy's coffin, and insisted on paying you more for it than you charged, and then after making that for poor ma and not let you pay one single cent."

"An' so I did—so I did—tell I found what a desateful creeter he were, a pertendin' to want Jane, when, lo an' be-hol', he's ben a-pesseeutin' o' the widder Rainwater; an' when he git her an' that plantation an' niggers, what chances have Ben Rainwater to s'pote anybody that'll take up 'long o' him? an I want nothin' to do 'ith none o' 'em, an' I want his k'yarcass kep' away from here."

"Oh, pa! pa! to think of your calling as fine a young man as Benny Rainwater a—a carcass!" Susan couldn't stand that. So she put her apron to her eyes. As for Jane, she had left already. "Very well, pa," said Susan, her apron still doing its needed service, "I'll have nothing to do with Benny. I have to do as you say; but such talk, and such—it's right hard, and 'special' on them that's done no harm in this blessed world."

Mr. Gillam had always been more tender with Susan than with Jane. He looked after her as she retired, and his heart might have softened somewhat but for his feeling what great, solemn duties he had to perform, both as a parent and as a man.

"Pa," asked Jane, who had returned to the room merely to put a single respectful question, "as you've forbid the house to Ben Rainwater, and as Mr. Griggs, if he has *any* self-respect, is not apt to come here again, I want to ask if you have any objection to Mandy and Morgan coming if they should ever feel like it."

"I got nothin' to do with Mandy an' Morgan Griggs— nothin' fer ner agin 'em. I don't bother myself 'bout whether *they* come er don't come."

"That's all I want to know," she said, with abject meekness; then again retired.

But for an occasional job in that line of which he was most proudly fond, there is no telling to what extent Mr. Gillam might have incommoded and perplexed those whose peace was dependent upon his conduct. As it was, while engaged in making a coffin, his mind, though not exhibiting that full resignation that used to be remarked on such occasions, yet kept within some sort of bounds his jealous resentments. If Mr. Griggs had broken his word and undertaken such a piece of work in that while, my patience! But Harmon Griggs—

However, I must return to Mr. Gillam. Now it came to pass that Miss Spears, having witnessed some and having heard other of the state into which Mr. Gillam had been put by the treatment that he had received at Mrs. Rainwater's —Miss Spears, good woman, peace-loving woman that she was, felt it to be her duty to do what she could to make matters at least a little better. The forbidding as fine a youth as Ben Rainwater to visit the house, the refusal on his own piazza to return the salutation of as respectable a man as Harmon Griggs, the leaving Mrs. Rainwater's house in what that lady described as plain and perfect a huff as anybody would ever wish to see—all this and more that had come within the knowledge of Miss Spears led her to determine to do whatever was possible in the circumstances to a mere stranger, who, though a stranger, had come to like both families, and to honestly wish for hearty reconciliation all around. Then she knew the Rainwaters and the Griggses all well enough to feel confident that they were not people to submit without some struggle to be warred against by even as passionate, determined a man as Mr. Toby Gillam.

With peace-making intent, therefore, Miss Spears rode over to the Gillams', and in the course of what conversation she had with the head of the family alone, she said that her cousin Sally had partially admitted to her that the extraordinary praise of Mr. Griggs on that fatal day was due to a little innocent desire on her part to tease. Mr. Gillam said that he could not see how that mended matters, and Miss

Spears, to be perfectly honest, had to admit that she coincided in this view—I should perhaps say, rather, this absence of view.

"But Cousin Sally always *were* a joky person, you know, Mr. Gillam; and as for me, I jest up and down, I did, an' I told Cousin Sally that *I* couldn't see wherein Mr. Griggs were *sech* a mighty, powerful, *tremenjuous* man, at leastways as fur as I seen of him yit; an' *as* for him *and* Cousin Sally, I couldn't say if Mr. Griggs *want* Cousin Sally; but I has my opinions about Cousin Sally's *never* of marryin' of *nobody*, exceptin' it's 'ith Benny's consents; an' I *do* know that when ole Missis Pate were a-jokin' of Cousin Sally not long ago about Mr. Griggs, Benny *he* got mad, an' he got up an' left the house, an' he *never* come back twell Misses Pate were *goned*."

"You think," asked Mr. Gillam, "that Ben would jes' natchel be agin his ma's a-marryin' o' *anybody*—any man-person, I mean, in co'se?"

"Well, now, Mr. Gillam, when you talkin' about *step-fathers* an' the *havin'* o' step-fathers, you know in genil how yearlin' boys *is*."

What further might have been said on this delicate subject between the two can only be imagined. But at that moment Jane came out into the piazza where they were sitting, and almost immediately afterwards Miss Spears said that she must be going back home. Mr. Gillam knew very well, of course, that he could easily enough cough Jane away; but just as he was clearing his throat for that purpose the guest gave him a look, went into the house, got her bonnet, came out again, mounted her horse, and home she went. She was so positive in her seriousness and silence that even when Mr. Gillam was parting from her at the horse-block they could only say a good-evening apiece.

That night in the family circle Mr. Gillam exhibited no moroseness whatever, and, to the surprise of his daughters, while unusually thoughtful, seemed rather cheerful in his thoughtfulness.

"I do believe," he said once, in a rather absent-minded way, "that Ben Rainwater's a sensibler feller'n I thought he was."

"I'm *so* glad, pa—" began Susan.

"Come now, come now, Susan; wait an' see."

When all had retired, that busy, scheming intellect revolved other possibilities in barter and exchange.

"Mr. Gillam are a great politicianer," the simple-minded Harmon Griggs used to say.

V.

Ben Rainwater was thought to be in a very embarrassing situation for as young a man as he was. There was his mother, a widow, and there were Mr. Gillam and Mr. Griggs, both widowers, and there were Susan Gillam his love, and Morgan Griggs his friend, and there was himself, in his heart opposed to his mother's marrying anybody at all. So what was Ben to do? Many people said they were sorry for Ben Rainwater, they were; and for their lives they couldn't see how he was to paddle his canoe just all alone by himself. But Ben kept himself collected, cool, and calm. He may have advised with the Griggses, especially Mandy, knowing, in spite of his nonage, that the female mind is more prompt with sympathy and sagacious in devices for such emergencies than the male. In all probability he also consulted his cousin Cynthy Spears, whom the Gillams and Griggses both knew that he thought a great deal of. Once, while at the Gillams' (for now since Mr. Gillam's partial letting down, he, accompanied by Morgan generally, went there right often), he said, in a somewhat distant manner, that if his cousin Cynthy had property, there was no telling what she might not be able to do with herself. For she was one of the best house-keepers, and one of the finest women anyway, that *he* ever saw in all his born days, and, in fact, nobody but him knew what a comfort *and* a consolation she was *to* his mother, especially here lately when the latter was afraid that she might be taking the heart-disease.

"What, Ben!" exclaimed every one of the Gillam family, simultaneously.

"Oh, well," said Ben, smiling sadly, "I can but *hope* it's not so. Ma's a little afraid she's gitting that or somethin'. Of course Cousin Cynthy an' me try to laugh her out o' the notion. But the difficulty is that when Cousin Cynthy's aunt, the old lady Pounds, dies—she's Cousin Cynthy's aunt on the tother side of the family—when *she* dies, and leaves Cousin Cynthy the prop'ty that everybody says she's actilly got in her will *now*, an' then Cousin Cynthy git married an' go away from our house, the *thing* is to tell what ma'll do in such a case. For she ben countin' on Cousin Cynthy takin' up her home along 'ith her."

It is probable that during his whole career Mr. Gillam never drew a longer breath than at these words. The muscles of his face worked with irregular violence, and his eyes grew watery with their heat. He stared at Ben hard for several minutes, then rose and abruptly left the room. Both Jane and Susan scolded Ben, though not harshly.

"Never you mind," said Ben, "you wait and see. News come to Cousin Cynthy only yisterday that her aunt was quite complainy."

If you will believe me, in less than a week from that very day, Miss Spears was sent for, and shortly afterwards a report came up from Buffalo that her aged relative had deceased, and by her last will and testament were bequeathed to Miss Spears, styled by the testatrix her well-beloved niece, two negro girls, an indefinite number of horses, cattle, and swine, and three hundred dollars in specie money.

"There it is, you see now," said Ben to the Gillams: "what ma's to do now with the heart-disease I can't see."

But Ben always declared that it was not himself, and he didn't know who it was for certain, that first started the report that Harmon Griggs, foreseeing the present state of things, had been having his eye on Miss Spears ever since she had been sojourning at Mrs. Rainwater's, and especially since the latter had been threatened by the heart-disease or some kindred malady, and that he had been waiting for the demise of Mrs. Pounds before proposing to appropriate to himself Miss Spears, together with her expected legacy, when every probability was that with the advantage of the hard cash that was known to be a part of it, he would enlarge his workshop and resume the coffin-making business upon a scale to which his former operations in that line were not to be compared. The morning after getting this intelligence Mr. Gillam said to his daughters at the breakfast-table, "Girls, I nuver slept not one single, blessed, everlastin' wink, not in the whole deternal night, last night. I'm a-goin' down to Buff'ler Creek neighborhood on a—on a little business, an' I mayn't be back in a couple or three days. Take keer o' things best you ken, an' don't be oneasy about me."

Brave man as he was, he had not the face to look at those motherless girls. They parted from him with as much respect and as few words as possible, and turned back to their thoughts and their business.

During all this tumultuous behavior Harmon Griggs remained calm until now. Whenever the two met, as they must, residing so near to each other, and to one objective point interesting to both, the younger man spoke just as usual, whatever might be the salutation, if any, that he received. Whenever the Gillam girls came to his house he inquired kindly after their father. But Harmon Griggs was now to show to Mr. Gillam and the rest of the world that he was not altogether the sort of man that he had been taken for.

When Jane, shortly after her father's departure, came all fluttering and flustered with the news, he smiled as men are wont when conscious of knowing what they are about, and sitting down for a while, rendered to the poor girl what consolation and counsel he could think of. Morgan happening to come in from the field, he also and Mandy cordially joined in all Harmon said. Accepting the consolation, she hesitated about the counsel.

"Oh, Susan, Susan, Mr. Griggs!" she said, almost wringing her hands; "what *will* become of poor Susan?"

Right there it was where Harmon Griggs showed the genuineness of his excellent character.

"Jane," he said, in mild solemnity, "you foller my adwices an' do what I tell you. We'll all take keer o' Susan, with Godamighty to help us. Don't you be oneasy about Susan. I've not a doubt *she'd* say you're doin' of right."

Jane at length felt that she ought to yield, and when she did, she said she felt a great deal better.

Then Harmon rose, retired to his chamber, dressed himself in a suit entirely new, came forth again, mounted his horse, and rode away.

VI.

A journey of twenty-five miles was something in that day for an industrious, home-staying man like Mr. Gillam; but he was one that was in the habit of going wherever he had business. Halting at the office of the clerk of the Court of Ordinary at the county-seat, he inquired of that officer if the will of the late Mrs. Jincy Pounds had been offered for probate.

"Why, law, Toby," answered the official, "the old lady Pounds didn't live in this county. She lived jes' on the aidge, but t'other side o' Buff'lo."

"My! my! my!" He rose immediately, and as he remounted his horse, cast his eye up the road by which he had come, in order to see if any pursuer was gaining on him. Then spurring, he proceeded briskly on his way south. He tarried for the night near the Buffalo Bridge, at the house of a farmer with whom he had some little acquaintance. There he learned that Miss Spears was sojourning for the present with a cousin near by who had been named executor of the will. Fortunately Mr. Gillam's host was one of the witnesses to that instrument, and he confirmed the report about the legacy, except that instead of two negro girls, three hundred dollars, and the other items, it should have been one negro girl, one hundred dollars, one mare and colt, two cows and calves, three sows and pigs, and her gig.

The legacy thus diminished subtracted at first somewhat from Mr. Gillam's ardor. But when he reflected on all that Harmon Griggs could do with that cash, and what a glory it would be if he could thwart the design of one who for so long had been an enemy to his peace, all his eagerness returned. Thankful in his heart as he was that his rival was a man of habitually slow motion, yet he felt the need of continued, prompt, energetic action, and so, immediately after breakfast next morning, he sallied forth, crossed the bridge, and repaired to the mansion of the cousin and executor.

Miss Spears, after a weak scream, declared, upon the honor

of a lady, that if *ever* a lady *was* surprised, that *present* lady was surprised at this visit of Mr. Gillam. But that man could see as plainly as the nose on her face, in spite of the regrets she must naturally feel for the recent departure of an aunt so dear, that she was gratified by an action at once so bold and so delicate.

"*Mister* Gillam, I always *knewed*, an' I *told* 'em I knewed, you *had* a heart, an' now I do know it, an' *not* a doubt."

To an inquiry of the visitor whether she expected any other man-person from her cousin Sally Rainwater's neighborhood to come down there shortly, Miss Spears vowed, and properly, I always thought, that she would *not* answer *that* question.

It is perhaps needless to say that such eager devotion and pursuit from such a man as Miss Spears had always known and always told them that she knew him to be, must prevail. But then, oh, *what* if his daughters should be opposed to having a step-mother *brought* there and put over *them!* She shuddered to *think* what they *would* say and *would* do when he *went* back home and *told* them he was engaged to *Cynthy* Spears.

"I'm not a-gwine thar 'ithout her," answered the audacious lover.

"Why! *Mister* Gillam!"

On the afternoon of the third day afterwards, at the point in the road leading northward where, about three hundred yards south of the residence of Mr. Harmon Griggs, the said road made a turn which was to continue for some distance beyond, three travellers might have been seen who were taking a brief rest. In a gig sat a gentleman and lady, who, in spite of the toil of travel, seemed to be in cheerful mood. On a stout mare rode a negro girl, apparently some thirteen years of age, whose face and form, though evidently fatigued, indicated patient endurance. The party had halted, it seemed, for the purpose of allowing the mare to rest and extend nourishment to her colt preparatory to a brisk course over the nice level stretch before them.

"Ride on, Lindy," said the gentleman to the girl; "trot up peert; we'll soon be thar now."

They moved again. The colt, strengthened and cheered by this last meal, dashed ahead, and in answer to the whickers from Mr. Harmon Griggs's horse-lot, gave one whicker himself, kicked up his heels contemptuously, then rushed on more recklessly than before.

It cannot be denied that as Mr. Gillam drew near home, however conscious of his greatness and triumphant felicity, he rather dreaded the meeting of those daughters, who, he believed that he had reason to apprehend, would not at first appreciate his effort to fill the place of the mother who had departed. He had tried to prepare them against sudden breaking forth into lamentations on his arrival by sending word, two days before, of the time and conditions of his return, with the request that they would have the house and everything else set to rights in the mean while. And to save his life he could not but feel some embarrassment when the house of his rival came within view. Clucking to the gig horse, he passed by it as rapidly as possible. He was surprised, however, to find the door closed, and not one of the white family visible.

"Why, hi!" he exclaimed, "what come of 'em all? Look like the whole tribe of 'em goned and flewed away."

A greater surprise awaited him at his own gate. In his piazza were not only Jane and Susan, but Harmon Griggs, and Morgan Griggs, and Mandy Griggs, and Mrs. Rainwater, and Ben Rainwater. In the yard every negro on the place was standing or held in somebody's arms. Not only so, but every blessed one among them, white and black, male and female, old and young and middle-aged, had on the very best things that to their names they possessed. Yet the sounds that greeted Mr. Gillam astonished him still more than the sight of this most unexpected assemblage.

"Howdy, pa? howdy, ma?" cried Jane.

"Howdy, ma? howdy, pa?" cried Susan.

"Howdy, pa? howdy, ma?" cried Morgan.

"Howdy, ma? howdy, pa?" cried Harmon.

"Howdy, Cousin Cynthy? howdy, Cousin Tobe?" cried simultaneously Mrs. Rainwater and Ben.

"Howdy, Cousin Toby? howdy, Cousin Cynthy?" cried Mandy.

"Howdy, marster? howdy, mist'ess?" bawled every negro time and time again.

It was perhaps well for Lindy that she had dismounted at the instant of attaining the end of the journey. For the colt, at the beginning of these tumultuous salutations, ran butting at his dam, and failing in his efforts to move her, stooped his head, squeezed himself through the space between her fore and hind legs, and fled with utmost speed back upon the way he had come. The anxious parent wheeled, and with affectionate but alarmed cries rushed in pursuit of the fugitive. Then Lindy, bent upon the recovery of these fellow-items of her new mistress's property, wheeled also, and—

But I *cannot* delay the account of events so much more important. The assembled parties rushed forth to meet the bridegroom and his bride, and a heartier wringing of hands, in my honest opinion, nobody ought ever to desire to be witness to. Mr. Gillam winked his eyes several times painfully, then gazed around him in speechless, abject wonder.

But for Mrs. Rainwater there is no telling what might have happened.

"Jane," said she, "take your ma in her room and help her off with her bonnet and travellin' things. Go on with Jane, Cousin Cynthy, bless your heart, and pull off and come back quick. Let's go in the peazzer, Cousin Tobe, and let me tell you the *good* news, and if you don't *say* they're good, you ain't the sensible good man I've always took you fer."

Letting her lead him in, he looked doubtfully at the chair that Susan had set for him. But being softly let down into it, he seemed partially thankful that it had not exploded beneath him.

"Cousin Tobe," said the lady, "could you of supposened, a smart, sensible man like you, that as fine daughters as you've got were goin' to stay single *forever*, and let you do *all* the marryin' in the family? If you could, all I *got* to say is, you was monst'ous liable to be mistakened. What you got to say to *that?*"

During this speech Mr. Gillam, whose legs were some distance apart, had lowered his eyes, and was painfully contemplating his feet, while the toes of both were scraping the floor right and left alternately, as if trying, in spite of the fixedness of his other members, to describe adjacent circles. At the question put by Mrs. Rainwater he lifted his head and looked at Harmon and then at Jane (who had now returned with her ma), as if he rather thought that he had some recollection of having seen at least one of them, possibly both, somewhere before.

"No, sir," said Mrs. Rainwater, "that's not the way of it. That's Missis *Morgan* Griggs, and *his* father have done a good part by him—give him two niggers an' other things accordin'. If you want to know who Missis *Harmon* Griggs is—and that 'stonished everybody else much as it'll now 'stonish you—thar *she* stand by her husband."

And she pointed to Susan, who, her cheeks covered with roses, laid her hand on Harmon's arm.

Already beyond any added stupefaction, he lowered his eyes again, and resting his elbows upon his knees, laid his chin upon his open palms, and seemed to be entering upon profound reflection.

"Come now, come now, Mr. Gillam," said his wife, "the girls have got married to suit theirselves, and you *can't* deny but what both of 'em has married well."

As if suddenly recalling something on which his mind used to dwell with moderate interest, he looked up and said,

"Why, hello, Ben! Why, why, why, whar was *you* in all thesen k'yarns on?"

"Cousin Tobe," resumed Mrs. Rainwater, "Ben's all right. One thing made us come over this evenin' was to invite you and Cousin Cynthy to him and Mandy's weddin' next Tuesday night, an' the infare I'm goin' to give 'em the next day."

"Cynthy," said Mr. Gillam, "don't it all beat— But— whar's your cousin Sally in all this mixtry an' minglin' up o' men an' childern, women an' boys? Whar's she?"

"Me?" answered the widow, laying her hand upon her breast. "Why, you know, Cousin Tobe, that *I* have the heart-disease;" and the whole grove echoed to the peal of her laughter.

Once more Mr. Gillam lowered his head and ruminated. Then lifting it, he said, "Harm Griggs, wuz you a-tellin' o' me the fack-truth when you said you wus done 'ith the makin' o' coffins?"

"I wuz, Mr. Gillam, solemn as ef my hand were on the Bible."

"'WUZ YOU A-TELLIN' O' ME THE PACK-TRUTH WHEN YOU SAID YOU WUZ DONE 'ITH THE MAKIN' O' COFFINS?'"

A smile by degrees overspread Mr. Gillam's face; he rose, and looking around, said, " Well, I got nothin' mo' to say fer nev' agin. Ef sech onbeknownst, an' sech onexpected, an' sech on-*possible* jindin' o' peoples satisfies you all, they satisfies me."

THE HOTEL EXPERIENCE OF
MR. PINK FLUKER.

"Mathematici, genus hominum sperantibus fallax."—*Tacitus.*

I.

Mr. Peterson Fluker, generally called Pink, for his fondness for as stylish dressing as he could afford, was one of that sort of men who habitually seem busy and efficient when they are not. He had the bustling activity often noticeable in men of his size, and in one way and another had made up, as he believed, for being so much smaller than most of his adult acquaintance of the male sex. Prominent among his achievements on that line was getting married to a woman who, among other excellent gifts, had that of being twice as big as her husband.

"Fool who?" on the day after his marriage he had asked, with a look at those who had often said that he was too little to have a wife.

They had a little property to begin with, a couple of hundreds of acres, and two or three negroes apiece. Yet except in the natural increase of the latter, the accretions of worldly estate had been inconsiderable till now, when their oldest child, Marann, was some fifteen years old. These accretions had been saved and taken care of by Mrs. Fluker, who was as staid and silent as he was mobile and voluble.

Mr. Fluker often said that it puzzled him how it was that he made smaller crops than most of his neighbors, when, if not always convincing, he could generally put every one of them to silence in discussions upon agricultural topics.

This puzzle had led him to not unfrequent ruminations in his mind as to whether or not his vocation might lie in something higher than the mere tilling of the ground. These ruminations had lately taken a definite direction, and it was after several conversations which he had held with his friend Matt Pike.

Mr. Matt Pike was a bachelor of some thirty summers, aforetime clerk consecutively in each of the two stores of the village, but latterly a trader on a limited scale in horses, wagons, cows, and similar objects of commerce, and at all times a politician. His hopes of holding office had been continually disappointed until Mr. John Sanks be-

"FOOL WHO?"

came sheriff, and rewarded with a deputyship some important special service rendered by him in the late very close canvass. Now was a chance to rise, Mr. Pike thought. All he wanted, he had often said, was a start. Politics, I would remark, however, had been regarded by Mr. Pike as a means rather than an end. It is doubtful if he hoped to become governor of the State, at least before an advanced period in his career. His main object now was to get money, and he believed that official position would promote him in the line of his ambition faster than was possible to any private station, by leading him into more extensive acquaintance with mankind, their needs, their desires, and their caprices. A deputy-sheriff, provided that lawyers were not too indulgent in allowing acknowledgment of service of court processes, in postponing levies and sales, and in settlement of litigated cases, might pick up three hundred dollars—a good sum for those times—a fact which Mr. Pike had known and pondered long.

It happened just about then that the arrears of rent for the village hotel had so accumulated on Mr. Spouter, the last occupant, that the owner, an indulgent man, finally had said, what he had been expected for years and years to say, that he could not wait on Mr. Spouter forever and eternally. It was at this very nick, so to speak, that Mr. Pike made to Mr. Fluker the suggestion to quit a business so far beneath his powers, sell out, or rent out, or tenant out, or do something else with his farm, march into town, plant himself upon the ruins of Jacob Spouter, and begin his upward soar.

Now Mr. Fluker had many and many a time acknowledged that he had ambition; so one night he said to his wife,

"You see how it is here, Nervy. Farmin' somehow don't suit my talons. I need to be flung more 'mong people to fetch out what's in me. Then thar's Marann, which is gittin' to be nigh on to a growd-up woman; an' the child need the s'iety which you 'bleeged to acknowledge is sca'ce about here, six mile from town. Your br'er Sam can stay here an' raise butter, chickens, eggs, pigs, an'—an'—an' so forth. Matt Pike say he jes' know they's money in it, an' 'special' with a house-keeper keerful an' equinomical like you."

It is always curious the extent of influence that some men have upon wives who are their superiors. Mrs. Fluker, in spite of accidents, had ever set upon her husband a value that was not recognized outside of his family. In this respect there seems a surprising compensation in human life. But this remark I make only in passing. Mrs. Fluker, admitting in her heart that farming was not her husband's forte, hoped, like a true wife, that it might be found in the new field to which he aspired. Besides, she did not forget that her brother Sam had said to her several times privately that if his br'er Pink wouldn't have so many notions, and would let him alone in his management, they would all do better. She reflected for a day or two, and then said,

"Maybe it's best, Mr. Fluker. I'm willin' to try it fer a year, anyhow. We can't lose much by that. As fer Matt Pike, I hain't the confidence in him you has. Still, he bein' a boarder and deputy-sheriff, he might accidentally do us some good. I'll try it fer a year, providin' you'll fetch me the money as it's paid in, fer you know I know how to manage that better'n you do, and you know I'll try to manage it and all the rest o' the business fer the best."

To this provision Mr. Fluker gave consent, qualified by the claim that he was to retain a small margin for indispensable personal exigencies. For he contended, perhaps with justice, that no man in the responsible position he was about to take ought to be expected to go about, or sit about, or even lounge about, without even a continental red in his pocket.

The new house—I say *new* because tongue could not tell the amount of scouring, scalding, and whitewashing that

that excellent house-keeper had done before a single stick of her furniture went into it—the new house, I repeat, opened with six eating boarders at ten dollars a month apiece, and two eating and sleeping at eleven, besides Mr. Pike, who made a special contract. Transient custom was hoped to hold its own, and that of the county people under the deputy's patronage and influence to be considerably enlarged.

In words and other encouragement Mr. Pike was pronounced. He could commend honestly, and he did so cordially.

"The thing to do, Pink, is to have your prices reg'lar, and make people pay up reg'lar. Ten dollars fer eatin', jes' so; eleb'n fer eatin' *an'* sleepin'; half a dollar fer dinner, jes' so; quarter apiece fer breakfast, supper, and bed, is what I call reason'ble bo'd. As fer me, I sca'cely know how to rig'late, because, you know, I'm a' officer now, an' in course I natchel *has* to be away sometimes an' on expenses at tother places, an' it seem like some 'lowance ought by good rights to be made fer that; don't you think so?"

"Why, matter o' course, Matt; what you think? I ain't so powerful good at figgers. Nervy is. S'posen you speak to her 'bout it."

"Oh, that's perfec' unuseless, Pink. I'm a' officer o' the law, Pink, an' the law consider women—well, I may say the law *she* deal 'ith *men,* not women, an' she expect her officers to understan' figgers, an' if I hadn't o' understood figgers Mr. Sanks wouldn't or darsn't to 'p'int me his dep'ty. Me 'n' you can fix them terms. Now see here; reg'lar bo'd—eatin' bo'd, I mean—is ten dollars, an' sleepin' and singuil meals is 'cordin' to the figgers you've sot fer 'em. Ain't that so? Jes' so. Now, Pink, you an' me'll keep a runnin' account, you a-chargin' fer reg'lar bo'd, an' I 'lowin' to myself cred-ies fer my absentees, accordin' to transion customers an' singuil mealers an' sleepers. Is that fa'r, er is it not fa'r?"

Mr. Fluker turned his head, and after making, or thinking he had made, a calculation, answered,

"That's—that seem fa'r, Matt."

"Cert'nly 'tis, Pink; I knowed you'd say so, an' you know I'd never wish to be nothin' but fa'r 'ith people I like, like I do you an' your wife. Let that be the understandin', then, betwix' us. An' Pink, let the understandin' be jes' betwix' *us*, fer I've saw enough o' this world to find out that a man never makes nothin' by makin' a blowin' horn o' his business. You make the tothers pay up spuntial, monthly. You 'n' me can settle whensomever it's convenant, say three months from to-day. In cose I shall talk up fer the house whensomever and wharsomever I go or stay. You know that. An' as fer my bed," said Mr. Pike, finally, "whensomever I ain't here by bedtime, you welcome to put any transion person in it, an' also an' likewise, when transion custom is pressin', and you cramped fer beddin', I'm willin' to give it up fer the time bein'; an' ruther'n you should be cramped too bad, I'll take my chances somewhars else, even if I has to take a pallet at the head o' the sta'r-steps."

"Nervy," said Mr. Fluker to his wife afterwards, "Matt Pike's a sensibler an' a friendlier an' a 'commodatiner feller'n I thought."

Then, without giving details of the contract, he mentioned merely the willingness of their boarder to resign his bed on occasions of pressing emergency.

"He's talked mighty fine to me and Marann," answered Mrs. Fluker. "We'll see how he holds out. One thing I do *not* like of his doin', an' that's the talkin' 'bout Sim Marchman to Marann, an' makin' game o' his country ways, as he call 'em. Sech as that ain't right."

It may be as well to explain just here that Simeon Marchman, the person just named by Mrs. Fluker, a stout, industrious young farmer, residing with his parents in the country near where the Flukers had dwelt before removing to town, had been eying Marann for a year or two, and waiting upon her fast-ripening womanhood with intentions that he believed to be hidden in his own breast, though he had taken less pains to conceal them from Marann than from the rest of his acquaintance. Not that he had ever told her of them in so many words, but— Oh, I need not stop here in the midst of this narration to explain how such intentions become known, or at least strongly suspected by girls, even those less bright than Marann Fluker. Simeon had not cordially indorsed the movement into town, though, of course, knowing it was none of his business, he had never so much as hinted opposition. I would not be surprised, also, if he reflected that there might be some selfishness in his hostility, or at least that it was heightened by apprehensions personal to himself.

Considering the want of experience in the new tenants, matters went on remarkably well. Mrs. Fluker, accustomed to rise from her couch long before the lark, managed to the satisfaction of all—regular boarders, single-meal takers, and transient people. Marann went to the village school, her mother dressing her, though with prudent economy, as neatly and almost as tastefully as any of her schoolmates; while, as to study, deportment, and general progress, there was not a girl in the whole school to beat her, I don't care who she was.

II.

During a not inconsiderable period Mr. Fluker indulged the honorable conviction that at last he had found the vein in which his best talents lay, and he was happy in foresight of the prosperity and felicity which that discovery promised to himself and his family. His native activity found many more objects for its exertion than before. He rode out to the farm, not often, but sometimes, as a matter of duty, and was forced to acknowledge that Sam was managing better than could have been expected in the absence of his own continuous guidance. In town he walked about the hotel, entertained the guests, carved at the meals, hovered about the stores, the doctors' offices, the wagon and blacksmith shops, discussed mercantile, medical, mechanical questions with specialists in all these departments, throwing into them all more and more of politics as the intimacy between him and his patron and chief boarder increased.

Now as to that patron and chief boarder. The need of extending his acquaintance seemed to press upon Mr. Pike with ever-increasing weight. He was here and there, all over the county; at the county-seat, at the county villages, at justices' courts, at executors' and administrators' sales, at quarterly and protracted religious meetings, at barbecues of every dimension, on hunting excursions and fishing frolics, at social parties in all neighborhoods. It got to be said of Mr. Pike that a freer accepter of hospitable invitations, or a better appreciator of hospitable intentions, was not, and needed not, to be found possibly in the whole State. Nor was this conspicuous deportment confined to the county in which he held so high official position. He attended, among other occasions less public, the spring sessions of the Supreme and County courts in the four adjoining counties: the guest of acquaintance old and new over there. When starting upon such travels he would sometimes breakfast with his travelling companion in the village, and if somewhat belated in the return, sup with him also.

Yet, when at the Flukers', no man could have been a more

cheerful and otherwise satisfactory boarder than Mr. Matt Pike. He praised every dish set before him, bragged to their very faces of his host and hostess, and in spite of his absences was the oftenest to sit and chat with Marann when her mother would let her go into the parlor. Here and everywhere about the house, in the dining-room, in the passage, at the foot of the stairs, he would joke with Marann about her country beau, as he styled poor Sim Marchman, and he would talk as though he was rather ashamed of Sim, and wanted Marann to string her bow for higher game.

Br'er Sam did manage well, not only the fields, but the yard. Every Saturday of the world he sent in something or other to his sister. I don't know whether I ought to tell it or not, but for the sake of what is due to pure veracity I will. On as many as three different occasions Sim Marchman, as if he had lost all self-respect, or had not a particle of tact, brought in himself, instead of sending by a negro, a bucket of butter and a coop of spring chickens as a free gift to Mrs. Fluker. I do think, on my soul, that Mr. Matt Pike was too much amused by such degradation—however, he must say that they were all first-rate. As for Marann, she was very sorry for Sim, and wished he had not brought these good things at all.

Nobody knew how it came about; but when the Flukers had been in town somewhere between two and three months, Sim Marchman, who (to use his own words) had never bothered Marann a great deal with his visits, began to suspect that what few he made were received by her lately with less cordiality than before; and so one day, knowing no better in his awkward, straightforward country manners, he wanted to know the reason why. Then Marann grew distant, and asked Sim the following question:

"You know where Mr. Pike's gone, Mr. Marchman?"

Now the fact was, and she knew it, that Marann Fluker had never before, not since she was born, addressed that boy as *Mister*.

The visitor's face reddened and reddened.

"No," he faltered in answer; "no—no—*ma'am*, I should say. I—I don't know where Mr. Pike's gone."

Then he looked around for his hat, discovered it in time, took it into his hands, turned it around two or three times, then bidding good-by without shaking hands, took himself off.

Mrs. Fluker liked all the Marchmans, and she was troubled somewhat when she heard of the quickness and manner of Sim's departure; for he had been fully expected by her to stay to dinner.

"Say he didn't even shake hands, Marann? What for? What you do to him?"

"Not one blessed thing, ma; only he wanted to know why I wasn't gladder to see him." Then Marann looked indignant.

"Say them words, Marann?"

"No, but he hinted 'em."

"What did you say then?"

"I jes' asked, a-meaning nothing in the wide world, ma— I asked him if he knew where Mr. Pike had gone."

"And that were answer enough to hurt his feelins. What you want to know where Matt Pike's gone fer, Marann?"

"I didn't care about knowing, ma, but I didn't like the way Sim talked."

"Look here, Marann. Look straight at me. You'll be mighty fur off your feet if you let Matt Pike put things in your head that hain't no business a-bein' there, and 'special' if you find yourself a-wantin' to know where he's a preambulatin' in his everlastin' minanderins. Not a cent has he paid for his board, and which your pa say he have a' understandin' with him about allowin' for his absentees, which is all right enough, but which it's now goin' on to three mont's, and what is comin' to us I need and I want. He ought—your pa ought to let me bargain with Matt Pike, because he know he don't understan' figgers like Matt Pike. He don't know exactly what the bargain were; for I've asked him, and he always begins with a multiplyin' o' words and never answers me."

On his next return from his travels Mr. Pike noticed a coldness in Mrs. Fluker's manner, and this enhanced his praise of the house. The last week of the third month came. Mr. Pike was often noticed, before and after meals, standing at the desk in the hotel office (called in those times the bar-room) engaged in making calculations. The day before the contract expired Mrs. Fluker, who had not indulged herself with a single holiday since they had been in town, left Marann in charge of the house, and rode forth, spending part of the day with Mrs. Marchman, Sim's mother. All were glad to see her, of course, and she returned smartly freshened by the visit. That night she had a talk with Marann, and oh how Marann did cry!

The very last day came. Like insurance policies, the contract was to expire at a certain hour. Sim Marchman came just before dinner, to which he was sent for by Mrs. Fluker, who had seen him as he rode into town.

"Hello, Sim," said Mr. Pike as he took his seat opposite him. "You here? What's the news in the country? How's your health? How's crops?"

"Jes' mod'rate, Mr. Pike. Got little business with you after dinner, ef you can spare time."

"All right. Got a little matter with Pink here first. 'Twon't take long. See you arfter amejiant, Sim."

MR. FLUKER FELT THAT HE WAS BECOMING A LITTLE CONFUSED.

Never had the deputy been more gracious and witty. He talked and talked, out-talking even Mr. Fluker; he was the only man in town who could do that. He winked at Marann as he put questions to Sim, some of the words employed in which Sim had never heard before. Yet Sim held up as well as he could, and after dinner followed Marann with some little dignity into the parlor. They had not been there more than ten minutes when Mrs. Fluker was heard to walk rapidly along the passage leading from the dining-room, to enter her own chamber for only a moment, then to come out and rush to the parlor door with the gig-whip in her hand. Such uncommon conduct in a woman like Mrs. Pink Fluker of course needs explanation.

When all the other boarders had left the house, the deputy and Mr. Fluker having repaired to the bar-room, the former said,

"Now, Pink, for our settlement, as you say your wife think we better have one. I'd 'a' been willin' to let accounts keep on a-runnin', knowin' what a straightforrards sort o' man you was. Your count, ef I ain't mistakened, is jes' thirty-three dollars, even money. Is that so, or is it not?"

"That's it to a dollar, Matt. Three times eleben make thirty-three, don't it?"

"It do, Pink, or eleben times three, jes' which you please. Now here's my count, on which you'll see, Pink, that not nary cent have I charged for infloonce. I has infloonced a consider'ble custom to this house, as you know, bo'din' and transion. But I done that out o' my respects of you an' Missis Fluker, an' your keepin' of a fa'r—I'll say, as I've said freekwent, a *very* fa'r house. I let them infloonces go to friendship, ef you'll take it so. Will you, Pink Fluker?"

"Cert'nly, Matt, an' I'm a thousand times obleeged to you, an'—"

"Say no more, Pink, on that p'int o' view. Ef I like a man I know how to treat him. Now as to the p'ints o' absentees, my business as dep'ty-sheriff has took me away from this inconsider'ble town freckwent, hain't it?"

"It have, Matt, er somethin' else, more'n I were a expectin', an'—"

"Jes' so. But a public officer, Pink, when jooty call on him to go, he got to go; in fack he got to *goth*, as the Scriptur' say; ain't that so?"

"I s'pose so, Matt, by good rights, a—a official speakin'."

Mr. Fluker felt that he was becoming a little confused.

"Jes' so. Now, Pink, I were to have credics for my absentees 'cordin' to transion an' single-meal bo'ders an' sleepers; ain't that so?"

"I — I — somethin' o' that sort, Matt," Mr. Fluker answered, vaguely.

"Jes' so. Now look here," drawing from his pocket a paper. "Itom one. Twenty-eight dinners at half a dollar makes fourteen dollars, don't it? Jes' so. Twenty-five breakfasts at a quarter makes six an' a quarter, which make dinners an' breakfasts twenty an' a quarter. Foller me up as I go up, Pink. Twenty-five suppers at a quarter makes six an' a quarter, an' which them added to the twenty an' a quarter, makes them twenty-six an' a half. Foller, Pink, an' if you ketch me in any mistakes in the k'yar'n' an' addin' p'int it out. Twenty-two an' a half beds—an' I say *half*, Pink, because you 'member one night when them A'gusty lawyers got here 'bout midnight on their way to co't, ruther 'n have you too bad cramped, I ris to make way for two of 'em; yit as I had one good nap, I didn't think I ought to put that down but for half. Them makes five dollars half an' seb'n pence, an' which k'yar'd on to the tother twenty-six an' a half, fetches the whole cabool to jes' thirty-two

MR. MARCHMAN'S PRESSING BUSINESS WITH MR. PIKE.

dollars an' seb'n pence. But I made up my mind I'd fling out that seb'n pence, an' jes' call it a dollar even money, an' which here's the solid silver."

In spite of the rapidity with which this enumeration of countercharges was made, Mr. Fluker commenced perspiring at the first item, and when the balance was announced his face was covered with huge drops.

It was at this juncture that Mrs. Fluker, who, well-knowing her husband's unfamiliarity with complicated accounts, had felt it her duty to be listening near the bar-room door, left, and quickly afterwards appeared before Marann and Sim as I have represented.

"You think Matt Pike ain't tryin' to settle with your pa with a dollar? I'm goin' to make him keep his dollar, an' I'm goin' to give him somethin' to go 'long with it."

"The good Lord have mercy upon us!" exclaimed Marann, springing up and catching hold of her mother's skirts as she began her advance towards the bar-room. "Oh, ma! for the Lord's sake!—Sim, Sim, Sim, if you care *anything* for me in this wide world, don't let ma go into that room!"

"Missis Fluker," said Sim, rising instantly, "wait jest two minutes till I see Mr. Pike on some pressin' business; I won't keep you over two minutes a-waitin'."

He took her, set her down in a chair trembling, looked at her a moment as she began to weep, then, going out and closing the door, strode rapidly to the bar-room.

"Let me help you settle your board-bill, Mr. Pike, by payin' you a little one I owe you."

Doubling his fist, he struck out with a blow that felled the deputy to the floor. Then catching him by his heels, he dragged him out of the house into the street. Lifting his foot above his face, he said,

"You stir till I tell you an' I'll stomp your nose down

even with the balance of your mean face. 'Tain't exactly my business how you cheated Mr. Fluker, though, 'pon my soul, I never knowed a trifliner, lowdowner trick. But *I* owed you myself for your talkin' 'bout an' your lyin' 'bout me, and now I've paid you; an' ef you only knowed it, I've saved you from a gig-whippin'. Now you may git up."

"Here's his dollar, Sim," said Mr. Fluker, throwing it out of the window. "Nervy say make him take it."

The vanquished, not daring to refuse, pocketed the coin and slunk away amid the jeers of a score of villagers who had been drawn to the scene.

In all human probability the late omission of the shaking of Sim's and Marann's hands was compensated at their parting that afternoon. I am more confident on this point because at the end of the year those hands were joined inseparably by the preacher. But this was when they had all gone back to their old home; for if Mr. Fluker did not become fully convinced that his mathematical education was not advanced quite enough for all the exigencies of hotel-keeping, his wife declared that she had had enough of it, and that she and Marann were going home. Mr. Fluker may be said, therefore, to have followed, rather than led, his family on the return.

As for the deputy, finding that if he did not leave it voluntarily he would be drummed out of the village, he departed, whither I do not remember, if anybody ever knew.

THE WIMPY ADOPTIONS.

"They make time old to tend them, and experience
An ass, they alter so."—*Mad Lover.*

I.

"When people begin on the adaptin' of other people's children, they is never any tellin' where it'll all end." This remark used to be made often by one of the most excellent ladies in our neighborhood. Long before its first utterance, and the events which I purpose now to relate, Mr. Lazarus Wimpy, after a courtship languidly extended through many years, married the woman whom gradually he had come to believe about as well fitted to promote his domestic well-being as any that he might reasonably hope to obtain. The fruits of this marriage, coming at equal intervals of two years, three weeks, and six days (an interesting freak of periodicity, Mr. Wimpy always thought), were, first, Faithy, a daughter, then Lawson, a son, lastly, Creecy, a daughter. Their dwelling, six miles west of the village, half a mile north from the public road, having, besides the usual two shed rooms in the rear, a small one at one end of the front piazza, stood upon a knoll, near the centre of the plantation of some four hundred acres of good, though rather rolling, land. Near, on one side, were the kitchen, smoke-house, dairy, and two cabins, quite enough for their small squad of negroes. On the other, outside of the yard, were the horse and cattle lots. In the rear was the garden, and in front, at the foot of the knoll, was the spring that ever since the settlement thereby had been the talk of the neighborhood, and the pride, though not boastful, of the family. There was hardly a homestead in that region that had not a spring of some sort near by, though the larger planters generally had wells dug in their yards for the sake of more convenience and sometimes greater coolness. But one attempt had ever been made to supplement the water supply on the Wimpy place. Miss Faithy used to tell of that in words that showed becoming compassion for the needy expert who proposed it.

"They come a man 'long here one day, with a bundle o' green switches under his arm, prewidin' that with ary one o' them he could tell where to git water the quickest and moest. I didn't laugh right out in the man's face, because my parrents never raised me to sech *as* that; but I told him, polite as I could, to foller me, if he choosed, a few steps. When he had laid eyes on our spring, an' when he have drunk a gourd I give him with my own hands, the man looked, he did, like he war 'shamed of hisself, an' I were that sorry fer him, I made him set down on the bench under the big sweet-gum, an' I went an' fetched some lightbread an' butter, an' honey, to go 'long of the jug o' milk were already there. He 'peared like he feel some better then; for he were a person of good, healthy appetites, an' the nex' I heerd of him he were stretchin' his switches on the Alfords' preemerses, an' no wonder; because they has nigh on to a hundred in fambly besides of stock, an' their spring have to be cleaned out every 'casional in the bargain. But *as* fer me, a body ought to try to not to be proud, an' that of the blessen's of Providence—yit I am not a person that I could invie them, no matter how many niggers, that has to drink well-water, for man an' beast."

Do I not remember that spring with its bold bubblings from the pebbly bottom, impatient of the great rock curb that delayed them to supply that economical family, before hastening to the creek a mile away, and the white oaks above, and the willows and sweet-gum below, under the last of which Mr. Lawson used to sit and watch the bees coming to drink, and whenever I and other children would be there revelling in the glorious refections extended by Miss Faithy, tell us tales of his huntings in the forests all around?

When I first knew these neighbors the parents had been long dead. The youngest child, lately widowed by the death of her husband, who, during the ten or a dozen years of married life, had spent the little property she had inherited, had come back to her native homestead. Her sister and brother had never married, and now were never so much as dreaming of such a thing. It was a harmonious family; that is, in the main. The younger sister, after her return, on occasions at first frequent, then at intervals of irregular duration, showed signs that she considered that she should be regarded as the head of the family, basing this claim upon the wisdom presumed to have come from marriage experience, a gift not possessed by the others, and which, at their ages, regarded by herself so very far advanced beyond her own, it was not to be expected that they ever would attain. But Miss Faithy, with more or less decision of mood and manner, ignored this claim, and held to the position to which she believed that by her age, if nothing else, she was entitled. She had inherited (from some remote ancestor, as seemed likely) energy to a good, not to say high, degree, and, as a general thing, she was able to express herself even with some animation, when believed proper, on whatsoever subject she felt herself competent to discuss. Contrariwise, her brother was mild and taciturn, though not gloomy, nor, strictly speaking, indolent. If he had been as active a person as his elder sister, it is possible that their estate, yet held jointly, would have been larger. But they both felt that the accretions had been enough for their needs; so the sister never complained, nor felt like complaining, at her brother's habitual pitch of the crop and other out-door work at a figure that would not hinder his indulgence in the pastimes of which, one especially, he had been fond from his youth. The lead in the household he had willingly yielded, since the death of their parents, to his elder sister. This submission, instead of diminishing her affection and respect for him, enhanced them; for the taciturn, yielding man will more often be appreciated at his just value than the loud and domineering. Habitually Miss Faithy consulted him in matters about which she was doubtful, and she sometimes said,

"Lawson may be a say-nothin' kind of person; but you git into de-ficulties in your mind, an' they is monst'ous few men their jedgments *I* ruther have. When you git down to the bottom o' Lawson, he's deep."

The ladies, especially Miss Faithy, were tall, somewhat gaunt, but not uncomely, full of health, first-rate housekeepers (especially the elder), hospitable, economical, given (notably the younger) to visiting among the neighbors, and always glad, even to acknowledged gratitude, when visited by them. The gentleman was of middle height, inclining of late years slightly towards stoutness, slow and low of speech, yet, if you gave him time, able to interest more than you would have expected. If he had been pressed to admit what he had most special fondness for, his answer must have been bee-hunting. In this sport he was as successful as fond. The number of bee-trees that he had found and reduced not even himself could have told. Whenever in his presence a bee rose from drinking at the Wimpy spring-branch, as soon as with wings outspread he set forth on his line, Mr. Wimpy would know if he were domestic or savage. If the latter, marking with his eye the insect's departure and latitude with a precision that no compass and quadrant could surpass, he would set out at his leisure, and afterwards tree him as infallibly as if he were already working in the Wimpy garden.

A peaceful, harmless life was that led in this household. What interruptions were made by the younger sister's ambitions were never important, and they diminished with the lapse of time. Not often was allusion made by the head of the family to her departed brother-in-law, but sometimes to Mrs. Keenum, her closest neighbor, she would talk about thus:

"People ought to try to be thankful, Betsy, that it were a blessin' the po' creetur leff no offsprings; an' if it wasn't a sin, a body might not feel like cryin' *too* much when he went; which Dr. Lewis told me in the strictest confidence, that nigh as he could come to his diseases, he thes give out from bein' of no 'count. An', which in case it is *not* the jooty of a person to talk too much about them that's dead an' goned, but what beat me is Creecy a-tryin' to fling up sometimes to me an' Lawson, of her onct a-bein' of a married person an' me not, to give her the k'yarrin' of the smoke-house an' pantry keys, like ef the livin' of thirteen year with sech as Reddin Copelin have made a wisdom out of her an' a ejiot of me. Yit we was thankful, me an' Lawson, when she could git back where she could git a-plenty to eat; an' ef the child knowed her own mind, she were thankful as we was. But its cur'ous how the gittin' of married of some women, makes no odds how triflin' the men they took up with, 'special' when they're widders, how they can consate that they must be the heads of people that's older than them, an' norate an' go on same as ef they be'n to a colleges somewheres, nobody knows wheres. I suppose it's a some consolation that ef they got nothin' else to brag about, they've had expeunce o' things which is worth more than them that hain't been calc'latin' on. Yit Creecy's a affectionate sister, an' in giner'l she give up when she see that I can't be conwinced she learnt that much from Red Copelin that I can't 'tend to my own business."

This was the only drop that was not sweet in the cup so abounding with peace and plenty. It was only a drop, and that not a bitter one. I remember that when I used to go there to carry or bring away some work (for Miss Faithy was a noted cutter and maker), I wondered that the whole family, instead of being mainly gaunt, did not all look like rotund stall-feds, and that I constantly, if vaguely, expected somebody from somewhere to come and fatten on this exuberant fecundity. And sure enough they did.

Even if I knew the precise ages of the members of this excellent family at this period, there are reasons why I should not tell; not that the two oldest would have objected to the revelation, but there are proprieties in cases of unmarried persons who have so remained for other reasons than that of extreme youth, throughout a somewhat extended period, that ought to be and, so far as I am concerned, will be respected. I pass on, therefore, at once to the Pringles.

II.

If anybody ever did know a more shiftless set than the Pringles, he must have been a traveller. They lived, such living as it was, in a log-cabin belonging to the Wimpys, situate near the junction of the public road with that leading from their place. Being nearer to these good people than anybody else, it was some relief to them when Mrs. Pringle died and Mr. Pringle was gotten away. Their children—Jesse, ten, and Milly, six years old—could then be taken care of with less trouble and expense than the whole family had inflicted heretofore. Miss Faithy, never laying claim to be an uncommonly charitable person, had fed and scolded, scolded and fed these imbeciles ever since they had been dropped there whence nobody, I believe, ever knew; and when the children had been left motherless, she said to her brother,

"Lawson, it's thes like they was two suckin' calves, with a dead mammy an' a-belongin' to nobody; er ef so be, their owner won't acknowledge 'em. But it's not goin' to do for 'em to per'sh thes so; fer the good Lord never wants sech *as* that, when it can be holp. Ef the Alfords would take 'em, or ef—but no use of *effin'* about it. They're nigher to us than anybody else, an' we've had 'em to feed tell now, anyhow, an' I don't know as we've missed or ben much worst off fer doin' of it. Me an' you, it seem to me, will thes have to take 'em, a prewidin' that Sol Pringle will take hisself off, as my opinions is he'll be ready an' willin' enough to do. You can, as it were, ruther *adap'* that Jes', an' me po' little Milly, or we can *adap'* 'em both j'intly; that is, of cose, tell they old enough an' big enough to help theirselves. It won't do to turn 'em out thes so in the howlin' wilderness. It'll be a trouble; but it seem like a jooty which a body *can't* dodge, an' maybe we won't go 'ithout a award some time *er* another ef we don't try to dodge it."

Her brother, as she knew he would, after solemn deliberation, yielded to the proposal.

250   THE WIMPY ADOPTIONS.

Mr. Solomon Pringle, in spite of appearances, had always spoken of himself as a person of lofty aspirations, which, but for the incumbrance of wife and children, he believed

MR. SOLOMON PRINGLE.

could achieve eminent success. He gave a resigned assent to the Wimpy proposal, that included his own perpetual withdrawal from the neighborhood, but he stipulated that he should not be hindered from sending to them such portions of his achievements elsewhere as his parental affection might urge. He shook hands all around, admonished his children to remember his precepts and continue to be good, accepted silently the money given by Miss Faithy for his household goods, apprized at double their value, then cheerfully departed westward.

These things occurred shortly after Mrs. Copelin, having nowhere else to go, had returned to the home of her youth. She did not heartily approve the advent of the orphans, and suggested the trouble, expense, and scarcity of room; but her sister answered decisively that they would come. As for the expense, they would be expected, when old enough, to work like the rest of the family; as for room, the boy could have a trundle-bed in Lawson's shed, and the girl sleep with herself; and as for the trouble, whoever counted upon living without some trouble in this world must have read the Bible to not very much purpose; and that as for herself, she believed that less trouble would be in taking than in turning backs against them that it did seem the good Lord had placed in the very path a body was treading. So they came, and if they did not improve, my, my!

"It nately did do a body good, Betsy," said Miss Faithy to Mrs. Keenum, some time afterwards, " to see how the po' little things did eat an' th'ive on it. People can see for theirselves the creases they come with in their jaws has goned cleaned away, an' their stomachs well as their jaws shows what a plenty of clean victuals *an'* washin' reg'lar do for them that was a per'sh'n' an' thes *a-rollin'* in the dirt. An', bless you, 'oman, I wer'n't *a-countin'* on the comp'ny they is; which Lawson is *not* a talkin' person, an' Creecy let on mostly what *she* learnt bein' a married person, that ain't interestin' to me as them children, that they'll talk everlastin', an' 'special' that Jes, which *he'll* rattle on tell the cows come home, ef you want him. But they're biddable little creeters, an' 'pear like goin' to be industr'ous. Thes betwix' us, I were little afeard at the first off-start that that Jes *might* take too much to lovin' bee-huntin'; not I got anything agains' bees, thes so; but we has now fourteen or fifteen gums, an' more honey than we know what to do with, an' the huntin' an' takin' o' bee-trees ain't what I should call the industrest an' ekinomic'lest practice for a boy that's got nothin' an' expects to *have* nothin'. But—an' oh it was right funny!—the first time he went with Lawson to a takin', he dis'membered what Lawson told him about dodgin' the things 'stid of fightin' 'em, an' they got at him so that Lawson sent him straight back home, an' that boy say he got no stomach for that business no more. But Milly—well, a body wouldn't o' believed it, but nothin' please *her* like follerin' Lawson up an' down, fishin' an' bee-takin', an' Lawson say she no more 'fear'd of a eel or a bee then him. It actuil seem like Lawson have a-dap' Milly 'stid of Jes. Well, them little things 'livens up the house more than a body could of expected, 'special' me an' Lawson. Even Creecy got more riconciled to 'em, 'special' sence she see how willin' they is to wait on her. They isn't no tellin', cose, not this soon, what the upshot of it'll all be; but I ken not *but* hopes the good Lord 'll let some good come out of it, for it do 'pear like He put 'em on us. Lawson say he hain't a doubts of *that*."

The years that elapsed until Jesse was nineteen and Milly fifteen had seemed to establish that it was a blessing to them to have been orphaned. Their gratitude had been evinced by strict obedience and the faithful performance of all tasks. Jesse, fully grown in stature, was a stalwart, right handsome fellow, and was now general manager of plantation affairs, the thoughtful habits of Mr. Wimpy having grown more and more settled. Milly was rather undergrown for her age, but round and plump, and in her way as industrious and as useful as her brother. She helped to make clothes for the family and outsiders. She ironed delicate, fragile garments with a nicety that Miss Faithy declared superior to her own, owing, Miss Faithy argued, to her having such little hands. Yet those same hands could work up as nice a pat of butter as was ever put into a bucket, and set at the mouth of that spring; and if it is necessary to say any more on that subject than that, I know not what it is. Although she had given up following Mr. Wimpy in his sylvan pursuits when Miss Faithy considered that they were less suited to her age and sex than those appertaining to the house and yard, yet occasionally, when work at home was not pressing, or it was thought that she needed the recreation, she would wander with him on fine days, and be as docile as he could wish to his lessons on the mild mysteries of the woods and streams.

Of education, two whole years, counting up all, had they gotten. The good people who had taken them in their destitution had reason to be a little proud of the results.

"That Jes," Miss Faithy would say sometimes, "he can fill a whole slate that full of figgers that Lawson, an' Lawson were *always* called good at them—even he say that same Jes can work a sum in intrust in more ways an' longer ways than *he* ever learnt. Now as for Milly, she mayn't have the head for actuil figgers like Jes; but, Betsy Keenum, you try to fool that child in the countin' o' what things will come to! An' she write a handwrite another sort to me or Creecy other, an' she can bound an' tell capitals to that, that sometimes I thes love to set an' hear how she do *ponounce* them names in jography, an' which some of 'em I do think on my soul they're the outlandishest. Ah, well, people oughtn't to brag; but it ain't ev'rybody's childern, an' them of their own flesht an' bloods, that is so very far ahead of them childern, an' the good Lord know ef we've missed what we tried to do fer 'em, me an' Lawson, we don't know it. Creecy—but Creecy have been married onct, you know, an' I've notussed—not *you*, Betsy, for marryin' never made you that kind—but it's cur'us how marryin', an' 'special' them that has come to be widders, can lay *sech* a stow on what they know more than me, which have kept singuil an' would do it forevermo', ruther than take up with sech as Red Copelin; but which he's dead an' goned, an' I got nary word to say agin him. But Creecy let them childern wait on her, coold an' calm; an' ef they was to leave that house, *she* mayn't know it, but I do, she'd miss 'em, an' 'special' that Jes, which it look like she never git tired callin' on him for one thing an' another, an' he's thes as obleegin' as if he belonged to her."

Within the last year or so Mrs. Copelin had seemed to have become fully reconciled to the presence of the orphans, especially the male, calling him "Jesse" instead of "Jes," and being condescending and polite to him to a marked degree. Her brother and sister had been called "Uncle" and "Aunt" from the beginning, but she had shown to the comers, in a manner that meant insistence, the wish to be addressed as "Miss Creecy;" for, ever during her widowhood she had felt and believed that she looked much younger than she was. Satisfied that if she should have the opportunity, she could make more out of some man than had been possible with the material of her late husband, she had been surprised, and to some degree disgusted, that such opportunity had not presented itself. The late increased cordiality between her and Jesse began to be remarked by Mr. Lawson and Miss Faithy; but they were not people to meddle in matters that they knew it was not their business to control. Lately, also, a nearly grown boy named Joshua Perkins had been coming to the house, and more often than he had been coming before the happening of an occurrence in which the family's feelings somewhat, Miss Faithy's considerably, had been hurt. Simon, the foreman, one morning at daybreak noticed a brindle dog sneaking from the sheep pasture, wherein was found, immediately thereafter, a favorite ewe and her lamb that had been killed. On Simon's testimony that, as well as he could judge with what light the dawn shed, it was Josh Perkins's "Watch," Miss Faithy sent a request to Josh to have the dog killed.

"My goodness alive!" exclaimed Josh, "the whole neighborhood's full o' brindle dogs. Got two over thar yourselves."

"And Josh Perkins, he *thes* 'fused to kill the varmint," said Miss Faithy to her brother.

"Oh, well, Sis' Faithy," he answered, "you know 'twere 'nigger everdence,' an' that not downright pine-blank."

Miss Faithy usually followed her brother's judgment when she had appealed to it, and so the matter was dropped. But when the youth's visits began to be more frequent than before, the good woman's mind took on an anxiety that she had never expected to feel.

III.

Mr. Lawson Wimpy has not been made very prominent in this history thus far. Indeed, he never became so except in cases which Miss Faithy, the head of the family, regarded too emergent for her individual control. During nine years he had pursued calmly the career that seemed to befit his meek, unambitious spirit. His interest in his favorite pursuit had received something of an additional spur during the period that little Milly used to accompany him; for we all have seen that the presence of childhood, especially young girlhood, innocent and dependent, serves to add activity to the gait and impart some juvenility to the heart of a man who otherwise might grow old faster than his years. After her withdrawal for the purpose of learning and taking becoming interest in things suited to her sex, a change very gradually came over him. Not that he gave up his piscatory habits or his bee-huntings to any very marked degree; for Lawson Wimpy was an honorable man, and one that always had wished to be consistent and true to his loves and duties. Many a time had he acknowledged that it was his nature, and he couldn't help it, to love a bee; and it was one of his few boasts that not many people ever took a bee-tree or a bee-gum with less sacrifice of life than himself, or left to those industrious insects more liberal allowance of the booty for which they were besieged. He would go so far sometimes as to say that it was a duty that people owed not only to themselves, but to bees *themselves*, to tame them out of their savage state, and reduce them from the wild tree to the peaceful gum, for that such reduction made them not only more useful, but more happy.

"My bees knows me well as they know theirselves; an' my opinions is they not only satisfied but reconciled to ruther bein' thar than in anybody's woods, makes no odds whose woods they is." .

In the abstract, therefore, he was little changed, if any. Yet within a year or so last past, his wanderings from home were less frequent, less distant, less protracted. More than had been his wont ever before, he sat in or about the house, and rendered help whenever needed and becoming in the house tasks of the ladies, such as filling quills for their spindles, reeling their brooches, winding their balls, warping their hanks, handing their threads, and threading their sleighs. Such services and similar were given especially to Milly, needful as the child was of what helps she could get. Often when Miss Creecy would call upon her for a gourd of water from the spring, he would go for it in her place, and that made such calls come at more reasonable intervals. His favorite seat outside of his dwelling was on a bench beneath a large, wide-spread sweet-gum that stood near the margin of the stream below the spring. Here for many years in suitable seasons he had been used to sit with face directed towards the adjoining woods, and watch the bees as they came to drink. Lately he had been conscious of feeling less lively interest in the thoughts that hitherto had occupied him mainly when in this quiet retreat, but he had not spoken of the change to anybody, not even to himself; and he had been thinking if it would not be well to rouse himself from this incipient supineness. One afternoon as he sat at this accustomed seat with a sense of something like revived interest in what used to be so dear, Joshua Perkins, who had asked for him at the house, proceeded to the spring. They had barely saluted when the visitor, seating himself, said abruptly, but with evident embarrassment,

"Mis' Wimpy, come to ast might I cote Miss Milly, sir."

Mr. Wimpy, not given to starting, did not then. Looking at Josh for possibly half a minute, he turned, and for some moments contemplated the spring, and for some more the adjacent woods over as large a part of the circle as his eyes could range without shifting his position, after which he rose, and, turning, looked up the hill towards the house. Then he walked several times the length of the bench on either side, closely scrutinizing Josh, back, front, sidewise. After several minutes he resumed his seat, and said,

"Josh Perkins, who you say—that is, you said anything to Milly?"

"No, sir, I has not."

"You has not?"

"No, sir; not nary word."

"I would of supposened not," rather as if soliloquizing, "bein' as she have only thes here a while back drap her pant'letts, an' him, I'll lay a jug o' honey, not cut nary one o' his wisdom-tooths." Then he asked, very pointedly,

"What you come to *me* 'bout it for, boy?"

"I hear Missis Keenum say that she have heerd Miss Faithy say nobody needn't ever go 'bout co'tin' Miss Milly 'ithout they first git the fambly's permissions."

"Well, my friend, did Missis Keenum tell you Miss Faithy was *me*, or that the fambly was *me*? Ef so, she were slight mistakened."

"No, sir; oh no, sir; no, sir," Josh answered, quickly, regretful for the possible mistake that had been made as to Mr. Wimpy's identity.

"Of course Missis Keenum—leastways I s'pose she did, an' so did I, she know you bein' of a man person an' the heads o' the fambly—"

"Now, boy, stop; stop right thar. I no sech a heads, an' I got nothin' to do 'ith — 'ith nobody's co'tin's; an' 'special' childern's. I got nothin' to say, an' I'm busy this evenin', ef that all what you come to see me about."

"Well, good-evenin', Mr. Wimpy. Glad you got nothin' agin me. Hoped you didn't."

"You knowed I didn't. Good-by."

"MISS' WIMPY, COME TO AS' NIGHT I COTE MISS MILLY, SIR."

After the youth had gone, and while Mr. Wimpy was marshalling the thoughts that were now on his mind, an incident, regarded by him ever afterwards more strange than any other throughout his whole history, occurred. A bee, fierce, swift as a bullet, came butting him plump in the forehead, then rebounding, sought the streamlet. After he had taken his fill, he rose again and made for his lair. Mr. Wimpy knew from his line that it was a new bee. I say not what that man would have done a year ago. He rose indeed with momentary alacrity, and noted with old-time precision the retiring beast.

"You little cuss, you! It were ruther the impidenst dar' I *ever* got from any o' your tribes; but—no, I got no time to be foolin' 'long of you now. You go to grass."

Now, why had he not time? He sat down again and asked himself that very question. The days were in the very solstice of summer; the wheat had been harvested. They were nearly through with reaping the oats; hardly a bunch of grass was to be seen in the cotton-patch; the field peas were up and doing splendidly, and the corn would get its laying by ploughing, and without need of haste, inside of a fortnight. For some time he continued to investigate himself. His sister Faithy had always said he was deep, and he knew he was. But the bottom of those profound depths was further than even himself had known or suspected. He rose at length, and without intermission of his soundings followed, with some hesitation, his legs, which took him first to the wheat-field. There, mounting on the fence, he whittled a splinter wrenched violently from a rail, and contemplated for a minute or two the fattening hogs rioting in the good gleanings. Then throwing away the splinter as if it were a thing unclean, he shut and pocketed his knife, and proceeding to where they were at work among the oats, he silently took from Simon's hands his scythe, made six enormous swaths, then, handing it back, returned to the bench under the sweet-gum, where he remained until called for supper.

"What did Josh Perkins want to see you about, Br'er Lawson?" asked Miss Creecy at the supper-table. "Did he 'pologize for not killin' that mean dog? He ought to."

"He never mention dog in my presence, Creecy — not once't. It were some business Josh *thought* he had with me, but he found he were mistakened."

"Somethin' on top of Br'er Lawson's mind," said Miss Creecy, when, quite earlier than usual, he had retired; "he never opened his mind exceptin' to answer my question the whole night, an' not answered at that; an' once't when he have retched for the biscuit, he come mighty nigh a-dabbin' his hand in the honey-bowl."

Miss Faithy had noticed the unusual absence of mind and taciturnity, but had thought best not to speak of it. Just at that moment his voice was heard from the doorway, and if rather sepulchral, yet, after giving an account of the remarkable occurrence at the spring, extending an invitation to Milly. As his coat was off, he stood in the dark.

"From the size of the lick the little rascal give me, I think they mus' be a power o' honey, an' I thought Milly, ef she feel like it, an' can spar' the time, might go 'long 'ith me."

"Law me, Lawson," answered Miss Faithy, "the whole back g'yard'n palin's is thes linded and bounded with bee-gums now."

"Besides," put in Miss Creecy, "I *did* want Milly, if Sis' Faithy could spar' her, to begin on the stitchin' of my new petticoat to-morrer, Br'er Lawson."

"Hold on, Lawson," cried Miss Faithy, as she heard him going back—"hold on; would you want to go, Milly?"

"Yes'm, if Miss Creecy could wait for the beginning on her petticoat till I got back."

"Yes, Lawson. Yes; the child need some ex'cise, anyhow."

Miss Creecy thought how much less difficult it was to get service from Jesse than from Milly. But she did not complain in words.

"Go 'long now an' enjoy yourself with your Unc' Lawson, an' don't git stung by none o' them bees," said the good Miss Faithy to her ward the next morning.

The hunters set out shortly after breakfast, Mr. Wimpy, besides his professional tackle, carrying the biggest bucket for the spoil.

"Why, Unc' Lawson," said Milly from behind, when, after a momentary glance upward, he began to advance from the spring, "seems to me you took mighty little sighting before you started."

"Never mind, Milly," he answered, without pausing; and if she had seen his eyes, even without experience in woodcraft, she would have known that their uncertain gaze was not apt to lead to a place that very careful search was necessary to find. Not only this, but looking not fully but somewhat over his shoulder as he leisurely proceeded, he chatted with her, directing his remarks mainly to the fact that it was an uncommonly fine morning.

When they had travelled near half a mile, they reached a small knoll, flat at its summit, whereon, besides towering oaks, was a pretty thicket of haw and crab-apple trees. At the bottom on one side was a spring. Here Mr. Wimpy came to a stop, and they sat down on a huge log that lay there.

"That bee belong some'rs about along in here," said Mr. Wimpy, indifferently. "My mind, arfter we started, got to runnin' on my parrents, an' it ben a-knowin' it weren't egzactly follerin' him on the line he made. Howbesomever."

Drawing from his pocket a small gourd, and rinsing it carefully, he dipped from the spring and handed it to Milly.

"*Well*, Unc' Lawson! a better gourd of water I *never* drank. I declare it's as good, I do believe, actual, as our spring at home."

"Thar now! I knowed she'd be obleeged to acknowledge it."

And he laughed as a man laughs after winning a long-contested dispute.

"Fact o' the business *is*," he said, after a brief enjoyment of his victory, "my father wanted to settle right thar whar you see them haws an' crab-apples, an' he begun on a clerrin'. But my mother she want to live closeter to the road; an' when he found the spring we has at the present, he let her overpersuade him; but he *allays* said ef Sis' Faithy er me should take notion to take other kimpanions an' sip'rate, right here were the place for them that moved away to settle theirselves; an' so the queschin in them ewents, not a-counting in Creecy, which have had her sheer — the queschin will be thes betwix' me an' Sis' Faithy, an' it'll then be which is which. Ahem!"

"Law, Unc' Lawson!" exclaimed Milly. "The *idea* of you an' Aunt Faithy a-separating! I never *dreamt* of such a thing, excepting one of you was to die."

Casting his eyes into the forest far as they could penetrate, he said, mildly, solemnly,

"They is sip'rations, Milly, an' they is diwisions, that

people ain't *allays* obleeged to die before they're fotch about. In cose Sis' Faithy, an' 'special' me, which is younger'n what she call fer, yit she, let alone me, might be counted on, by good rights, to live fer lo those many a year. I'm not talkin', an' I don't know as I shall ever be talkin', about myself, though I don't egzactly say them words; *but* ef Sis' Faithy—mind, I say *ef*, Milly—an' ef she was to do like some like Creecy expect to do, an' maybe *Jes*, for all I know, then an' in those ewents, when Sis' Faithy have took a kimpanion, the queschin in that solemn hour will be thes betwix' Lawson Wimpy an' his lone self, an' it'll be what's what, thes so, pine-blank an' p'inted, an' nothin' else."

He then turned and looked Milly in the face. Now, the fact was that Mr. Wimpy had not the slightest suspicion of any wish or expectation of his elder sister to marry. Later on it was asked him how it had gotten into his head thus to frighten a timid, dependent child, and he answered, coldly, boldly,

"Instinc'. 'Tweren't nothin' but instinc'; the same like what a bee have."

"Oh, Unc' Lawson," said Milly, much disturbed, "how can you think such things about Aunt Faithy? I can't believe—"

"Ef you'll 'member, Milly," interrupted he, apparently cold as the water from which they had just drunk, "that I was only thes a-supposen' about Sis' Faithy, an' then a-astin' o' myself, what was what in them cases."

Milly, looking back with some anxiety, said,

"Hadn't we better go back, Unc' Lawson, sence you missed the bee-tree?"

"Well, maybe yes," drawled the man, with an unconcern that seemed perfectly heartless. "Possible we well go back. I hain't give up that bee, howbesomever. The bee don't live can give me sech a dar', right plump in the forrid, an' I not trace him to his den, some time er 'nother when I in quindition to projeck, as I knowed I weren't today. Sis' Faithy, you know, Milly, know nothin' o' sech as the present convisashin, an' onlest you think it's the best to tell her about it—fer in things that is both dilicate an' interestin' at the same times it mayn't always be best; that is, in cose, my meanin's is, not ontwell they're fotch out by the warious circum'ances an' sichiations, so to speak; ahem! we'll perceed on back, ef you ruther."

"Yes, sir, Unky; I *know* Aunt Faithy an' Miss Creecy needing me this minute."

Not willing to return entirely empty, and as the season was late for honeysuckles and jessamines, Mr. Wimpy would linger to gather a good supply of red-buds, sweet-bottles, and Carolina pinks.

If Miss Faithy had been in laughing mood, oh, how she might have gone on at sight of the results of a hunt so boastingly set upon. As it was, the returning party found her in the act of applying to her lips the blowing-horn. Laying it aside, she almost pushed Milly into the house, saying,

"Go in, child; go in an' try to prepar' for what's a-comin'." Turning to her brother, she said,

"Lawson, my gracious me! Josh Perkins have come by here on his *way* from town, an' he *bring* the news that Sol Pringle have got back, an' have *employed* lawyers to sue fer Jes an' Milly, an' damidges *to* boot."

"The everlastin'!" But instantly recovering his poise, he took his sister by the hand and led her to the spring. From all that I could gather of the talk and counsel then and there had, in no previous family emergency had more earnest, wise thoughts ascended from the great deep of Lawson Wimpy's being. Not fully comprehended at first, and therefore not fully satisfying, yet Miss Faithy, when

THE RETURN OF THE BEE-HUNTERS.

she rose and started back for the house, felt that if there was nothing else for an unhappy one like herself to be thankful for, she ought to get upon her knees for having such a brother.

IV.

The head of that family used to declare that "tongue could not begin to tell the egzitements of that night, nor the follerin' day." I confine myself to a few facts and conversations.

The subject of all thoughts was not one for discussion in family conclave. There were some points that had been submitted by Mr. Wimpy at the spring that involved delicacy, and if manageable at all, would be managed only by talks in couples. Jesse and Milly had their talk, so Jesse and Miss Creecy. Here Jesse showed that he felt himself to be a man with a man's courage, and Miss Creecy said that she would back him to the utmost. A brief talk Jesse had with Mr. Wimpy, in which each hoped he understood the other. Poor Miss Faithy, after her first talk with her brother, was so shaken up that she could not speak, except mere irregular snatches of words, first to one, then another. However stirred away down in his depths, Mr. Wimpy's surface was calm. Just before retiring he said, generally,

"If Creecy weren't sech a rapid rider, I'd be willin' fer her to git on Dolly to-morrer an' go to town, an' ef it took a day or two, to stay thar an' gether what's to be gethered about Josh's news. People don't know how to *ack* tell they see whar they *stan'*. But Creecy sech a rapid rider."

Now, Miss Creecy was fond of going to town, and especially on her brother's riding nag. So she answered:

"Dolly know I never ride her to hurt. I'll go ef people want me."

"Be it so, then," said Mr. Wimpy, in quick answer to Miss Faithy's doubtful look.

They retired early. After weeping in each other's arms until Milly fell asleep from exhaustion, Miss Faithy, disengaging herself, rose, and when not upon her knees, paced the hall room and piazza for several hours. Occasionally she tiptoed to her chamber door, and listened as if to be reassured if Milly were still there and still asleep. At length she lay down again, and placing one arm under Milly's neck, and the other across her breast, sank into the sleep that, in spite of tribulation, comes to the good and charitable. Long before all except her brother had awakened, she was up and dressed. Approaching softly to call Mr. Wimpy, he issued from his chamber, with face, as on yesterday, newly shaven; and if that man ever did the like before on two consecutive days, nobody ever heard of it.

"Lawson," she said, in subdued but resolute tone, "I want Storm kep' onchained to-day, an' I want the hounds to stay about the house."

"Cert'nly, Sis' Faithy, ef you say so; but I s'pose people *ought* to know that dogs, no marter how bitin' they is, can't thes by theirselves keep a' officer o' the law off a place whar the jedge send him."

"I know that well enough; but they can keep off robbiers an' house-breakiers untwell people can gether their senses to find out what to do."

"What I told you yistiday, Sis' Faithy, *at* the spring is the onlest way that is lawfuld an' effecuil. Jes an' Milly, though they ain't actuil *childern*, what people *call* childern, yit they're what the law o' Georgie call *minders*, an'll be minders tell they're one-an'-twenty apiece; an' Sol Pringle, a-bein' of their natchel fathers, can lay in his claim o' titles to 'em; *a-thout* they marries theyselves off, an' in which ewents them titles has nother law ner gospil."

Lord Thurlow could not have laid down in firmer tones the law of estoppel.

"But, Lawson," Miss Faithy insisted, "in the *name* o' goodness, what good an' what consolation to *me* would be fer Milly to git married an' go from this house; an' as fer Josh Perkins, which you say he want her, why, the child despise Josh Perkins in her sight, an' she say—"

"She do, do she?"

"Yes, she do; an' as fer Jes an' Creecy, Milly say she don't believe that so; an' ef it was, that no business o' mine; fer you know how hard it is to git along with Creecy now, when she nothin' but a widder, an' what would it be—"

"Say Milly don't take to the idee o' Josh?" He did not appear to have heard his sister's last remarks.

"No, she don't; an' she say she'll thes die ruther'n she'll other have Josh Perkins, or leave me to go 'long with her pa."

"Don't Milly know then, Sis' Faithy, that Josh Perkins not the onlest marryin' man-person in the *world?*"

Mr. Wimpy looked as if he suspected that Milly must have taken Josh Perkins to be Deucalion.

"I don't s'pose she do, in cose; but the child nothin' *but* a child, an' her head not been runnin' *on* men, an' my laws! when she were a-layin' on that bed arfter cryin' of herself to sleep, she look like a blessed angel."

"My, my, my, my, *my!* *That* don't seem to do then; an' as you say, Jes an' Creecy a-jindin' poplars, even ef they did jind 'em, would be monst'ous little consolation to me an' you. An' Jes is a—I tell you, Sis' Faithy—Jes Pringle's a *man,* an' ef he have the chance, he'll take—I come nigh a-sayin'—he'll take his place among the people o' this whole section o' country."

"What *is* to be done in sech a case?"

"Sister Faithy, my adwices is to say not one word to nobody—not untwell Creecy git off to town, an' arfter that fer you an' Milly to have a talky-talky betwix' yourselves here at the house, an' me an' Jes will go to the spring. For in the case we got on hand, the warious seck er people can talk to more adwantages, an' 'special' on subjecks that's dilicate, an' skittish to boot; that is fer a while; an' Milly, by good rights, ought to try to find out that they is in cose other an' defferent people besides of Josh. As fer Jes—Jes in cose know his own mind. Better go in now. I hear 'em a-movin'. Try to be calm, Sis' Faithy, an' 'special' try to be coold."

After breakfasting at sunrise (their usual hour), as Miss Creecy was mounting upon Dolly, her brother said,

"Lemme see. This is a Chuseday; I'll look fer you a Thursday night, though I has my doubts ef you can pick up ev'rything about them solemn perceedances before a Friday. But, Creecy, do don't ride Dolly too rapid, an' ast Mr. Leadbetter to see that she's fed an' give water reg'lar. Howsomever, good man like him won't let a po' beast suffer. Good-by."

The auxiliary influence of a broom in her hand to a woman of spirit, when feeling that she has been treated or threatened wrongfully, was always remarkable. I could not say how many times in imagination Miss Wimpy swept Mr. Solomon Pringle out of that house and piled him up in a heap on the ground to be burned, the while she made Milly sit in full view on the piazza. Milly looked sad, like the daughter of Epimetheus after the flood, still there were signs upon her face of innocent hope. Her Aunt Faithy was too full for much utterance beyond frequent painful ejaculations, some shorter, some longer than this:

"My laws of gracious mercies! Ef that child is took away from me it'll thes kill me."

When not another speck of dust was to be seen, still holding her broom, she took Milly's hand, and drawing her up, said,

"Come, child, less go to the spring where your Unc' Lawson is. I hope to the good Lord Lawson got some senses left. I hain't."

Hand-in-hand they set out. As soon as they appeared Jesse rose, and walking rapidly up the acclivity, met them under a white oak with low-hanging limbs.

"Milly," he said, "Unc' Lawson want to talk to you on some partic'lar business. I don't know as I ever thought as much o' Unc' Lawson as I do this mornin'. Aunt Faithy, I want to speak a few words to you, if you please, ma'am."

His face was flushed. Miss Faithy, as she afterwards often declared, "thes knewed somethin' were on his mind."

"Aunt Faithy, I made up my mind not to go with pa no more, an' I'm a-goin' away from this place 'ithout you say I sha'n't, an' that is ef you'll have me."

"Have what?" she gasped. "My laws! what do that Jes mean?"

"I mean ef you'll have me for your husband, to love you, an' work for you, an' take keer of you, an' fight for you, an' die for you, an' do ev'rything upon the top o' the blessed ground for you."

She caught with one hand at a limb, that swaying to her pull, it looked as if she must fall. Jesse was extending his hand to help, when she instantly recovered herself, and raising her broom, cried in a tone not loud but most threatening,

"You Jes; you Jes Pringle! don't you put them hands

on me. Who? What put that in your head, Jes Pringle? Lawson? I didn't think Lawson keered that little—"

"Aunt Faithy," quickly interjected the youth, "*that* Unc' Lawson didn't. He never hinted sech a thing! an' he nev-

"'YOU JES PRINGLE! DON' YOU PUT THEM HANDS ON ME.'"

er dreamt o' sech a thing tell I told him last night. I ben a-lovin' you ever sence I ben here, an' a-wantin' to marry you for this two year an' better."

"Well, I always did believe this world were comin' to a'

end, before people was a-calc'latin', an' now it's done done it. Bless my soul, where's Milly? I forgot all about that child."

"Milly down at the spring, settin' by Unc' Lawson under the sweet-gum, an' ef she have the sense I think she have to git out an' keep out a shower o' rain, thar whar she goin' to stay an' settle herself a endurin' life."

"What! the world a-comin' to a' end thar too? Jes Pringle, go 'long; go 'way. Don' say nothin' more to me now, boy. I got no senses to talk back at you. I'm that 'shamed o' myself I got to go an' hide. What *will* Creecy say? The good Lord know, I thought ef it were anybody here that boy were *that* foolish an' crazy about, it were Creecy. Go 'long, Jes; go 'way. I don't say go *clean* away, but go 'long off som'rs by yourself, an' combit yourself to the hands of the good Lord, an' ast Him to let you know ef you *in* your senses, er ef you done gone ravin' distracted."

She strode on to the house weeping and striving, but striving in vain, not to look back at the lover who steadily followed.

V.

Betimes the next morning Jesse Pringle set out for the county-seat to attend to a little matter of business that Mr. Wimpy and himself thought might be despatched as well now as later. Not very long after his departure, Mr. Wimpy made a brief but pleasant visit to the Rev. Mr. Sanford, who dwelt near by, a highly respectable and much-beloved minister of the gospel. The visit was returned about nightfall on the same day, the excellent gentleman accompanied by Mrs. Sanford in the gig, and followed by their grown-up son and daughter on horseback. The rest

I think proper to let be told by Mrs. Faithy (*née* Wimpy) Pringle, as was done some weeks afterwards to her friend Mrs. Keenum.

"What I went through with them two days before they was wound up by Br'er Sanford in the presences of *them* witnesses, I never had expected sence the days an' hours I was borned. Flustered as I were when I first heerd of Sol Pringle's comin' to claim them childern, it were nowhars like I was flustered when Jes named what he did; an' I were that 'shamed *an'* mad, ef I *had* of had my strenkt, I'd of hit him with my broom, which I were holdin' *in* my hand to help me to 'fend off *some* of the troubles that was on me about the losin' of Milly. But thar, Betsy, were whar I were lackin'. When that boy, that Jes, fasten them eyes of his'n on me, an' named what he did, Betsy, Betsy Keenum, I were that weak an' that charmed that it wouldn't of ben defferent ef it have ben a rattlesnake; an' it struck me suddent as thunder that I loved the boy and didn't know it, an' ef I had, I'd of died before I'd of acknowledge it. An' then, lo an' behold, thar was Lawson *at* the spring a-werryin' Milly thes like Jes a-werryin' me *under* the white oak. An' Milly, poor little thing, she helt out an' declar'd she thes wouldn't 'ithout her Aunt Faithy say so, an' she done the same 'ith Jes. An' I driv' Jes off, an' Milly she runned from Lawson; but they followed us plump in *to, the, very, house*. An' I pleaded an' *pleaded* 'ith Jes, that ef it have ben the will of the good Lord, I were old enough to of ben his own lawfuld mother. An' Jes he come back at me amejiant, an' he say, that as sech were not His will, it fuller as a natchel conshekens it *were* fer me to be his lawfuld wife. An' Lawson then he up an' say he never heerd a more clinchiner *argiment* than Jes have use, an' that he have me whar I couldn't cherrip. An' it did look like the boy did. An' *so* we had it *up* an' down all day long, Creecy, she gone to town, an' *nobody* to help stop their pessecutin' untwell finiul me an' Milly, to get some peace *in* our mind, we thes had to knock under an' give our consents. *An'* then Lawson, Jes him a-backin' him up, argy that we well have the business settled accordin' to the law *an'* the gospil, so Creecy could git riconciled quicker to the way things was a-goin', an' Sol Pringle could see for hisself that as for his claim o' titles to them minder childern, he were at the end of his row, an' a-barkin' up the wrong tree."

The bride paused, and after a brief rest resumed:

"An' yit, ef you'll believe me, child, a-notwithstandin' all I ben through before, when I hear Br'er Sanford an' them a-comin', an' me an' Milly settin' thar with our white frocks on, an' what few taslets we could *gether* up, an' Milly, she were coold, same as a cowcumber, but *me!—Betsy* Keenum, I were that 'shamed that ef it have ben lawfuld an' decent, I'd of not let Jenny lit candles, but of ast Br'er Sanford to pe'form his cer'monies in the dark. An' I *do* think he use the pootest words about marryin' bein' honerble an' to the app'intment o' Scripter. An' *when* he put up that pra'ar I couldn't of holp from cryin' of I'd of ben a-dyin' 'stid of beginnin' on a new life."

After another brief pause she continued:

"But I'm thankful that before so very long I got another sort more riconciled an' compoged in my mind. An' them come quicker when Creecy an' Mr. Pringle—look like they done it so quick to spite me an' Lawson—but tell you the truth, me an' Lawson was glad when they married suddent that way, because, bein' his sons-in-law and daughters-in-law both, we was bound to support him, an' we settled 'em back on the place whar we give Creecy agin, an' it 'pear like they livin' very kintented in thar mind, a-knowin' me an' Lawson not goin' to let 'em suffer. Lawson already a-buildin' by our other spring, whar he showed Milly the very mornin' of the day the fracases begun. Oh, he's deep, Lawson is! Him an' Milly calm an' gayly as two young pullets, or, ruther, him bein' a man person, I'll say two young kittens. It please Lawson an' make him laugh when Milly ketch him by the jaw an' tell him she wouldn't want him to be a day younger. But Jes know I don't want no sech talk about me. Yit Jes good to me as he possible can be. Ah, well," she ended, wiping her eyes, "I can but hope the good Lord 'll send His blessin' on a poor sinner in the takin' *sech* a venter at this time of life. He know how many times I drap on my knees what little time I had before it all taken place, an' He know what my daily pra'ars is now to the thone of grace."

THE STUBBLEFIELD CONTINGENTS.

"What should discontent him,
Except he thinks I live so long?"—DENHAM.

I.

Mr. MAPP STUBBLEFIELD and his sister Cynthy dwelt together at their hereditary home a mile north of the village. Their joint estate consisted of about twenty negroes, five hundred acres of land on this and three hundred on the other side of the creek, besides plantation stock and some money at interest. The smaller tract had been occupied for some years by their cousins, Mrs. Polly Stubblefield and her son Wiley, who yet owed the greater part of the purchase-money.

By the last will and testament of their father the property had been bequeathed to Mapp and his sister jointly, with right of survivorship to the whole in the event of either dying without issue; but such decedent was empowered to dispose by will, and not otherwise, of his or her moiety to any wife or husband whom he or she might leave.

Neither the brother nor the sister had ever been entirely satisfied with the terms of the will. Mapp, who from early childhood had evinced an eager love of ownership, had been heard often to say that, being the younger and a man, he ought to have been left over half, and the sole management of the whole. His sister, well knowing his disposition, had always regretted that her interest had been complicated with the coutingencies annexed.

They were very unlike. Mapp, somewhat under middle height, was stout, strong, loud and voluble of speech, and light, sometimes even jolly, hearted. Miss Cynthy was rather tall, spare, taciturn, and of late habitually pale. He was far from believing such a thing, yet she was quite superior to him in understanding, and especially in intelligence. Visiting little, she was quite a reader for those times (forty years ago), while he had gotten, he doubted not, a far greater wisdom from contact with the world, and from discussions, in which few men were more fond to indulge.

The one intimate friend of Miss Stubblefield was her cousin Mrs. Polly. With her she spoke occasionally of her conviction that her brother had always counted upon succeeding to the whole estate with an eagerness that had been ever increasing, and becoming more and more painful to her to contemplate. In her young womanhood, now more than twenty years gone, suspecting the purpose of the frequent visits of a young man named Norris, Mapp had treated him with such rudeness in her presence that he abruptly ended his attentions. None knew whether or not there had been any affair of the heart. After that, young men seldom came to the house, and the few who did were known, or confidently believed, to be without matrimonial intentions. Mapp, especially when at home, habitually spoke of marriage as a state of bondage to which a free person would act wisely to not become subjected. Not that he did not pride himself, when in society, upon his gallantry to ladies.

"Oh yes; oh yes. Nobody love fun with girls more'n what I do. But *marryin'!* Ah, that's a gray hoss of another color, you know; an' on which subjics I've got yit to see the female to which and to who I've said even the word *beans*."

Merry, even jocund, as he could be, yet he was liable to subside suddenly into great depression. A severe toothache, a drought in summer, an alarmingly grassy cotton patch, the insolvency or absconding of a debtor, however small, was enough to bring on such a condition. Never what might be called harsh to his sister, he had lately been growing quite considerate of the few wishes she uttered. This change was due partly to what he seemed to believe a very rapid decline of her health, caused by a cough, and her consequent increase of sadness, that gave him a consciousness of manful and brotherly compassion for one whose few and evil days appealed for support, and partly to the fact that he was beginning to revolve upon other duties that he owed possibly to society, certainly to posterity. He had even styled himself the "residiary legatee o' the prop'ty," and now when the contingencies respecting it had lapsed into long-desired certitude, he reflected that he might become even somewhat tender with one whom he assumed to regard as an aged invalid, especially in view of the fair prospect that was now to open before his own robust, perennial youth.

The Pritchetts dwelt about a mile away, on the Polly Stubblefield side of the creek. Miss Lorinda was heiress-apparent of four hundred acres of land and ten or twelve negroes. This young lady, about twenty years of age, stout, somewhat commanding of presence, though quite amiable, Wiley Stubblefield, now in his twenty-fifth year, had a decided notion to marry. What might have been done in time by a youth, tall, very handsome, industrious, honorable, as Wiley, but for certain accidents, could only be conjectured. What these accidents were will appear from the following conversation between him and his mother:

"And you say, my son, the widder Flynt have fooled your cousin Mapp, an' he have sot in at the Pritchetts'?" asked the mother. "Um hum! I knowed he'd bait his hook thar ef the tother fish 'scaped it, and ef so you well hang up your fiddle, for in that an' which ewents old man Pritchett (an' he's head thar, cert'n shore) will put him through. Made out like he was tryin' to help you? Aha! Jes' the defference between him an' your cousin Cynthy, an' which she have too much sense, *an'* principle too, to meddle, or 'tend to meddle, in sich business. Mapp Stubblefield think he's pow'ful smart, gittin' fixed up at last in them calc'lations he's been makin' all him and his sister's life, an' a-always makin' her out sickly, an' old as Merthooslum to boot, an' which he know to be to the contrary."

"How old *is* Cousin Cynthy, ma? Ever since that time, away long ago, when I accident'ly called her Aunt Cynthy, she never seemed to like me much."

"And which you no business to of done, because them kind o' accidents hurts female persons just as bad as when they're done o' purpose. As for Cynthy's age—Cynthy Stubblefield never made a practice o' goin' about noratin' about *my* age, an' I'm not a-goin' to do deffernt. But she's young compared 'ith some, an' not nigh as old as her own brother want to make her out, he know for why. Ah, law me! But it's no business o' mine, and you'll find that the Pritchetts no business o' yourn."

She proved to have been a true prophet. During the fixing of the preliminaries, the Pritchetts, who were excellent people, were properly touched by the affectionate manner in which the suitor spoke of his poor declining sister.

"A-not'ithstandin' I'm to be an' is the residiary legatee o' the whole prop'ty, yit I can't but feel—ah! nobody know how *I* feel—about po' sis' Cynthy."

When alone with his sister he was wont to speak of his approaching marriage as a mournful duty, in order to hinder the property from descending to the collateral line—a result which, if their father had foreseen it, he would have grievously deplored.

"I like Rindy, brother, and hope it will all be for the best," said Miss Cynthy.

"It's jest obleeged to go right, sister, 'ith them that love the Lord."

He felt suddenly some moisture in his eyes and a pleasant warmth in his nostrils. He was ever fond of trying to quote Scripture, especially on solemn occasions, and now he felt that he was as affectionate a brother as any aged, sickly, forlorn maiden sister ever had.

"Poor Wiley!" she said, after some moments of compassionate abstraction.

"Good gracious, laws o' mercy, sister!" he answered. "Wiley! I'd 'a' never put in thar if— Oh, Wile Stubblefield!—he nothin' but a boy. Time enough for him. He'll do well in time."

"I suppose so—at least I hope so," she said, languidly.

II.

The wedding and the infare were attended, of course, by Wiley and his mother. The latter, plucky, hearty, independent woman that she was, enjoyed everything. Wiley was somewhat cool, though not wanting in expressions of good wishes. Such a disappointment hurts a candid, single-minded youth more than one of bolder ambition. Mr. Pritchett, generally rather complaining, had now his jokes and pleasant prophesyings, and everything passed off well. After the infare the newly married started off in the gig on a tour (then very rare) to Augusta, which, with its five or six thou-

MAPP AND CYNTHY.

sand inhabitants, was the pride of all middle Georgia countryfolk. Mr. Stubblefield, expensive as it was, acceded to his bride's proposition the more readily, perhaps, because he prudently thought that the first transports of the enormous happiness he was destined to impart might be better extended over a wide space and among vast multitudes than partaken in one quiet mansion, and witnessed by only a poor invalid.

A week afterwards, on the evening of the return, when they were a few miles from home, the bride said,

"I'm glad sister Cynthy seem so friendly. You think she'll like the present I bought her, Mr. Stubblefield?"

"Nary doubt about that, honey. Sister know how to knock under when she know she's obleeged to."

"I've often wondered why such a smart, good-looking woman never married."

"My goodness gracious, child! in them ewents I'd 'a' never been the residiary legatee o' the prop'ty."

"Of course not."

"Well, that's jest what I never wanted."

A sadness, the first since the marriage, came over the wife's face, which the husband did not notice, or which he ignored.

"It's jest as 't ought to be, Rindy. Jest as our parrents would of wanted. Sister 'll be all right. She ain't one o' them kind that jest grabs holt an' tells people how she love 'em, like — like me, aha! Go 'long, Jim; whut you stop fur, sir? We'll all have to bar an' *fer*bar fur a short time, mo' or less, when the prop'ty 'll be palmed off whar it belong. Git up, Jim."

The travellers were welcomed becomingly. Mrs. Stubblefield, in answer to questions, enlarged upon the greatness of the city, the crowds of people, wagons, and other vehicles, the certainty that any careless person would be crushed in those multitudinous throngs, and (you wouldn't believe it, but) the crossing that great bridge, and taking view, brief and hazardous as it was, of the strange tribes that got their living somehow (goodness knew, she didn't) on the Carolina shore.

"An' don't you know, sis' Cynthy, that everybody knew we were just married? *I* said 'twas because we looked an' behaved so quare; but Mr. Stubblefield said them Augusty people know everybody the minute they lay eyes on 'em."

"An' you say, Rindy, your nice present was brother's choice?"

"Yes indeed, sister," said Mapp. "I thought how lonesome you wuz, an' I told Rindy I knowed you'd ruther have somethin'—ah—dilikit, an'—ah—"

"Mourning, eh?"

"Ne-o; not adzackly *moanin*', sister; but—ah—dilikit—dilikit, you know, sister."

"Thank you. Very kind in both—very kind."

When they were in their own chamber, Mrs. Stubblefield said, "I told you I didn't think she'd like that frock pattern an' trimmings."

"Well, well, well, with her bad health, an' at her times o' life, I should suppose she'd be a-reflectin' that death's a molloncholy sound, as the hyme-book say."

"Mis-ter Stubblefield, you talk like sis' Cynthy— She may outlive you and me both."

He stared at his wife, but said no more on the subject.

Two days afterwards Miss Stubblefield went to see her cousin Polly.

"An' how *do* they 'pear to start, Cynthy? Do tell me."

"Oh, right well, Cousin Polly—loving as usual; particularly brother Mapp, though he's rather serious sometimes —for him, at least. I'm going to love Rindy. Childish as she is, yet she's considerate, and she's straightforward, which somehow poor brother can't be. Think he didn't make

Rindy get me in Augusta a mourning frock pattern and trimmings!" Then she smiled faintly.

"My goodness gracious, patience everlastin' me!" exclaimed Mrs. Polly. "Cynthy Stubblefield, it's none o' my business, but *I* should let people know that I weren't nother a widder ner a old-fashioned piece o' chainy to be hid away on the shelf; not ef Polly Stubblefield know herself, she wouldn't."

Notwithstanding a little estrangement between Miss Stubblefield and Wiley, caused, as he believed, by his unfortunate remark, yet she had been ever an indulgent creditor, while Mapp had exacted considerable yearly payments or excessive interest. The society of the two ladies must now become more frequent and close, when one must bear a sadder, if not more complaining, part, and the other a consoling and advisory.

The next night after this last-mentioned visit Wiley said, "Ma, coming from town this evening I saw Cousin Cynthy walking in the road by the gate. She looked better, and was chattier, than I've noticed in a long time."

"Did—did you? The child's blood's up."

Then she told about the present, and hinted her belief that Miss Stubblefield, in her opinion, would not much longer brook Mapp's selfish calculations.

"Ma, you don't mean—"

"Yes, sir, but I do."

"With her cough, and her age?"

"The marryin' o' people, Wiley Stubblefield, my expeunce is, don't allays 'pend on thar healths ner thar times o' life. It 'pends, my expeunce is, on a powidin' people, two at a time—my meanin's is, in co'se—consatin' they ruther change thar kinditions than keep single. Cynthy Stubblefield ain't the aigeable person Mapp make out. An' as for her cough, I've knowed warous people to have 'em a constant, an' yit outlass a many another that hadn't ner didn't: like old man Lazenberry, an' which his own wife told me he ofting hacked an' racked of a night so that even the dogs couldn't sleep, an' went to barkin' an' howlin', an' that for fifty year, an' *he* retched eighty-sebn. An' besides, Cynthy told me herself her cough were a heap better; an' I've told her freekwent it were jes' a habit she got into thar stayin' by herself, an' ef she'd peruse round in s'iety like other girls she'd git over it intire. Cynthy know well as me an' you what Mapp been a-countin' on, an' silent, say-nothin' person as she is, she's the smartest 'oman I know anything about. You heerd me."

III.

None who knew the Pritchetts had ever even dreamed that the wife, who was many years younger than her husband, would decease before him. Yet this event occurred a few weeks after the wedding. The daughter's sorrow was doubtless the sadder from remembering that her mother, though submitting without complaining words, had not favored her marriage. Far more pronounced were the lamentations of the father. I may not dwell on that period wherein the stricken widower was heard to cry out, time and time again,

"I jes' tell you what it is, folks, ef thar's anybody can stand sech a racket *always*, they ain't me ner I ain't them."

Mr. Stubblefield made every effort within the scope of his genius to comprehend the situation, and had to admit frankly that he could not. Nigh overwhelmed by such a shock upon the fitness of things, yet he knew he had duties to perform, particularly to his desperate father-in-law. At first Mr. Stubblefield endeavored to dwell, and did dwell, on the mercy that such an affliction had not befallen until now, when the excellent man was so far spent in years that he might safely hope to rejoin his beloved companion in a very short time, more or less.

"Law bless my soul, Mapp Stubblefield!" Mr. Pritchett would answer, looking with wondering face at his consoler, "whut — whut you preachin' sich talk as that to me fer?"

Mr. Stubblefield would have convinced him that afflictions were blessings in disguise.

"Don't b'lieve 'em. Leastways ain't so 'ith me. May be so 'ith tother people; ain't so 'ith me, cert'n shore. Talk 'bout my jindin' along o' Sooky? In co'se I want to do that, an' go to hebn too, *when the time come.* But I ain't ready to go thar *now*, Mapp Stubblefield, an' I ain't *now* a-countin' on goin' *nowhars*, whar I got to die befo' I git thar. The man talk to me like he done got his lisons an' gone to preachin', like I were a Methooslum, when he know my wife dyin' were a accident, an' he no chicken hisself. *The* good Lord!"

Disappointed in arguments from so high authority, Mr. Stubblefield's fertile mind resorted to others with the desperate wailer. Mr. Pritchett was reminded that, at all events, if he had lost as good a wife as any man or any set of men ever had, yet that in the very nick of time, so to speak, he had gained a son-in-law, who, without wishing to compare himself with the various sons-in-law of various people, that is, square, according to the scale, you may say, yet he was willing, open and above-board, to leave it to time *and* eternity to say who was who, and what was what, in the various matters and things in general of a man who, so far as *he* was concerned—

"Mapp Stubblefield," the mourner would break in hereaabout, "want know whut you 'mind me of, 'ith your million o' multiplyin' words? You 'mind me o' the harricane I heern ole people tell about that tore everything up pooty nigh in creation. You well go 'long home; I'll work my case 'ithout your help."

Mr. Pritchett's good native physical constitution was a faithful support to his afflicted mind. In time he rose from his ashes, put off his sackcloth, got him new clothes, even linen and broadcloth, and one Sunday while at the house of his son-in-law, among a great number of others, made to Miss Stubblefield the following remark: "I tell ye what's a fack, Cynthy, I hain't felt as young an' active not in ten year; an' not only so, but I feels myself as much a man as they in genil makes 'em."

These words were not so unexpected by Miss Stubblefield as by her brother. Yet even before the death of Mrs. Pritchett he had noticed with interest incipient color in his sister's cheeks, somewhat more elasticity in her step, a slightly enhanced pronouncement of language and manners, and an increase in attention to dressing. One day when she had gone to Mrs. Polly's he said to his wife: "I've heerd folks say figgers won't tell lies. 'Tain't so. Who'd of thought your pa 'd outlass your ma? an' which *she'd* 'a' been satisfied to stay at home an' take keer o' the prop'ty. An' look at sis' Cynthy, ef you please. Rindy Stubblefield, this here sum we've got have got whar it's to be ciphered out by the *Double Rule o' Three*. Understan' me?"

"Don't say *we*, Mr. Stubblefield. *I've* got no sum, and my advice with you is to let your sums and your calc'lations go, and let the good Lord manage such matters as you're ciphering about as He pleases, and which He's certain to do, whether you let Him or not."

That very night at the supper-table Mr. Stubblefield,

while carefully spreading the butter over his biscuit, said, "Rindy, how young your pa do look!"

She made no answer. The sister, raising her cup of coffee contentedly, said, "Yes, very young, considering."

"An' *as* for his *gaits*—that man's gaits is even younger'n his looks. I see him hop over a ditch in his cornfield yistiday same's a hoppergrass—a heap activer than *I* could, not to save my life."

After this and similar domestic chats, Mr. Stubblefield felt some increase of confidence in the veracity of numbers, and it grew apace.

On one of Mr. Pritchett's visits (which were becoming more and more frequent) Miss Stubblefield was at the gate, about to mount her horse for a visit to Mrs. Polly.

"Mayn't a feller have the pledger o' keepin' company 'ith you as fur as Missis Stubblefield's gate?"

"Certainly, sir, and go in, if you please. Cousin Polly is a hospitable woman, you know, and always glad to see any of her friends or mine."

Feeling that the Stubblefields over the creek had been a little hurt in their feelings, the old man was gratified by the opportunity of meeting them under so safe conduct. On the way he would have told of some thoughts that had been forming lately in his mind with great rapidity, but for a respectful brief allusion of the lady to his late wife. Knowing Miss Stubblefield to be a stickler for proprieties, he reflected that he might make surer progress by hastening slowly. Mrs. Polly was not a person to harbor resentments. Very fair, tall, stout in proportion, constant work in rather pinched circumstances had not impaired her health, her cheerful courage, nor much of her native comeliness. Mr. Pritchett was highly pleased with the reception, the dinner to which he was invited to remain, and everything else.

SHE STROLLED WITH WILEY ABOUT THE YARD.

It was polite in Miss Stubblefield, for half an hour or so after dinner, to leave him and her cousin Polly together, while she strolled with Wiley about the yard, the horse-lot, the cow-pen, looking at the poultry, the colt, and the young calves. Wiley was touched by the deportment of his cousin, softer than its wont. He did not doubt that it was meant to conciliate him towards Mr. Pritchett, the gracious reception of whose pronounced attentions he had seen. So when that gentleman was taking his leave, in a manful way he expressed his pleasure from the visit, and asked him to repeat it.

"Ef I don't do it, Wiley," answered Mr. Pritchett, "people may call me a liar and welcome."

During the family chat that night Wiley said, "Ma, it looks like Cousin Cynthy is going to take Mr. Pritchett. Don't you think so?"

"I ain't no prophic, Wiley. Her mind's makin' up for somethin', cert'n shore. Ef it's to take up 'ith him, you 'n' me got to pull up stakes, for Cynthy couldn't help us even ef she wanted, because the law, as you know yourself, give the husband every blessed thing a woman got, etsep the close on her back. Law mercy me! I wish I *war* a man jes' onnly for the present time bein'."

"Good gracious, ma!"

"Oh yes, I know it'd be good gracious; and I'm that pestered I don't know, ner neither do I know whut to want to be, ner whut to want to do."

IV.

The words that could not longer be suppressed were spoken by the impetuous lover. In accordance with becoming usage, Miss Stubblefield asked time for self-examination and for counselling with her only confidante, Mrs. Polly. Mr.

Pritchett hoped that his anxiety might not be strained too far, and prudently hinted that persons at their time, with thoughts of making hay, ought to avail themselves of all, beginning with the earliest, sunshine that presented itself.

"Mr. Pritchett," she said, at the close of this interesting interview, "delicate matters ought not to be talked about generally. If brother does not already know of your intentions, he will not find them out from me."

"Blame Mapp Stubblefield!" said he, resentfully. "He want to preach to me to git ready to die! Coted Scripter on me an' every hyme in the hyme-book. But yit he's pow'ful fer you an' me to jine in the banes. Keep prop'ty in the fambly—see?"

"I see, I see. Good-by."

As soon as he reached home Mr. Pritchett sent a negro boy to Mrs. Polly's with the following message:

"Sim, take this bastit o' Muscoby duck-aigs to Missis Polly Stubblefield, an' tell her my respects of her, an' tell her a-knowin' she have none but puddles, I has sont her these here; an' tell her they'll hatch under a puddle well —howsomever, she know that. Go 'long. K'yar the messenge right, break none of 'em, you git a biscuit."

The following day Miss Stubblefield spent at Mrs. Polly's. As Wiley looked at her, so improved in health, so cheery of words, and trying (he suspected) to be so cheery of heart, he felt what a sin was this sacrifice of the innocent by the selfish, and he was glad that pressing work called him to the field. A long talk his mother and cousin had. Sometimes there were tears, occasionally smiles, subdued as usual, on Miss Stubblefield's face, but hearty on the round, smooth, ruddy face of Mrs. Polly. The guest was about starting homeward when Wiley returned from the field. She delayed a few moments, hoped that cotton would bring a good price the coming fall, suggested his putting in as much small grain as possible, and, at a degree of distance that evinced both delicacy and kindness, expressed willingness to help him, when so needed, in planting and harvesting. He thanked her in few, simple words, set her upon her horse, and as she rode cantering away, looked at her until she was out of sight. In the usual after-supper conference the mother said,

"Ah, laws of mercy me! Ef I could be king o' this country for about three weeks, I'd stop *some* o' Mapp Stubblefield's projeckins."

"Ma," said Wiley, petulantly, "can't Cousin Cynthy take care of herself? I *can't* believe she's afraid of Cousin Mapp."

"It ain't that she's afeard o' Mapp, Wiley, but the child's jes' wore out 'ith his calc'lations, an'—an' 'ith lonesomeness."

"Well, ma, don't she know Mr. Pritchett's not the only man in the world?"

"Cynthy Stubblefield ain't a person to traipse and pe-ruse around a-huntin' for 'em, but she know well as anybody thar's warous wocations o' men persons, yit she have respects of herself, an' she not run arfter 'em. Now as for Mr. Pritchett, nobody have never denied that he were a good husband ontwil his kimpanion were tuck away. Cynthy know that, an'—an' yit—one thing— *Ef* she did like, or ef she didn't— There! I no business—" She paused, and looked down.

"Liked what, ma? Do tell me what you mean by such talk."

"Him a-sendin' o' me o' them duck-aigs."

"Law, ma, do hush!"

"No, Wiley, I shall not hush, ef even that were the onnlest way for a child to talk to its parrents, an' you know I never counted on him a-sendin' me them duck-aigs, no more'n o' thar drappin' spang out the moon under old Mollie, an' which she gittin' ready to go to settin' on that very day of our Lord, an' it look 'most like a marracle, an'—"

"Oh, ma, you needn't take on so. I didn't mean to *order* you to hush; I was just surprised at Cousin Cynthy making anything out of nothing."

"'Tall'd oaks from little aco'ns grows,' as I've not onnly heerd, but I've saw printed." She looked for several moments at him as he sat silently gazing into the small lightwood fire; then drawing from her bosom a paper, she said, before handing it to him, "Ef a angel from hebn had a-told me so, my feelinks wouldn't of been worked up powerfuller. Read that paper, boy."

It was their joint promissory note to Miss Stubblefield, on which the mother's name was erased and a credit of half the amount then due indorsed in the payee's well-known hand. Wiley laid his head upon the table, and when she heard his first sob she shouted, in a rapture of thankfulness.

"Yes, she say no matter what happen, me 'n' you got to keep this place; an' she done it as she were startin' home, an' before I could gether up my senses to thank her she put her blessed hand *on* my mouth, she *varnished from* the sight, she marchted *to* her horse, an' *as* she e-*loped* away I couldn't keep *out* my mind them passages o' Scripter, 'Oh, turn, *sinner*, turn; why *will* ye die?'"

The next day Mr. Stubblefield, coming in from the field, said, "Ah! Wiley been here, eh? Um hum! Say he talk mostly 'ith sister? Aha! Want to git her to git your pa not be too brash on him 'bout his note. I don't blame him. Scripter say git friends fer yourself when you has the chance."

Wiley had been over to thank his cousin for her most

generous kindness to his mother, and he did so in a way unsatisfactory to himself; yet out of the struggling words of simple gratitude a good woman like Miss Stubblefield can sometimes "pick a welcome" above that imparted by

> "the rattling tongue
> Of saucy and audacious eloquence."

V.

On that same morning Mr. Pritchett rode to Mrs. Polly's, who, after the salutation, said, "And I do think, Mr. Pritchett, it were the dilikitest and the dimestickest thing, as I told Cynthy. I were no more a-countin' on that settin' o' them Muscoby duck-aigs, though she know herself, and can't denies, I been a-wantin' to git in the breed of 'em."

"Glad you liked 'em, mum. Cynthy say anything 'bout 'em? Ast anybody's adwices about me, mum?"

"Now look here, Mr. Pritchett, Cynthy Stubblefield, female though she be, nobody but a lone female, she know how to paddle her own canoes, and in co'se I could see mighty plain that she have things on her mind; but she's one o' them that allays *would* take her time about tellin' her secrets an' makin' up her mind up; an' as for the sendin' a neighbor jes' one lone settin' o' duck-aigs, in co'se Cynthy *ought* to of knowed that there were nothin' o' the kind, nary thing, and—"

There she stopped suddenly, and pressed her lips closely together. The guest smiled, and sat out his morning visit with only occasional allusions to Miss Stubblefield, to which Mrs. Polly rather vaguely and mysteriously responded.

"Joe," said Mr. Pritchett to his horse, as, after having mounted, he rode away, "women's women, Joe. Hit ain't jes' one; hit's all of 'em."

It was well for Mr. Pritchett in the end that such a present, artfully managed, as he believed, had been sent to as good a woman and as affectionate a cousin as Mrs. Polly. Yet, as it was, he found Miss Stubblefield (for he had gone there straightway from Mrs. Polly's) rather distant in manner, comparatively, though she said that she was not quite well. The visit was less satisfactory than he had hoped, and when he had taken his leave, being anxious and lonesome, instead of going home, he returned to Mrs. Polly's. It very soon appeared what a stanch, sensible, true-hearted woman Mrs. Polly was. For in two days' time all misunderstandings were adjusted, and everybody was perfectly cheerful, even bright, except Wiley. Wiley, poor fellow, sincere, deep-feeling man that he was, could not but feel rather cool towards Mr. Pritchett for a while; yet when he saw that matters were definitely settled, he became, if not entirely cordial, at least entirely respectful.

After this Miss Stubblefield rose to a cheerfulness that surprised her brother, sometimes even humming snatches of merry tunes while at her work. For now she was making her needle fly, both at home and at Mrs. Polly's, who was a famous cutter and fitter.

"Rindy," said Mr. Stubblefield, "I never knowed sis' Cynthy try to sing before, exceptin' of a hyme, an' not makin' but monst'ous little o' them, for why, she never 'peared to have no heads ner woices for singin', like me; but blame ef I didn't hear her to-day in the g'yard'n, blazin' away on 'Betsy Baker.' Jes' as the Scripter say: when people, young or old, git to waxin' fat, they goes to kickin'. Hit's a-gainin' on 'em, shore. They talk to you any? They don't to me. I hinted to your pa, but he say he don't want no g'yardyeen, an' I had to let him drap, I did."

"Pa knows, Mr. Stubblefield, that I'm obliged to think he might have waited a little longer—"

"Good gracious, laws of mercy, Rindy! When a person is once't dead—"

"Stop that, Mr. Stubblefield. You think nothing of my feelings because you've got your own projects. They've neither of 'em said a word to me, and I'm glad they haven't."

One morning at the breakfast-table, when the meal was nearly over, Miss Stubblefield said, "Brother, I'm going to spend the day with Cousin Polly. Don't be uneasy if I do not get back to-night. I'm busy with some things she's helping me about." She blushed deeply.

Her brother smiled, and said, "All right, sister; take good keer o' yourself," then left the table and the house.

Putting some things into a large basket, and despatching them by a negro boy, she took her sister-in-law's hand, saying, "Good-by, dear, dear Rindy. I hope—I do hope the good Lord will bless us all."

Tears came into the eyes of both, and they were clasped for a moment in each other's arms.

The disrespectful remark made by Mr. Stubblefield touching the veracity of figures, he had often told his wife that, as a man of honor, he withdrew. He had indeed trembled at the death of his mother-in-law, and until the easy, rapid coalescence of the widower with Miss Cynthy relieved him of all apprehension. After he had gotten into his bed that night, his wife, who was yet sitting up reading her Bible, heard him muttering, "I'm like the feller that were shot at by a double-bar'l, by George! and jes' skipped bein' of hit. Yes, sir, Fractions was too little for that sum. The figgers that done the business were the Double Rule o' Three."

After awakening next morning, Mr. Stubblefield was suddenly attacked with illness so violent that a messenger was despatched in great haste for his family physician. This gentleman, a man of capacity, though bluff in manner, on arrival approached the bed, where the patient lay flat upon his back, his face covered with a handkerchief, underneath which ghastly moanings were uttered. The wife, pale and sad, had risen at his entrance and retired.

"Hello, Stubblefield!" said the doctor, uncovering his face and feeling his pulse. "What's all this racket about? Pulse good as mine. Where's your pain?"

"In my bres', doc," he answered, feebly; "not my *actil* bres', doc, but the feelinks inside thar."

"Hippo, by George! Hippo again."

"My laws, man, don't begin 'ith the cotin' o' yer everlastin' hippo on me, when I'm ruined, an' broke, an' busted, an' sick, an' mighty nigh dead. The Izzleites has run away 'ith the Phlistians. Rindy's pa goned an' married to Polly Stubblefield; an' sis' Cynthy she goned an' tuck up 'long o' Wile!"

The doctor, in deference to Mrs. Stubblefield, who at that moment re-entered, repressed the laughter he would have uttered.

"Well, Stubblefield," he said, "this is no case to put a man like you, just married, flat on his back. You got to divide with Wiley. That's all right, of course. Don't doubt Mrs. Stubblefield will say the same."

"I've said it to him, doctor; and I begged him not to send for you."

"Aha! I knew it. Stubblefield, you ought to get down on your knees every day and thank God for such a wife."

"Sh-sher!" said the husband, turning his head away.

"Confound such a creature!" muttered Dr. Lewis, as composedly, yet with a flush upon his face, he looked down

"I GOT NO PHYSIC FOR SUCH A CASE."

upon the utterer of the insult. Taking his leave abruptly, he turned when he had reached the door, and said, "Stubblefield, I got no physic for such a case. Mrs. Stubblefield is the doctor for you, if you'll ever find it out. Good-by."

The disappointment of Mr. Stubblefield's calculations had not been produced as capriciously as may have appeared. Mrs. Polly had never dreamed of wedding Mr. Pritchett until that good man, with the promptness of lovers at his age, feeling the necessity, in his limited remnant of sunshine, of proceeding without unnecessary delay to his haymaking, turned from the fair field whose gates were shut upon him to the next adjoining. Mrs. Polly rejected him at once, saying she would marry neither the king's son nor the king himself, unless she could foresee some good to come to Wiley by such marriage. Now Wiley had been indulging in two blessed emotions—pity and thankfulness. He scarcely knew all of what was on his mind on the morning of his late visit to his cousin. Eagerness to rescue her from a destiny with shameless selfishness planned struggled with what he felt to be due to Mr. Pritchett. When he found that she never had even thought of making such a marriage, something in her face and something in his own heart led to the offer of himself.

"Oh, Wiley! Wiley! I am far—I am entirely too old for you; but—but I've loved you all your life." Then she would have fallen but for his strong arm.

The very next day Mr. Pritchett, who had traded with Mapp for the promissory note, came to Mrs. Polly's, and the paper with innumerable cancellations was thrown with a force approximating violence into her lap. "Now what?" said he, with the manner of a mower whetting his scythe.

What *could* Mrs. Polly do besides crying with an overflowing breast? Wiley was reluctant to view this unexpected turn in the proper light; but he prudently submitted at last to the inevitable.

After their return from Mrs. Polly's, whither Mrs. Stubblefield had virtually dragged her husband in order to make their congratulations, she said,

"You see, Mr. Stubblefield, people have to let live as well as live themselves. As for you and me, we've got to get away. This place is not big enough to be divided, and sister's the oldest, and it'll suit her and Wiley both to keep it. Besides, it's best for us to get out of this neighborhood."

It was always remarkable how soon some women in emergencies can become heroines. The influence obtained by this woman, had it been earlier, might have been salutary. He accepted without thanks the several advantages accorded him in the division, and having purchased a plantation several miles south of the village, removed there, saying over and over, both before and while on the way to his new home, "I feels adzackly like the Izzleites when they was tuck pris'ners." The reflection that his calculations were to begin again on other contingencies and a diminished slate weighed heavily upon him, and he became yet more prone to compare himself with noted Scripture characters who, once great, had fallen into low estate. His wife, generally, not always, patient, kept up as well as she could both him and herself. Lately he had been getting some comfort from morning drams, and was moderately thankful for that. He seldom visited his relations, but his wife did, and not often returned without some substantial token of their affection, especially from her step-mother.

Once they heard that Wiley's wife was in poor health.

"Um hum! Didn't I tell you so? The Scripter say they's time for all things, and some they ain't, an' her takin' up 'ith Wile jes' to spite me were one that warn't."

"Mr. Stubblefield," she answered, with a sick smile, "yes; there is a time for all things, and one, you might think, seems to me, for you to quit complaining of other people's doing what they please with their own. There was a time for ma to die, and for pa to marry again, and that to one of the best women in this world—"

"In—mortal thunder!" he broke in. "Whyn't she let your pa *give* me some niggers 'stid o' *sendin'* 'em to help 'sport—"

"Stop right there, sir!" she said, with panting breast. "Don't say what you were going to say yet; not quite yet. The time came for sister Cynthy to marry, and she done it to suit herself, not you; and if you, her own brother, are not sorry for her poor health, I AM; for she's just as good as your cousin Polly, and been a true-hearted sister to me."

She looked at him in silence for several moments. He did not know, and might not have been much concerned if he had known, the anguishing disgust in her heart.

"Then the time came for *me*, poor me, to marry, and—"

But here the sense of wifely loyalty broke her into tears and silence.

V.

"Time it is that brings the roses." Not, indeed, had they bloomed in Mr. Mapp Stubblefield's garden, but in another a bud sprang forth one morning, bringing ineffable gladness. Wiley Stubblefield, little Wiley, I mean (for the mother, when told it was a boy, said such was to be his name), came at his Heaven-appointed time.

"Is it—is it a healthy child, Simon?" gasped Mr. Stubblefield to the neighbor who brought the news on his way from town.

"Healthy? Erleb'n pound, old man Pritchett told me; an' he say he have a woice that he ken mighty nigh hear him holler plum over to his house. He say he call him marster, he do. 'Pear like old man proud o' his gran'son. I knowed it would mighty nigh kill him," said the man to his companion, after they had left. "Mapp Stubblefield been a countin' on gittin' his sister's prop'ty, twell he got to think heap more o' that than he do o' his own."

At the illness that now ensued Mrs. Stubblefield herself sent for the physician.

"Hello, Stubblefield! Hippoed again! Who's married now?" asked Dr. Lewis.

"Tain't marryin' this time, Doc. It's worse; it's offsprings: its pedigrees."

"Whose—pedigrees, as you call 'em. Yours?"

"Na-oh. You know I got no pedigrees, nor no nothin'. It's Wile Stubblefield."

"Hurrah! Good for Wiley!"

"Doc Lewis, has you got any feelinks?"

"Few; but don't have them for just one man, dry so."

"Oh, Doc, I *nuver* calc'lated on thar k'yar'n thar spite agin me to that lenth; an' jes' to have thar pedigrees taggin' arfter me for whut little I got; an' arfter news come she were gin out in her healths, an' I got no pedigrees to my name, an' old man Pritchett palmin' his daughter on me for support, and Cynth Stubblefield— My laws! it beat old Sairey. Want know my symchums, Doc Lewis? It's like the childern o' Izzerl when they sot down 'mong thar harpies an' cried on the Bablom river."

"My sakes!" said the doctor, as Mrs. Stubblefield appeared for a moment at the door and turned away again; "worse off than I thought, Stubblefield. Took them fellows and their—what you call 'em—harpies?—some time to get over it, didn't it? I not much of Scriptorian, you know."

"*Four hundred year!* I knowed," he said, in mournful

triumph, "you'd be scrous when you got the symchums o' the case."

"More time 'n you got, cert'n." Feeling for his pulse a moment, contracting his brows, he moved back his chair a space, and said,

"Made your will, Stubblefield?"

"Will! Doc! my Lordamighty!"

"Because folks tell me your wife gets nothing from you except by will, and it would be a shame for fine widow like her—"

"My laws! They goin' to kill me, Doc, shore 'nough?"

"Stubblefield, death with you only matter of time. 'Tain't a case of *homicide*. I should rather call it *suicide*. Killin' yourself with nobody's help except your own mean, selfish fooleries. 'Rithmetic on the brain killin' you; told you so often. Godamighty don't stand such as that; wonder you never found that out, everlastingly quoting Scripter. Leave your wife without a cursed cent, when you might keep off some of the hottest o' the fire by doing a man's part by her! But, good woman as she is, I don't doubt she'll pale you in to keep—hello, behind there!—the cows, and hogs, and dogs from trampling on you."

At the close of this speech Dr. Lewis was standing on a step of the piazza, having overturned a chair while backing from Mr. Stubblefield, who at the mention of the word "will" had risen in haste, thrown on a few clothes, and with suppliant hands was following him as he grew more solemnly eloquent during his hazardous retreat. At that moment Mrs. Stubblefield came out, bonneted, a bundle wrapped in a handkerchief suspended from her arm.

"Dr. Lewis, I'm again glad you came, because I wanted you to hear what I have to say to this man."

Her face, pale at first, began to redden.

"When I married him—for what God knows; but pa thought best, and I thought I loved him well enough—but if I'd known how he'd been treating his sister, and calculating about her, I tell you, as I've told him, I'd have died first, as many and many a time I've wished I had. But *I've* been expecting no blessing, Dr. Lewis. Not me. Yet I'm thankful that sister Cynthy have such a husband as she has, and an offspring to comfort her. You want to know what else I'm thankful for, and 'specially since I heard the words he spoke to you a little while ago? Oh, my Lord!" She put her disengaged hand to her face, red-hot with grief and shame, then, pointing to her husband, said, "It's because no child was sent to ME; for me to see him raised, and see what he was to be taught, and him take it and follow it, or grow up a man ashamed of the parents who brought him into the world. Oh, Mr Mapp Stubblefield! I've told you God Almighty would disappoint your calculations; but I've never told you that many, many, many times on my knees I've prayed him to send no child to me. Bless His holy name!"

Turning again to Dr. Lewis, she said,

"And now, after this, can I live here? *No!*"

This last word was uttered in a scream. The men stood aside, as, passing, she walked rapidly to where her horse was tied, led him to the block, hung her bundle over the horn of the saddle, mounted, and rode away. The husband, gazing at her with bewildered eyes, said,

"You reck'n—Doc, you reck'n the gal's in yearnest?"

"Earnest? You Godamighty, God— Go in the house, Mapp Stubblefield. If you stay in my sight another minute I'll poke a vial o' laudanum into you, or kill you with rat-pizen—you God—"

He turned, rushed for his horse, and galloped furiously off.

* * * * * * *

"Cheap, Fann—cheap, but strong," said Mr. Stubblefield the next week to the keeper of a drinking-shop. "I want her for my stomach's sake, as the 'Postle Paul 'p'inted to—to some of 'em over thar, I disremembers who. Give me your cheapest, that have the strenk I'm arfter."

Mr. Fann, after reflecting, looked slowly around and said,

"Right thar, in that thar bar'l thar, Mr. Stubblefield, is a article o' whiskey that the man I got her from told me a man that know how to load and aim 'ith ken knock a squ'r'l from top o' a pine-tree a hunderd yards, her an' *he* call her rifle-whiskey. I ain't a-sayin' if that's so; yit I has sometimes taste her, an' a man have to handle her keerful. A leetle of her go a fur ways, ef that whut you want, an' she's ruther the cheapest article in this whole—synagogue, so to speak; yit I can't but adwise a man to handle her keerful, same as he'd handle aggyforty."

The decline was so rapid that in six months Mr. Stubblefield became as a helpless idiot. Then his wife returned, and though never recognized, nursed him throughout. He grew to regard Mr. Pritchett as Abraham, his sister as Sara, and Wiley the prince who had interfered between them.

"Old Sairey," he would mumble—"she 'n old Aberham was sisters one time. No: no: they wus brothers; that's whut they wus. And that tother feller. Lemme see. Whut *war* his name? my, my! Seem like my ric'lection not good like it used to wus."

Thus his poor remnant of understanding dwelt upon one theme.

HISTORIC DOUBTS OF
RILEY HOOD.

> "'Tis far off,
> And rather like a dream than an assurance."
> *Tempest.*

I.

Mr. Francis Hood, a man of thirty-five, rather small, high-tempered, and impulsive, was married to a tall wife, who, though of much mildness of speech, had quite enough of courage for all necessary purposes. What he regarded his chief virtue was veneration for the aged—a virtue that he professed to fear might die out before long.

"Childern," he would say, "ain't raised like they used to be. They think they smarter not only than grown people, but *old* people, an' they'll 'spute thar words like *they* knowed all about it, an' old people knowed nothin'; an' they want the hick'ry, that whut *they* want."

These allusions were understood to have been made to occasional reports of what had been said by some of the boys in the neighborhood about certain statements of his grandmother, whom he had ever held in the very highest reverence. A native of the upper part of North Carolina, whence, after the War of Independence, the family had removed to Georgia, now a widow of fourscore, she resided with her granddaughter, Mr. Hood's sister, a mile distant. Ever a great talker, she had grown more and more fond of discoursing upon noted events that had occurred in her youth, and her reminiscences had begun lately to be received with some grains by all except her dutiful grandson. A few of these even Mr. Hood possibly might have felt himself at liberty to doubt somewhat if given by another than his grandmother. As it was, he regarded it his pious duty to accept and to defend all.

He had never so much as dreamed that his son Riley, now twelve years old, and with some little schooling, could have the audacity to controvert, and to her very face, any narration of the stirring times of which she spoke, and of some of which she was a part. Therefore few things could have astonished and disgusted him more than her telling him one day, while calling at his sister's, of Riley's having lately left the house after disputing with her about things that had happened right where she had lived, and scores on scores of years before Riley Hood was born, or ever so much as thought about.

"I did not, I did *not*, on my blessed word, gran'ma; I wouldn't of believed it of the impident. He'll not do it agin while *I'm* a-livin'."

Cutting short his visit, he returned home. Incensed as he was, he intended to be as cool as possible, and he was gratified on entering the house to find that Mrs. Hood was in the backyard engaged in some out-door business. In a voice low and unconcerned as he could put it, he called Riley, who was standing near his mother. Having ordered him to a seat on the top step of the front piazza, he took a chair, and with his back to the door thus began, in tones that painfully resisted the constraint put upon them with every word:

"Gittin' too smart, my young man, an' a danger of too big for your breeches. People tells me you so smart you got 'way up 'bove gran'ma, an' she acknowledge she know nothin' compar'd to you."

Riley, knowing what was safest, answered not, except with looks partly avoiding, partly penitent, and for the rest suppliant.

"Yes, sir, smarter'n *gran*'ma! that all the fambly ben a-lookin' up to from all—from all *generations*, sir, exceptin' o' you, sir. Now, sir, I'd be that proud that they ain't everybody I'd even speak to, ef I could believe *you'd* ever live to come anywhars nigh a-bein' as smart a man as your gran'ma —er as smart a 'oman—that is, as a—whutsonever—"

Here, feeling that Riley would laugh if he dared at this confused comparison, he grew more incensed and louder.

"Oh yes, sir; you want to laugh, do you? But you know who's who now; an' it ain't gran'ma you can conterdick an' run over, not by a jugful. Whut you got to say, sir, 'bout takin' up gran'ma 'bout the Rev'lution War? I want it quick, an' I want it squar', up an' down."

Riley looked up humbly, and seemed trying to find words adequate to express his remorse for obstructing transmission of the events of that historic age.

"Frank."

The sound was low; for Mrs. Hood's voice, like her husband's, was in inverse ratio to her size. But it had this peculiarity: the lower it sounded, the more it meant sometimes to convey. She merely called her husband's name, and paused in the door-way. He winced. He had never quarrelled with his wife. He loved her too well for that. Then he knew that she dearly loved his grandmother, always treating her respectfully and affectionately. He winced; but this served to enrage him more towards Riley, whom Mrs. Hood, as he well knew, had never upheld in anything approaching insolent behavior. During the remainder of this tripartite conference the boy never opened his mouth, Mrs. Hood spoke only to Mr. Hood, and he only to Riley. Stiffening himself yet more, and setting his chair so that his back was squarely towards the door-way, the accuser proceeded:

"Yes, sir; lemme hear 'bout your conterdictin' o' gran'ma 'bout the Rev'lution War, that everybody, exceptin' of you, an' not a-exceptin' o' your own blessed mothers, acknowledge to her a-knowin' more 'bout them times than anybody in this whole settlement, er anywhar around; an' it's left for you, you little—"

"Frank," said his wife, lowly, almost suppliantly, from behind, "it were only that gran'ma she insisted that Guilford Court House were in Virginny, an' Riley—an' the child say he done it polite—he corrected gran'ma, an' he say that sister Patsy say she think he were right in a-saying it were in North Callina."

Mr. Hood slid himself down somewhat in his chair, threw back his head, stretched out his legs, letting them rest wide apart on his heels, and looked scornfully at his son for several moments.

"Riley Hood," he then broke forth, "wuz *you* thar? I must supposen you wuz, an' that you had the layin' off of Old Virginny, an' North Callina to boot."

"Oh no, Frank; Riley, you know, if you'll rec'lect a minute, is thes twelve year old; an' this was in the Rev'lution War, before the child were borned, or, as to that, me an' you uther."

"I'd s'pose then, sir, nobody could never of *altered* them lines."

"But then, Franky—"

These beginning words were almost inaudible. Now the softer her words the more difficult, as Mr. Hood knew from experience, to maintain a course to which she was opposed, and he saw the importance of becoming yet more indignant and magisterial.

"Ho, yes, sir; it's *Franky* now, is it, sir? you impident—"

"Oh no, Franky; by no means. It ain't Riley. The child have too much respects of his father to call him *that*, as he know well enough he better have. It's me, an' I was goin' on to say that when gran'ma—an' bless her heart, *she* know how *I* love *her*—but when she went to put Yorktown, whar the British give up, right thar by Danville, an' make the Jeems River, an' the Staunton, *an'* the Roanoke all a-empt'in' clos't to whar she lived an' intoo one another—"

"You inconsidible or'nary!" cried Mr. Hood, in profoundest, angriest disgust, "them towns an' them rivers all b'longs to you, don't they, sir? *You* built 'em, and *you* run 'em, an' you—the goodness laws of mercies! Whut *is* this generation o' boys a-comin' to?"

With a prudence commendable in the circumstances, he pocketed both hands, as if in apprehension of their seizing upon and throttling the audacious monster beneath him.

"Yes, indeed, Franky, an' when gran'ma went on to make Gener'l Washinton whip Julus Cæsar at the Cowpens, an' the child—an' he done it respeckful—but he *told* gran'ma that Mr. Cordy say, an' *he's* a school-master, you know, that Julus Cæsar were dead an' buried before Gener'l Washinton ever even started *to* the Cowpens—"

"Aha! aha! aha!" ejaculated Mr. Hood, in rapid sequence, adroitly changing his method of attack. "I jes' now see whut's ben a-troublin' *your granduous* mind. It's gran'ma's *lies*. Ye are jealous of 'em, is ye, sir? Want 'em all for yourself, do you, sir? Needn't be a-lookin' behind me. Look straight *at* me, sir. Who wuz it denied eatin' them green May-apples ontwell they swelled you up 'ith the colic, an' you had to holler an' peach on yourself, an' your ma had to pour a cupful o' castor-oil an' ippercac down you, an' scall you in a tub o' hot water to boot? Who done *that?* I think it must of ben gran'ma. Who that penned up old billy-goat an' the little peach-orchid boar, an' they fit an' fit ontwell long arfter the sun sot, an' they never *did* quit twell nary one could see whar to put in his licks? Couldn't of ben nobody *but* gran'ma, as nobody *here* would own knowin' nothin' about it. Who that tried to git out o' pullin' White Face's calf's tail through the auger-hole in Jim mule's stall, an' were tyin' a knot in it when old Aunt Peggy come on you, an' you knowed I knowed, nigger as she wuz, she weren't goin' to tell no lies fer you ner agin you! *I* wouldn't be surprisened if old Aunt Peggy weren't mistakened, an' gran'ma done that too."

"No, Franky; you whipped the child well for them, an' I were glad you did, for he deserved all he got. An' it's not that gran'ma want to tell *lies*, nor Riley want to make out she do; for he's obleeged to know, like everybody know that know gran'ma, that she have ben as straightforwards an' truth-tellin' woman as ever lived or died, twell now she's old, an' her riclection's a-failin'; an' Riley, which to my certain knowledge actuil *dote* on his gran'ma; but when she went on about Gener'l Greene comin' up of a suddent on Nepoleon Nebonaparte, why, you see, my dear Franky—"

Mr. Hood, who for some time had sat with his hands clasped behind his head, and hammering with the heel of one foot the toes of the other, groaned in anguish, rose, rushed down the steps, turned round, and, as he retreated backward, shouted, in a terrific voice,

"Riley Hood, from now out, gran'ma's lies none o' your

20

business, sir. She shall tell many as she *pleases*, sir. An' sir, I give you the hick'ry ontel you can't squeal, ner squirm, ner—"

"Frank! Frank Hood!" screamed his wife, pointing towards the gate, "for gracious sake, look behind you?"

Turning, and seeing his grandma, he wheeled, rushed back to the house, through the back door, made for the field, and did not return until dusk.

II.

The reflections of Mr. Hood during the remainder of the day were so uncomfortable that he became uncommonly fretful towards the hands. He had left his poor grandma to fight her battle alone; yet somehow his recent defeat made him feel conscious that if he had remained he would have been unable to render to her assistance of any importance. But he could not but hope that his wife, regarding the great difference between the age of her assailant and her own, especially in her own house, would be as forbearing as possible consistently with her evident resolution to protect her offspring. The points of history in dispute he knew not precisely how to regard. Being almost without any education, he did not feel himself competent to judge, though he must have some apprehension that his grandma may have mixed Cæsar and Bonaparte rather too much with the thrilling scenes that she had been relating to Riley. Later he found himself growing sorry for his wife, in spite of his knowledge of her sufficiency in ordinary contests, and he began to sympathize with her in a possible first defeat; for he loved her with all his heart.

I leave him for a while to his various ruminations.

The old lady, whose approach had been observed so late, aiding her steps with a cane whose head towered above her own, stood for a moment at the gate, seemingly much surprised at the loud cries and singular actions of her grandson. When he had fled, she slowly advanced up the walk. Like his father, Riley retreated, but only into the house. His mother met the visitor half-way.

"What Franky ben a-fussin' so about, Betsy, honey?" asked grandma. "I heerd him a-hollerin' an' a-bawlin' clean in the lane. What could of made him bile over so brash? Any o' the niggers make him mad?"

"Come in, gran'ma. Howdye? Glad to see you; *that* I am, you dear, precious gran'ma. Now you set right down in that rockin'-cheer. There, now; give me your bonnet. Warm this evenin', ain't it? 'special' walkin'. But you do look *so* well and peert, gran'ma."

"I'm mod'r't', honey, thank the good Lord. But you hain't told me what ail Franky, an' I ken but be oneasy what make him mirate 'ith his woices so heavy, an' run back'ard so rapid."

"Franky, gran'ma, were then a-scoldin' of Riley for denyin' of some—but which the poor child is sorry enough for it, an' never meant any impidence at all; an' ef I ever see a child that love an' have respects of his gran'ma, it's him. Riley! Riley!" she called, "here's gran'ma come to see us. Weren't that good in her? Come out an' tell her howdye. But first you open the top drawer of my bureau, an' take out an' fetch here that new cap you made me make for her; an' you handle it keerful precious, an' whatever you do, don't rumple it. Yes, ma'am; an' ef you'll believe me, gran'ma, that boy, here this very mornin', thes *made* me put down my work, an' go to makin' that cap he have made me promuss to make for his gran'ma, an' he bought the meturials hisself out of the store, an' paid for 'em out of his own cotton money; an' he het the iron for me, an' he set by an' watched me the whole blessed time I were at it tell I finished. Riley think a heap of his gran'ma, Riley do."

The boy soon appeared, holding modestly in his hand the new cap.

"Why, Godamighty bless the child!" exclaimed the old lady; "I don't know whut could of got *holt* o' Franky to be bawlin' that way at sech a fine boy. Franky ought to be 'shamed o' hisself, an' ef he hadn't of tuck hisself off so quick I'd of give it to him good fer doin' of it. Come here, my child, an' let gran'ma hug him." Riley accepted the embrace gratefully. "He's a smart boy, an 'll make a man, ef he lives, shore's your borned. Why, Betsy, honey, you mayn't know it about that boy, but he know a'ready right smart 'bout the Rev'lution War; an' whensonever he come to see gran'ma, gran'ma goin' to make it her business to p'int out to him more about them awful battleses. Gran'ma know all about *them*, because she were borned an' raised right thar whar they wuz fit, bless the child's heart. An' as for Franky, ef he ain't afeared to let *me* lay *my* eyes on him before I go back home to Patsy's, you tell him from me that I say I'm older'n him, an' by good rights I ought to know a good child an' a smart child when I come up 'ith him, an'— But laws me, Betsy, honey, ain't you ben married long enough to found out before now what kind o' creeters men folks is? An' that many's the time they think they got to rip an' t'ar round, an' make out like they want to break everything in a thousan' small pieces, when a 'oman, ef she'll only jes' keep her temper fer the times a-bein', an' let him do his bilin' a while by hisself, arfter while, when he's biled over, he'll swage down an' git cooled all over agin? Ef you hain't, I tell you that now, because you young, an' got your life to go through 'ith. It's the natur' o' the seck o' the nuniversal men people o' the good Lord's yeth, an' us women has to put up 'ith it the best we ken. They're borned that way, an' made that way. They don't allays mean nothin' by thar cavortin', no more'n a horse allays mean by his snortin'—why, bless my soul, thar's a rhyme—an' bless the child's heart for not a-forgittin' of his old gran'ma! Ef it don't 'mind me o' the time, an' it war when Gener'l Greene cum a-ridin' by our house—"

The narration, which there is not space to give, was listened to with deepest attention and respect. When the visitor was gone, Riley said to his mother, "Well, ma, gran'ma, for me hereafter, she may make as many histories an' jographies as she want, an' go by 'em wharsonever they'll take her. She may have the Atlantic Ocean an' the Gulf o' Mexico, both of 'em, a-empt'in' in the Jeems an' the Staunton all in one place, 'ith the Roanoke flung in to boot, an' I'll not try to hender 'em. She may even pit Gener'l Washinton an' the old man Noah agin one 'nother right at the door o' the ark, for me, an' I'll stan' aside an' let 'em fight it out theirselves, her an' them."

"I think I would, if I were in your place," she answered.

When Mr. Hood came home his face had never worn a more pleasant, affectionate expression. One would have thought that it would have taken days and days to work such a change. He was extremely anxious to hear account of the last battle fought by his gran'ma, and he had come prepared in his mind, like a loyal husband, to lift up, if sorely wounded, the wife of his bosom, and comfort her to the extent of every resource he had within him. No allusion for quite a length of time was made to the visit; but he was thankful to notice the moderately cheerful responses made by his wife to his most cheerful remarks. He did not speak a word to Riley, nor seem to be even aware of his presence, during the whole evening. After the latter had gone to bed, he said, "Oh, Betsy, my dear, I thought I saw gran'ma comin' as I left for the field this evenin'."

"Yes, she were here."

He waited for more in vain.

"Gran'ma fetch any news?" he asked, at length.

"No, not *new* news. She did tell some things not egzactly like I've heard her before about Gener'l Washinton, Debonaparte, an' them, but she were mostly took up 'ith the praisin' an' huggin' of Riley, an' the expressin' her opinions about men persons that flies into vi'lent passion in their families when no 'casion for it."

When she had told him the whole story, he said, "Well, *apun* my soul! What *is* a feller to do in sech a case?"

"Why, they is nothin', Frank, ef you want to know. Nothin'. Because the' ain't nothin' to do nothin' about. Riley meant no disrespects of his gran'ma, an' which you ought to of knew, but he'll never conterdict gran'ma again, no matter how her riclections gits all mixed up, because the child don't natchel want to be thes eat *up* bodacious alive by his own father about Julus Cæsar nor nobody else. I knewed they weren't no 'casion for sech a harricane, because I knewed gran'ma, if she hadn't done forgot a'ready she'd forget all about it soon as she see that new cap, an' I were glad you weren't here when she let out on you."

He reflected for some time; then, in a friendly tone, said, "I sposen then gran'ma an' all thinks I ben making a cussed fool o' myself; an' I ain't shore in my own mind but what I has."

The contradiction that he had hoped for did not come.

Yet, when, after several cordial assurances of self-reproach, she kindly admitted that he was nobody but a man person, but as such he was in her opinion as good as the best of them, and to a certainty the dearest little fellow in this blessed world to her, he kissed her, kicked up his heels, and gloried in the occasion that had led to words that, coming not often, were the more welcome when they came.

MR. THOMAS CHIVERS'S BOARDER.

"He would have made them mules, who have their provant
Only for bearing burdens and sore blows
For sinking under them."—CORIOLANUS.

PART I.

I.

To one of the counties bordering on the head-waters of the Ogeechee River came, many years ago (from the northwestern portion of North Carolina, he said), Ticey Blodget, bringing with him a few slaves, and money sufficient to make the first payment on the purchase of a considerable body of first-rate land. About twenty-five years of age, rude in manners and speech, but tall, well-shaped, and rather handsome, he mingled little in society at first, and seemed intent mainly on subduing the forest that belonged to him, and getting rich with all possible speed. His residence, a little way removed from the public road, was on the first rise as one travelled east a mile distant from Ivy's Bridge, where were a store and a blacksmith's shop. Two miles farther on, close by the road, not far from the ford on Long Creek, dwelt the Chiverses, a widow, with a daughter Margaret, seventeen, and a son Thomas, fourteen years old. The mother, who had a life interest in the estate, consisting of a dozen negroes or so and several hundred acres of land, died about a year after the coming of Mr. Blodget, and then it was that he made known to Margaret his wish to marry her—a wish that he declared he had entertained ever since he first had set eyes upon her. Mrs. Chivers had not liked the new-comer, partly on account of his general rudeness, but particularly because of the reputation that he had made, soon after coming into the community, of being unduly close and hard with his negroes. But his prompt, persistent pursuit, his good looks, that peculiarly receptive state of young maidenhood when in grief for recent sore bereavement, the minority of her brother—all these were favorable, and he married her. In the division of the estate the homestead fell to Thomas, who, some time before his coming into manhood, intermarried with Miss Maria Brantly.

Among the Chivers negroes was a man named Ryal, who though now of middle age, seemed to have lost none of his extraordinary vigor and activity. He was of great size and physical strength. He had been for years the leader in all work, and admitted by everybody to be the most valuable slave in the county. He wielded the axe, the maul, the hand-stick, the hoe, with a dexterity that it was very interesting to see. With the plough he could run across a fifty-acre field a furrow straight as a carpenter's ruler. Rough jobs of carpentry and smithing he did in a manner sufficient for most plantation uses. He was as honest and humble as he was powerful and adroit, and with him yet was the cheerfulness of youth. He had lost apparently none of his love for the Corn Song, and persons more than a mile away from the shuckings in autumn nights could distinguish among a hundred his roar, whether leading or joined in the chorus.

Whatever sincerity may have been in Mr. Blodget's avowal of love at first sight for Margaret Chivers, there was no doubt that since the first day on which he had seen this negro at work he had eagerly wished to be his owner. With a youth like Thomas Chivers, simple-minded, accommodating, withal devotedly fond of his sister, it was easy to have the man assigned to her husband's portion, and even at a figure below his market value.

To his new master Ryal, though he would have preferred to remain at the old place, yet transferred without reserve the loyalty that he had practised always theretofore, and the services that he rendered were incalculably important. Besides the work done by his own hands, his judgment in pitching and tending crops, their regulation according to the varying conditions of the seasons, their harvesting, the care of domestic animals and plantation tools—all services incident to his position—made him of highest value to his master, who was fond, even to boasting, of the pride he felt in owning a piece of property that other people coveted.

"Mr. Blodget 'pears like he were prouder o' gittin' Ryal for his nigger than o' gittin' Margie Chivers for his wife," said Mr. James Lazenberry one day to Mr. Ephraim Ivy, one of the deacons at Long Creek meeting-house.

"Yes, it seem so; and the reason is, Jemmy, that he understand the value o' Ryal, and that o' Margie he don't; and a pity he don't. If he did, she might git some o' the worldy and keer-nothin' savage out o' him. He's a rusher, shore, but sometimes people rushes too rapid."

It might have been supposed that for a servant so efficient and faithful the master would have felt some, yea much, of the affection that was not uncommon among slave-holders, pioneers as they were in a new and most fertile region. He had always lived hard. When I say that, I mean that, with exception of a few indispensable things not of home production, he lived upon mere necessaries. Yet of these he kept abundance, and dispensed them right freely among his negroes; for he knew well enough that if a beast cannot do satisfactory work with insufficient food, no more can a man. His slaves and his teams, therefore, looked as if reasonably fed, and the former were clothed rather comfortably in materials raised and manufactured on the plantation.

In return for these supplies he exacted service to every degree that was possible, and he punished with severity all real or suspected derelictions. As for affection, he was without it, or with such only as he had for his beasts. All he regarded as chattels, belonging, with whatever they did or could possess, exclusively and absolutely to himself, and subject to his unlicensed control. After marriage his character grew more and more pronounced. His wife, a delicate woman, submitted to his wilful rule, visited almost none, worked hard both when well and when sick, unless when sick to bed-prostration, and so continued to do through fifteen years. Sickness in a beast Mr. Blodget could, because he knew he must, tolerate, and even, to a degree, be tender withal as something that was inevitable. But sickness in human beings, sometimes in the case of his wife, always in that of one of his negroes, he resented, and physicians' bills he regarded one of the chief curses to a planter's life. His own health had been good always, for, besides being of a strong constitution, he was of temperate habits. It often requires much thoughtfulness on the part of such a person to be properly sympathetic with weakness and suffering. This man never did find out what that was.

He grew richer with great rapidity, and with the increase of riches became more set in his ways and less regardful of public opinion. Sometimes, when met with one or more of the neighbors at the Bridge, he would run on about thus:

"Whut I got, gent'men, ef I understands my business, is *mine*, and it ain't nobody else's. I worked fer whut I got, exceptin' whut come by my wife, an' the law give me that, same as I worked fer *it*, too. A good law; 'twern't fer which some men might of got married, but not me. An' my prop'ty, all of it bein' o' mine, whut I does 'ith it, er whut I does not 'ith it, is *my* business, which ef I didn't have sense enough to 'tend to it, the law could 'p'int me g'yardyeens, an' which they could feed me 'ith a spoon er cut up my victuals fer me like a egiot. I never meddles 'ith t'other people's business myself—not me, I don't; an' it natchel disguss me when I see t'other people a-meddlin' 'ith whut ain't theirn ner don't concern 'em. An' *as* fer them doctors, they gits thar livin' out o' the foolin' o' people in an' thoo thar wives and niggers, an' 'special' niggers, which everybody that know anything 't all about 'em, know they're full o' deceitfulness as they are o' laziness, and they ain't a-goin' to work when they can keep out o' the retch o' the cowhide by a-pertendin' to be sick. My niggers knows I know 'em, an' they fools me as little that way as the next man's niggers, though I do git fooled sometimes, because they're cunnin' as they're mean an' dev'lish. But it ain't often. I allays keep on hand a jug o' castors-oil an' one o' as'fedty. They despises to take 'em, an' 'special' when thar 'lowance o' victuals is shet down on 'em when they layin' up. As fer people a-dyin', why everybody *got* to do that when thar time come, spite o' doctors, which they can't keep thar own selves from doin' that, an' which *that* ought to show people by good rights how they can be fooled by 'em. *Tharfore* Tommy Chivers, an' sech as him, may spend most o' whut they can dig out the ground on doctors, ef it suit 'em. But as fer *me*, I ain't a person that is willin' to have to lose a nigger, an' arfter that to have to pay a doctor fer helpin' to kill him."

This last remark was known to be meant for Dr. Park, who had been heard to say that on at least two occasions a negro child had died on the Blodget place because, as he confidently believed, he had not been called to it in sufficient time. This young man boarded and kept his office at the residence of Mr. William Parsons, a mile beyond Long Creek. He was a native of the county, a graduate of the medical college at Philadelphia, and with notable success had been practising his profession for three or four years in a circuit extending many miles on both sides of the river.

II.

A just regard for decorum demands of me, now at least when the brother of Mrs. Blodget was thirty years of age, the husband of a wife and the father of children, to style him *Mister* Chivers, although, to the best of his recollection, never during all his previous life had he been so addressed; not even by the woman who had married him, nor by any one of the several sweethearts who before her had received his special attentions, nor by any of his acquaintance of any age, sex, color, or condition. This omission was owing partly to the smallness of his stature, mostly to the simple-hearted, merry-hearted boyishness that had been with him in childhood and now remained with him in all its freshness. He was a favorite to the degree of being beloved of everybody that had the heart to love truly, unselfishly, anything. White folk called him *Tommy*, and negroes *Marse Tommy*. Although a very industrious man and a thrifty, he had not increased his property to a degree at all approaching his brother-in-law's, who had often laughed at him, sometimes to derision, for his lack of ambition in that behalf, and specially for his indulgence to his negroes. This treatment he had borne without complaining, partly on his sister's account, partly because it gave him little concern. The more he knew of Mr. Blodget the less he regarded his opinions upon most subjects. There were times, no doubt, when he felt like remonstrating with what seemed to him wrong in the treatment of his sister; but, convinced that such action would produce harm instead of benefit, he had never done so.

Yet people used to say that Tommy Chivers, what there was of him, was all man, every inch of it, and they were wont to recognize it as fully sufficient for any man's needs and duties. He worked diligently, and required his negroes to do likewise. But he never exacted a service that was not reasonable, he fed and clothed amply, and was as careful and considerate with the sick and infirm in his household as a man need be. His family, white and black, loved him dearly, and, small as he was, regarded him equal to the greatest. If he was careful in the spending of money, he was of undoubted integrity, and withal notably accommodating to persons of every class. Whenever he went to the Bridge or on a visit of not more than two or three miles, he usually walked, always carrying a cane, but rather, as it seemed, as a companion and ornament than for the purpose of assisting his legs, that were as agile as they were short. This cane had been manufactured of white-oak by his own hands with much elaboration. About an inch and a quarter in diameter throughout its length of thirty inches, except the handle, that was round, it was squared and its edges neatly notched. Through a hole in the handle a cord of stout leather was run, making a loop, from which dangled a tassel of twisted silk. The fondness indulged for this instrument led to its reception of a name. It seldom was allowed to touch the ground, except by accident, but when not employed for special purposes usually hung by its loop from his left arm or rested calmly upon his shoulder. The special — that is, the most special, though not avowed — purpose for which Bobby (for that was its name, bestowed in a particularly felicitous moment) was carried was to mark time, so to speak, to his owner's music. For Mr. Chivers was a noted whistler, not so much of known airs as others of his own composition. These airs, it is possible, might not have been competent to undergo the test of the strictest grammar of music; but they were so satisfactory to his own taste that he seldom travelled, if alone, without giving utterance to some of them. In these whiles Bobby, high-lifted, was flourished with a vigor and a rapid variety that would have been in no shame in the presence of the costliest jewelled *baton* in the hand of the leader of the grandest orchestra in this country or any other. These airs — the original I am now speaking of — were given names also. They were taken mainly from the feathered tribe. There were the *Markin-bird*, the *Cat-bird*, the *Thrasher*, the *Joree*, the *Yallerhammer*, the *Sapsucker*, the *Settin'-hen*, the *Hen-and-Chickens*, and roosters *Game*, *Dungle*, and *Dominicker*. It was not worth while to argue with Mr. Chivers that some of these birds, such as the yallerhammer and the sapsucker, were not singing birds; and that as for the setting-hen, she during the period of incubation seemed disposed to silence, solemnity, and meditation, and not to the utterance of music of any sort. Mr. Chivers's imagination, exuberant as his spirits, opened wide the mouths of all, and the discoursings of these humbler songsters were represented by his whistle with a vivacity equal to those of the proudest.

His avowed reason for never travelling entirely alone was the need a little fellow like himself had to be never wholly unprepared for the assaults of dogs and other vicious animals, and he claimed to wish for no better fun than to play, as he phrased it, "a chune on a bitin' dog's head." It was after a noted victory that he had achieved one day over a fierce cur that the thought first occurred to give a name to his dear companion.

"It were Bill Anson's *Rattler*. He follered Bill to the Bridge one Sadday mornin', an' my 'spicions is he were fool enough to think the Bridge belong to his marster same as his home-place, an' it were his business to g'yard it jes' the same. Er he may of ben one o' them fool cur-dogs that they can't learn nothin' 'ithout whut's beat intoo 'em. Anyhow, as I were a-walkin' up to the sto' the same mornin', a-whistlin' like I 'casion'ly does to ockepy my mind, that *Rattler* he see me, an' I allays thought he tuck me fer a boy that wanted to sass an' make game o' somebody, mayby him, an' so he come a-tarrin'. Bill, he were in the sto'. I says to myself, 'I'm man enough for you, you imp'dent, oudacious son-of-a-gun.' Look like the ornary cuss aim first at my throat, an' as he ris I dodged an' let him have my stick back o' his head. He tuck a turn he did an' made for my bres', an' I fetched him on the jaw a wipe that wheeled him half round. That didn't satisfy him, an' he turned an' made a surge at my legs. I begin to git sorter riled in my mind then, though I wer'n't actuil hot mad, because I knowed the creetur got no better sense, an' Bill were a mighty good neighbor. Howbeever, as he come agin I tuck him backhanded on his t'other jaw, an' *as* he whirled I grabbed him by one o' his hind-legs and I played the *Yallerhammer* on his hide to his satisfaction. When I turned him a'loose he forgot his marster were about, an' he struck a bee-line for home, a-yelpin' every jump. Then were the time I name my stick Bobby; an', tell the truth, I got so I think a mighty heap o' Bobby, much as I do o' some folks, monst'ous nigh, in an' about."

III.

Unhappy as it seemed for her only child that had survived infancy, yet some people said that they thought it a blessing to Mrs. Blodget when she fell into her last sickness. In the coarse society of her husband she had dwindled, first in spirit, then in health. He had never abused her directly. He had behaved towards her rather as if he felt some pity along with his contempt for the weakness that could not withstand and thrive under the brutality that as he knew pained and disgusted her. His evident displeasure, with no degree of sympathy for any of her complainings of physical infirmities, had led her, whenever it was possible, to withhold them. Dr. Park felt ever an earnest interest in her case, and he had often admonished her husband of the importance of exercising particular care, otherwise she might fall into a decline that could not be arrested. An abrupt, thoroughly honorable man, he was disgusted at the little heed that was paid for such admonition.

"Blodget is the cussedest fellow—please excuse my language, Mr. Ivy. I suppose he loves his wife. Ought to. Worth dozen of such as him. But I can't scare him about her, no matter what I say. Curious fellow! He makes gods of his land, niggers, and money, and sets, seems to me, mighty little value on the best piece of property he's got."

"The row Mr. Blodget's a-weedin' now, doctor," answered the old gentleman, "is one that, short or long, will come to a end, an' when it do, my opinions is to the effect that Mr. Blodget 'll be disapp'inted."

A few days afterwards the physician, on meeting Mr. Blodget in the road, said,

"Mr. Blodget, I saw your wife yesterday at Tommy Chivers's, and from what, in answer to my questions, she told me about herself, she's what I call a sick woman, and needs uncommon, special, most particular care taken of her, and prompt medical attention. Good-day."

Mr. Blodget looked at him as he rode on, and, ignoring the insult conveyed by his words and manner, muttered,

"That's the way with you all, you 'special', that's the proudest an' ambitiousest of 'em all. You'll ketch up 'ith women when they gaddin' about, an' persuade 'em they're sick an' wantin' a doctor; an' it's off'n the case that what sickness they got comes from jes' sech projeckin' as that."

Yet he was put into some apprehension. At his return home that night he said to his wife,

"Doc Park say you sick. Never told me about it. Wonder you never told me 'stid o' him. Whut's the matter? Send for him if you want too. I told him some time back that I were done spendin' money on old Ryal, an' I s'pose he think he must make it up somehow. But, in co'se, in *co'se*," he emphasized, as if conscious and regretful of the hardness of his last words, "send for him. I want him to come to you, ef you need his medicine."

"Mr. Blodget," she answered, "I am sorry you stopped Dr. Park from coming to see Uncle Ryal. He needs his attention more than I do. I hope I am not as bad off as the doctor seems to think. *I* shall not send for him—that is, for myself; but I do hope you'll let him keep on coming to Uncle Ryal."

"That, I tell you agin, I—sha'n't—do."

Two days afterwards Hannah Blodget, now thirteen years

old, said to her father, as he was about to leave the house after breakfast,

"Pa, ma needs to see Dr. Park, and if you don't send, I'm going for him myself."

The courageous sense of duty that had been gradually developed in this girl had gotten from Mr. Blodget, as it usually does from such men, a respect such as he had never felt for her mother, and he was beginning to stand in a sort of indefinable awe of one who was beginning to show that no force short of physical could either coerce or restrain her when prompted by the sense of honor and duty that she had inherited from her mother. It was for this that her father had yielded more ready consent that she should go across the river to Dukesborough, where she boarded and went to school. It was now a Saturday, she having come the evening before on her monthly visit home. At the startling speech Mr. Blodget turned and said,

"My Godamighty, Hannah! I'm not agin sendin' for the doctor, ef your ma need him. I told her some time ago to send fer him, if she wanted him, and she wouldn't do it."

"She wasn't the one to send for him, pa. I wish to the Lord I'd not gone the last time to school. If I'd been here I'd have noticed how badly she needed Dr. Park, and *I'd* have seen that he came here."

"Name o' God, Hannah! I didn't know. Tell Aaron to git on mule Jack an' go for him."

It is just to say that he had not suspected that his wife's case was emergent or very serious. After its sort, he had considerable affection which a woman so faithful, who yet kept a good share of the beauty of her young womanhood, could not entirely fail to inspire in a husband.

The physician came; but the subtle malady by which she

had been attacked had gotten beyond human skill to arrest. Before her death she obtained a promise—and she knew how willingly it was given — that Hannah, when not at school, might dwell with her uncle for at least a year or so. Then she solemnly warned him against the neglect of Ryal. Her death affected him deeply; but, as in the case of other providential distresses, the feeling that was excited most was resentment. At the burial in the homestead graveyard he showed that he had been painfully shocked. To Mrs. Parsons, who ventured to offer some religious consolation, reminding him of the humble yet trustful faith in which his wife had lived and died, and of the sure mercies of God, who never afflicts except out of love, he answered, angrily,

"Don't see why *my* wife should be tuck an' t'other people's left. See no reason ner jestice in it myself. Now, how my house and smoke-house is to be kep' from havin' every blessed thing stole out of 'em, I can't see."

"Humph!" muttered, not quite audibly, the lady, turning away; "he's meaner than I thought."

Hannah's face was tearless. The affliction seemed to have made her a woman, and one whose grief was not of a kind to be expressed or exhibited in tears. As they were beginning to disperse she happened to observe Ryal leaning against a tree, his great breast sobbing, yet in silence. Running to him, she kneeled at his feet and wept sorely for a brief time.

"Dar, den; dar now, honey," he said, lifting her up tenderly. Then she dried her eyes and turned away.

"No, no, Aunt 'Ria," she said, as Mrs. Chivers expressed surprise at her movement towards returning home, and besought her to remain. "I won't stop here to-night. I wouldn't feel right to leave pa by himself yet. I'll come over when I can get things straightened out a little at home."

"But, Hannah darlin'," began Mr. Chivers, "it won't do, it won't begin to do at all, for as young a girl as you—"

"Now, Uncle Tommy, you may just hush right up. I *can't* stay away from home yet awhile; and it's no use to say anything more about it."

When she had gone he said to his wife, "'Ria, her mother dyin' have made a grown 'oman out o' Hannah, blamed if it hain't."

"She need to be grown, with the father she have."

"That she do."

If Mr. Chivers had had in his repertory a mournful air he surely would have tried to solace his sadness with its rehearsal, as he turned away and began on a walk towards the creek. Even as it was, the *Joree* poured, though very, very mildly, as he went slowly on; while Bobby, unused to strains at all lugubrious, modestly, humbly hung low.

Few words passed between father and daughter that night. If he felt any surprise at her insisting on returning home, he did not exhibit it. If he sympathized with her bereavement, he had no knowledge of how to console. At supper she took the head of the table, and, as if she had long been so accustomed, presided with calmness and efficiency. Her father regarded her occasionally with a curious, anxious expression, but said almost nothing during the meal. When the table things were put away by Mandy, the house-girl, she got her mother's Bible and read it for a considerable time, while her father paced the piazza. Several times he paused while passing the window, through which he could observe her, and looked as if he would like to talk with her; but he could not find satisfactory words with which to begin. Perhaps he had some notion that Hannah was in such company as himself could not be expected to enter. When bedtime came he turned into the house and said,

"Hannah, you goin' to call Mandy or one o' the other gals to sleep in your room, ain't you?"

She shut the book, rising, laid it back on the table from which she had taken it, then, lighting another candle, answered, "No, sir, pa. I don't need anybody."

She retired to her chamber, and for the first time in all her life closed the door. This action astonished him greatly, for heretofore she had been notably timid at night, and had always insisted, with permission, on keeping open the door leading from the chamber in which her parents slept to her own. When she had shut herself in the darkness he looked as if his astonishment had become fright. He wished that she had not returned home from the burial; for he felt more lonesome, he thought, than if she had stayed at her uncle's and himself been entirely alone. It seemed to him that Hannah was with her mother, or nearer being there than with him. Returning to the piazza he promenaded, though with greater silence and slowness than before. Several times he crossed to the porch looking from the dining-room to the negro quarters, paused there for a few moments, then resumed his walking. Finally, after repairing there again, he called a negro lad, and when he came said to him in a low tone, but as if he wished to be emphatic,

"Aaron, you go git your blanket and fetch it here, and you lay yourself down in a corner of mine and your mistess's room; an' whatever you do, you mind about not 'sturbin' your Miss Hannah."

In another corner of the chamber stood a bed, on which he reposed sometimes when it suited him to rest alone. Hereon he laid himself some time after Aaron was wrapped and asleep.

IV.

Within these last fifteen years Ryal had oldened much; for no man, however endowed by nature, can crowd during an extended period all the work of a much greater without falling into premature decay. Incessant hard labor and difficult responsibilities had made him, now sixty, appear to be seventy years old, and to have the infirmity of one yet more advanced. Such had been his devotion to his master's interests that as long as was possible he had not heeded, but instead had ignored, the ever-repeating warnings of decline, and often been actually fretted by their persistence. Instead of yielding to them, as a humane master would have required that he should do, he even had often undertaken more than was habitual, and it was pitiable to see how he vainly strove to equal the service of his prime by efforts to surpass it. Day and night he continued to go, until rheumatism set in and he must stop.

In all this while not a word of sympathy or compassion fell from the mouth of the man to whom, in the disposition of Providence, the humble slave had been consigned. Mr. Blodget had always maintained that negroes by their nature were liars and thieves, and that every performance of duty by them was due to the apprehension of detection and the punishment that would follow its neglect. It is ever true that those of one race who are least worthy of its privileges, obligations, and destinies vaunt themselves higher above those of an inferior. Mr. Blodget verily believed that his negroes had no more affection for him than he had for them, and that in their case the best, the only just discipline was that which made them feel that they were never trusted to perform any task from a principle of duty, but that the cowhide or other punishment would be sure to attend every defalcation. With one time excepted, he had never laid this instrument upon Ryal, and he had the audacious meanness to tell of this instance to a knot of men at the Bridge not long after his marriage, and to admit that he had done so for no reason whatever except because he thought it well for the negro to understand at once, for good and all, to whom he belonged. This castigation, wholly, confessedly, avowedly undeserved, was submitted to without any louder or more bitter complaining than would have been uttered by a goodly horse that had known nothing of the cause of its infliction. The exuberant strength, diligence, activity, and faithfulness of the negro had hindered repetition, and little as the master knew it the slave felt for him much affection. I have sometimes wondered at the strong attachment shown by negroes towards masters who seemed far from deserving it. Yet with that race the feeling of family was always strong, especially among the most home-staying and industrious. Slaves of hard masters have been heard to laugh with contemptuous incredulity, not always real, at those belonging to the more humane, when the latter were boasting of their greater privileges and enjoyments. Ryal had always felt great pride in his master's successes, and every trust that had been assigned to him had been executed with a fidelity and efficiency that were simply perfect.

For all this Mr. Blodget felt no more gratitude than for the work of his beasts or the accumulations of dollars that he had invested in the purchase of other slaves and put out at usurious interest. He was not a type of his neighbors and countrymen. On the contrary, he was an exception, known and talked about far and wide. That such a man would cease to take proper interest in a slave after he had ceased to be valuable, however important the services of his foretime, was natural as in the case of an aged ox or a worn-out ox-cart. With the negro's continual failures, therefore, he found continual fault; and when he saw him exhausted, though far from being a man capable of murder, he wanted him to die. Mrs. Blodget, with the means at her disposal, had provided as well as she could for his needs, and done what was possible to assuage his grief from the consciousness of being of no further use to his family. On the day before she had taken to her bed in her last sickness, when, having carried to him some delicate morsel from her own table, he complained of the trouble he was inflicting, she said,

"Uncle Ryal, you *must* not talk in that way. You have done your part in this family—the good Lord knows you have, over and over again; and if I had had my way, you should have had long ago the rest you needed and the care that is so important to you. It hurts my feelings to hear you talk as you do. Then you know, Uncle Ryal, that sickness comes of God's will, and it isn't right to complain of that or any other affliction that He sends. I am far from being well myself, but I cannot complain, because it is of God's will. Don't you see?"

"Bress your heart, Miss Margie, my good, precious mist'ess! I'll try to not kimplain nary 'nother time, an' I'll try not to cry no more—dat is—dat is," he continued, trying to dry with his sleeve his flooding eyes, "arter dis one time. Godamighty bress you, my good mist'ess! Now you go 'long back in de big 'ouse, honey, an' take good keer yourself. Whut *would* Miss Harnah do if you wus to git down sick, an' 'special' ef you wus to drap off an' leave her? It natily skeer me to even think about sich a thing."

"God will take care of her, and you too, Ryal, if you trust in Him. Sometimes I think, mayby, it would be better for you both if—but God knows what is for the best. Don't you forget. People may make mistakes, and they do; but God never does. His will be done! I want you to feel about that as I do. If you will put your trust in Him, He will not forsake you when you need His help most. Good-by now. I'll come again to-morrow to see you, if I'm well enough; and if not, I'll send Hannah. She'll be home to-night, and I know she'll want to run to see you soon as she can. Good-by. God bless you!"

She took his hand, and holding it a few moments, turned and went back to the house. They never met again on earth. The old invalid mourned her sorely. No wonder he leaned his feeble frame against the tree in the graveyard and wept tears that were the better part of those simple obsequies.

V.

The being of a man like Ticey Blodget, after the loss of such a wife, must change for the better, or it will tend to the worse with increased rapidity. The society of such a woman, though frail in health and subservient to a degree as to be regarded almost a nonentity, yet pure in heart, God fearing and compassionate, will not fail of exerting some influence upon a husband, coarse even as Blodget, however unconscious of and however disdainful to admit it; and when it is withdrawn, unless the warning and the lesson are heeded, he must relapse into the evil vulgarity that was his normal condition, and then descend headlong on the way to ruin.

Hannah put off removing to her uncle's, lingering in order to see what arrangements would be made by her father for the management of his house affairs. To her great surprise, instead of assigning this to Hester, the sister of

Ryal, an elderly woman who, equally with him, had been trusted by her mother, Mr. Blodget evinced, although he did not openly announce, his intention of appointing to the office Ryal's daughter, Mandy, about sixteen years old. Her father, who had been a widower for some years, had had much trouble, even with Hester's help, in controlling the wilful temper of this his only offspring. Lately, however, he had been much gratified by being told by her and Luke, a steady young man on the place, that with his consent (which he eagerly gave) they had agreed to become man and wife. The prospect of this match had been cordially favored by their mistress; but after the latter's death Mandy, with the levity marked among females of that race, began to grow cold towards Luke to a degree that grieved and offended her father much, and, as had been his wont, he reproached her severely, and she had the cunning to appeal to her master for protection. If Ryal had died along with his mistress, Mr. Blodget, it is possible, might have escaped some, at least, of the unhappy consequences that ensued. But Ryal lingered, and he might linger for very many years; and the sight of him, as did to Haman that of Mordecai the Jew sitting at the king's gate, made him feel that all that he possessed availed him nothing. It cannot but be intensely painful when a man, however coarse, has to endure a long-continued presence of one to whom, if he does not thus feel, he knows that others regard him to have been grossly ungrateful. In the defection of Mandy from her lover Mr. Blodget hoped that he saw an opportunity. The value of this was enhanced in his estimation when Ryal, for the first time in his life, and then with utmost humility, undertook to remonstrate with him for tolerating Mandy's behavior, that, especially since she had been expecting to be put in control of the business of the house, had grown in insolence and become at last insupportable. He got for his pains a cursing and a threat of expulsion from the premises.

The continued presence of Hannah embarrassed her father somewhat, and delayed open announcement of his purposes. He wanted her to repair to her uncle's, and his hope was that by some means Ryal should be made to follow her there. But one day, to his surprise, she said to him that, after much reflection, she had come to the conclusion that it was best for her to remain where she was and take charge of the house. The proposal startled him greatly.

"The very *idee* of sech a thing!" he said, angrily. "What could of put sech a notion as that in your head, Hannah?"

"Pa, I *think* it would be as well for me to keep the house as Mandy, and I *know* it would look more respectable. Another reason is, that if I go away, Uncle Ryal will not be attended to as he ought."

"Who told you that Mandy—" he began in an excited tone; but he stopped, walked up and down the piazza for a few moments, and then, with what mildness he could employ, said, "Your poor ma, Hannah — my Lord, how I do miss her! — but she jes' broke herself down complete a-waitin' on that deceitful nigger, which he's now gittin' to be as impident as he's deceitful. It look like she keered more for him, an' 'special' when he got no 'count, than for them that helt up and kep' up at their work."

"Pa," answered Hannah, and it was apparent that she spoke under pressure of not less constraint than her father, "ma knew that she owed too much to Uncle Ryal—and in all my life I never heard you till now call him deceitful and impudent—she knew she owed too much to him to let him suffer, if she could help it, for anything she could do, and get for him what he needed after he had broken down in working for her family."

"I'd like to know," he said, doggedly, "if he ain't *my* nigger, er ef he war'n't till he got so no 'count that it make no deff'ence who own him now."

"Yes, sir, pa. I have heard that the law gives a man all his wife's property. Uncle Ryal at yours and ma's marriage became your property, and he is yet."

"Yes; well, I shall 'tend to that nigger accordin' to how he behave hisself, and do sech work as, spite o' his deceitful talk and k'yar'n on about his cussed rheumatiz, I know he can do. But if he bother with me, and ondertake to give me his jaw about *my* business, I'll cut down his rashins furder than they're cut down now, and, more 'n that, I'll give him the cowhide in the bargain."

"And that," she said, in low, trembling tones, "when what you call "jawing" about your business is nothing but the poor, dear old man's trying to do you a service that, if you'd take it, would be worth to you more than all he ever did for you before, in warning you against his own, only child, who, with your very own consent, treats him as badly as you do." Raising her voice high, she continued: "Oh pa, pa, pa! I wonder a man, *so* soon after his wife has been put under the ground, can use such words when talking about a servant who he knows—for I heard her tell you so—was on her mind in her dying hour. It is a *shame* —a shame against God!"

Her face reddened and quivered with the anguishing indignation that burned in her breast. He rose, and glaring fiercely upon her, said, in a low, husky voice,

"Lookee here, Hannah Blodget, you know who you talkin' too !"

"Yes, sir," she almost screamed, as hot tears poured from her eyes. "I am talking to my own *father*, to the husband of my dead *mother*, and to the master of a poor negro whom, now that he is old and broken down, he intends not only to neglect but to *outrage*. That's who I'm talking to!"

Muttering a curse, he moved towards her, his hands extended as if to grasp her. She rose quickly, and covering her face with her hands, cried aloud,

"O my mother! O my God!"

He turned abruptly away and immediately left the house.

Hannah went to her own chamber, took out and wrapped in a handkerchief a few articles of clothing, and, after a brief visit to Ryal, set out on foot and alone for her new home. As the old man stood leaning upon his staff, looking after her departing form, Mandy came flaunting where he was, and asked,

"Whar dat gal prancin' off ter?"

"You imp'dent hussy, you! You darsn't to call your young mist'ess dat way!"

"Whut I calls dat gal er nobody else no business to you," she answered, perking her face insolently towards his. He raised his hand, but she eluded his grasp and ran off laughing to the house.

"Wish to God you never had o' ben borned!" he said, in hopeless anger and shame.

A few minutes afterwards Dr. Park, who had been visiting a patient beyond the Bridge, rode up to the gate, and seeing Mandy in the piazza, said, "Hello, Mandy! tell your Miss Hannah to step out to the piazza a minute, if she pleases. Tell me first how your daddy is. Never mind; Hannah 'll know better than you about that. Ask her to step out. Be quick about it."

"Miss Hannah ain't here, doctor."

"Ain't here? Why, Tommy Chivers told me two hours ago, as I rode by his house, that she hadn't gone there yet. What do you mean?"

"I reckon she gone thar now, sir. She lef' here I 'speck it ben no more 'n jes' about a quarter of a hour ago. She never told me whar she were goin'."

"Didn't she tell her pa?"

"Dat I don't know, doctor. Marster he lef' for somewhar not long befoe she did."

"Nobody go with her? Ride or walk?"

"She went right dar out de gate wid a bundle on her arm tied in a han'k'cher, by herself, a-walkin'."

"Didn't her pa know she was going?"

"Don't know, sir."

"You don't, eh? What *do* you know? Can you tell me how your daddy is? I've no idea you can. I'll go see for myself." He alighted, hitched his horse to one of the red-oaks near, and walked rapidly to Ryal's cabin. In a few minutes he returned, and as he was passing the house called to Mandy, who did not immediately answer.

"You Mandy!" he roared, "have you got *deaf* since you got so big? Why *don't* you answer and come out here?"

She came, looking as if she had used very great haste.

"Ah, ha! Come at last? Look at me, Mandy, and try to have sense enough to remember what I tell you. If you don't 'tend better to your daddy than you've been doing since your mistress's death, the devil will get you certain. I rather think he's got one of his paws on you now. I know you didn't have much sense, but I didn't think you quite as big a fool as it looks like you're bent on making of yourself; but if you don't want the devil to grab you in short, and that before you can say 'Jack Roberson,' you attend better to that daddy of yours."

VI.

When Dr. Park left Mr. Blodget's, with what speed that was consistent with due regard for the good horse that had borne him already over a space of many miles that day, he rode along the road leading to Mr. Chivers's. Overtaking Hannah when she had made two-thirds of her way, he cried,

"Tommy's right. You *are* a grown woman, or at least take yourself to be one. You must have been reading about that girl that with wands and jewels and crosses, and so-forths, went clipping it along by herself all over the country and nobody took her up. But I tell you now that such travelling as that in a country big as this is and full of wolves won't do for a girl with nothing but a bundle of clothes on her arm. Where you migrating to? It's to be hoped you'll tarry a while at your Uncle Tommy's, though there's no telling where a girl that's been made a woman all of a sudden will fetch up after she once starts."

He dismounted, shortened the stirrup-leather on the hither side, brought over the other, and, holding forth his open hand, said,

"Put your foot in that hand and mount."

"Doctor," she began to remonstrate, "I'm not tired, and how can I ride on a man's saddle, and—"

"Lookee here, Hannah, if you're already *done* grown, you aren't so big and heavy that I can't *put* you on that horse if I have it to do; in which case I'll have to take you in my arms. Put that foot in this hand, and catch hold of Bill's mane, if you don't want to be hugged."

She obeyed; he lifted her to the saddle and walked by the horse's side the rest of the way.

"Blow for your Marse Tommy, Sooky," he said to the cook, when Hannah had alighted and gone into the house.

Sooky took down the conch, whose blast (only one she wound), long, clear, sonorous, commanding, made soon appear her master, who came, as usual, with hurrying tread. The physician, leading his horse, met him as he came along the road, and climbing the fence, they seated themselves upon a rider.

"How's your crop, Tommy?" asked the visitor.

"Oh, in the grass turrible, Doc."

"Umph! umph! And you know, Tommy Chivers, that it's the cleanest in the whole neighborhood. Astonishing how some folks, and they not the worst in the world, will complain and try to fool people about their crops. If I didn't live so close to you I suppose you'd try to deny getting that good rain that came day before yesterday."

"No, indeed, Doc; but yit — and I were monst'ous thankful *fer* the rain—but yit we couldn't run the ploughs tell this mornin', and the press o' work is that—"

"That I want to try to help you out a little. I made Sooky blow you up because I wanted to talk to you about taking a boarder. I just left Hannah at the house."

"A boder, Doc? You jokin', 'ithout you call Hannah a boder, which *I* don't, ner do 'Ria, and we both ben havin' our mind pestered why she haven't come along on, as her mother wanted and expected. I s'pose Blodget thought he have a use fer her fer a while tell he got things sort o' straightened up. I never went over to inquire, for I didn't have so powerful much to do 'ith Blodget while sis' Margie were alive, an' sence then nother me ner 'Ria 'pear like we got the heart to go thar, though 'Ria said this very mornin' that ef Hannah didn't come to-day she were goin' over thar to know what the reasons was. But, Doc, we don't call Hannah no boder, no more 'n one o' our own childern."

Dr. Park moved himself a trifle, and looking sidewise at Mr. Chivers, said,

"Tommy, the dickence is to pay over at Blodget's, as I knew it would be. I'm not talking about Hannah, but somebody else as a boarder, and I was never in more dead earnest in my life."

"Idee o' my takin' boders! when my house hardly big enough for them that's in it now. That *is* funny, Doc."

"The boarder I'm talking about now won't be for your *house*, Tom Chivers, though that is far too big for a fellow of your size. I'm now talking about old Ryal."

"What? thunder, you say! Can't Tice Blodget take keer of his own niggers? He ought to; he makes 'em work hard enough."

"There's a difference, Tommy, between *canning* and *wonting*. Tice Blodget's like that old fellow Cato, of whom mayby you've read. If you haven't, I'll tell you that he was a fellow who, when one of his slaves got too old or too sick to work, he got rid of him like he would have done with a worn-out horse."

"Who you say he wus, Doc?"

"Old Cato."

"Whar did *he* hold out at? Anywhar's in Georgie?"

"Oh! no. He was of Rome, in Italy, away over the Atlantic Ocean."

"Well, wharsonever he wus, he were, to my opinions at least, he were a mean an' a infernal ole cuss."

"Been just my opinion always, Tommy. But then he was a heathen, and Ticey Blodget, even if he ain't a Christian, as a good many of the rest of us poor devils ain't, yet he ought to know better."

"Ef Tice Blodget ain't a heathen, whutever sech folks is— But whut about old man Ryal? Have Blodget driv' him off?"

"Not quite; but it amounts to it, and I promised his wife to do what I could in seeing him taken care of."

"So did I, by gracious! though sis' Margie know I wouldn't let old Uncle Ryal suffer if I could help it. In course, Dr. Park, if Tice Blodget drive him off, and the old feller can't do no better, I'll do the best I can for him. 'Deed, if he is driv' off, I rather he'd come here than go anywheres else; for pa and ma both thought a heap o' Uncle Ryal. But I sha'n't call him no *boder*, Doc, no more 'n I call Hannah a boder. The very idee o' sech a thing!"

Dr. Park again shifted his seat, looking the while rather angrily at the space he had lately covered; then in a tone somewhat disappointed, sad, distant, said, as if soliloquizing, "I'm afraid I'll have to make other arrangements about the poor old fellow."

Mr. Chivers was impressed sensibly by these words. Drawing up his cane and applying his mouth to the handle end, he let it hang down between his legs, and placing his fingers carefully in a row as if on a clarinet, he meditated as he moved them up and down with great rapidity. To an imaginative person it might have seemed as if he were essaying by this means to personate the shepherd on the Grecian urn, and

"Pipe to the spirit ditties of no tone."

Suddenly his visitor broke forth thus:

"Tom Chivers, I don't care what you *call* old Ryal when he gets here. What I want to have understood is that you shall not, at least with my connivance, feed, clothe, and wait on other people's negroes for nothing. Ticey Blodget is responsible in all this business, and I am going to make him see it to his cost. Mrs. Parsons would let me take him there, but being a family negro I thought perhaps you'd rather—"

"In co'se, in co'se, Doc," said Mr. Chivers twice in quick succession, "if the poor old fellow have to forridge on other people besides of his lawfuld owner, I'm the one for that. What I were a-thinkin' about—"

"I know what you were thinking about, but that is what I don't intend to allow. Ryal sha'n't *forage* on you, as you call it. The law of the State don't allow a man to throw off an old negro as he would an old mule, without paying for it."

"I never heard of any sech law, and didn't s'pose they'd ever be any needcessity *fer* sech a law."

"No; because it is the first time in this section that there has been any occasion to resort to it. I didn't know of its existence until yesterday, when I went to see the old man Ivy — who, you know, is one of the judges of the County Court—in order to ask him if he didn't know of some way to head off Tice Blodget in his devilment. Mr. Ivy got down the 'Digest' and showed me this law, which I copied. Here it is." Taking from his pocket a paper, he read as follows:

"AN ACT TO COMPEL OWNERS OF OLD OR INFIRM SLAVES TO MAINTAIN THEM. Approved December 12, 1815.

"SEC. 1. From and after the passing of this act it shall be the duty of the inferior courts of the several counties in this State, on receiving information on oath of any infirm slave or slaves being in a suffering situation from the neglect of the owner or owners of such slave or slaves, to make particular inquiries into the situation of such slave or slaves, and render such relief as they in their discretion may think proper.

"SEC. 2. The said courts may, and they are hereby authorized to, sue for and recover from the owner or owners of such slave or slaves the amount that may be appropriated for the relief of such slave or slaves in any court having jurisdiction of the same; any law, usage, or custom to the contrary notwithstanding."

"Good law," said Mr. Chivers, heartily; "but what I was thinking about is how to go about makin' charges for what little poor old Ryal 'll eat."

"Well, what I've got to say is this, that if you don't, I'll take him somewhere else, which I know you don't want done."

"Cert'nly not, Doc Park; but it look mighty nigh like chargin' my own father; blame if it don't."

"There's got to be a contract about it, Tommy," said the doctor, looking away for a moment, "so figure away on your calculations. I consider myself the agent of the court now, and things must be done up bang. So fire away and make it a plenty. I'm coming to see him every day, and I mean to pile it on him to the full—visits, mileage, and medicine. What do you say to ten dollars a month for yourself?"

"Ten dollars a month! Law, Doc Park! he can't eat three, to save his life, not if he was a well man."

"You don't think of what I'm talking about, man. I'm not talking about your *meal* and *meat*. I want old Ryal to have *luxuries*. He needs them to build him up from the condition to which his master's meanness has reduced him. He's got to have tea *and* coffee, chicken *and* batter cakes, biscuit *and* fritters, pancakes *and* dumplings, rich as butter and sugar can make 'em, pie *and* custard, tarts *and* pudding, cream *and* preserves, lemon-syrup and — yes, *syllabub*, by blood!"

"Laws of mercy, Doc Park! Talk about all sech as that fer a nigger! Why, we don't, me an' 'Ria, jes' for ourselves, we don't have p'wye more 'n three or four times a week."

"That," said the doctor, as in contempt for such niggardly abstemiousness—"that makes not one speck of difference in the case I'm putting to you now, Tom Chivers. I want old Ryal to have *all* those things; of course not exactly all at one meal, but as many as he fancies, *three—times—a—day*, with snacks thrown in between whenever he wants or thinks he wants them. I know I can trust Mrs. Chivers about that."

"Law, yes. 'Ria love to feed."

"That's what I knew. I rather thought, until hearing how you've been going on in this case, that *you* were a little stingy, Tommy, but I find I was mistaken."

"Doc Park," said Mr. Chivers, not noticing this remark, "you talk like you want old Uncle Ryal fed up an' pompered up the same like—like, in fac', he were a fightin'-cock."

"The very *word* I've been trying to think of ever since I been talking to you, by George!" said the doctor, heartily, rising, and descending to the ground. "That confounded rail kept it from coming to me. Gemini! You make your fence-riders sharp as razors. Now see here, my fine landlord, besides all that, and more too that I shall add as I can think of them hereafter, I want you to go to the Bridge and buy the best flannel in the store, and let Mrs. Chivers have made up some shirts and drawers, and from time to time I'll let you know what else I want done for him. I tell you it's going to be an expensive business to keep the old man on the line of living I want him put."

Mr. Chivers played thoughtfully with the tassel of his cane, and revolved the questions that had risen in his mind. After some moments he looked at his visitor, and, with the firm voice of a man who was determined at length not to yield to an insidious temptation, said,

"Doc Park, I don't keer *how* you feed him, you can't

make it come up to them figgers. Now you jes' look at the itom o' meal, and which a peck a week is the highth that any *well* nigger can go, I don't keer whut his stomack ner his appetites is. Thar's one itom."

"Look here, Tom Chivers. Look straight at me, sir. I got no time to follow you up with your *itoms*, as you call 'em. All I want is for old Ryal to live like a lord—*and* a fightin'-cock, both; and when we see what the cost and the trouble will be to you, and especially to Mrs. Chivers, we can settle on the price. But it sha'n't be under, or much under, ten dollars, else you and I got to have a fight—that is, provided I can ever catch you without that stick. By-by. I got to go to Jim Lazenberry's before dinner."

He remounted and rode away. Mr. Chivers descended, and as it was not long before his dinner-hour, and specially as he wished to report to his wife the conversation just held, he proceeded on towards the house. The physician, hearing the whistle that he was lifting cheerily, checked his horse for a moment, and turning his head towards the musician, soliloquized:

"Tom Chivers! if I had the making of a world, to some folks, probably to a considerable majority, I might give longer legs, but I swear I wouldn't make a single one of 'em any more of a man."

PART II.

I.

Mrs. Chivers agreed with her husband that the figures named by Dr. Park for the board of old Ryal, in the event of his being cast upon them, were high; but she determined to come as near earning them as possible. She was a noted feeder to white and black, home folk and guests. Mr. Wilcher, the sheriff, used to say that he couldn't help from loving to have a dinner-hour catch him as he was riding by Tommy Chivers's house on his official business.

On the night of the day when Dr. Park and Mr. Chivers had their last conversation, the man Luke, having come there clandestinely, reported that his master, acting on Mandy's account of her father's motion to strike her, had given Ryal notice that he should withdraw his rations. Thoughts upon the responsibilities likely to be devolved upon him as a boarding-house keeper, so far outside of his habits and expectations, hindered Mr. Chivers from finding sleep until an hour later than usual, and he did not awaken on the morrow until nearly sunrise. Bouncing from his bed and slipping into his clothes — a thing that he could do in less time than most men would consume in putting on mere trousers — he issued forth from his chamber, and learned with some surprise that Hannah, with his wagon and Jim, his gig-horse, had set out by the dawn for her father's in order to bring away the exile.

"What!" he exclaimed, "that girl *is* a grown woman, sure enough. Somethin' got to be done with her, cert'n."

Without a moment's delay he set out, and the woods, as he passed along, echoed the reproductions of their various songsters. Hannah had intentionally provided against the possible meeting of her father and uncle that she knew both would rather avoid, and had sent by Luke instruction to Ryal to repair early to the opening of the grove in front of his master's place, where she would meet him. She was half-way on her return when Ryal exclaimed,

"Dar come Marse Tommy. A body don't need to lay eyes on Marse Tommy to know he somewhar about."

"Hello, Hannah!" cried her uncle, when they had met.

"Caught a runaway nigger, er have Uncle Ryal found a lost child?"

"Bofe un 'em, Marse Tommy, I reckin," said Ryal, smiling sadly. "No; 'taint dat way," he added, solemnly. "De Lord in heb'n sont her to fetch me to you, a-knowin' I couldn't git to you by myself. Mist'ess told me befoe she died to put my 'pen'ence on de Lord; it look like I have to put some 'un it on you, too, Marse Tommy."

"All right, all right, Uncle Ryal. You welcome at my house as you used to be. But, Hannah, dad fetch it all! it look like you told the truth when you told 'Ria you feel like you got so you 'fraid o' nothin'. Howbeever, no danger in Jim. He's gentle enough. Drive ahead. Git up, Jim. No, I don't want to ride, exceptin' these two ponies I always k'yar under me. Move on. Move up. Straighten that trace, Jim, and make 'em git a good breakfast for you all. You want yourn, I know, whether the balance of 'em want theirn or not, and I'm keen for mine. Geet up, sir!"

As they trotted on, the invalid said,

"Moust'ous good man, Marse Tommy. Mist'ess allays said he wouldn't let me suffer if he could hep it."

"Uncle Ryal," answered the child, "he's the best man in this world, I believe, not excepting Dr. Park, and hardly excepting old Mr. Sanford."

A room, not expensively garnished indeed, but cleanly swept and comfortably appointed, awaited the boarder. It had been occupied by two half-grown lads, who declared that they were proud to give it up for that purpose and take narrower quarters elsewhere; for Ryal at all times had been a favorite among black and white. The old man's outfit in furniture was far beyond satisfactory; and if the negroes on the place had not been used to the greatest abundance, they might have envied the sumptuous *ménage* that Mrs. Chivers or Hannah set before him several times a day. As it was, the younger children of both races, though not exactly hanging around, were wont to be within convenient call for tidbits of chicken-pie, custard, and I could not say what all, that were sure to be saved for them.

On the day after his arrival Mr. Chivers repaired to the Bridge, and, although his usual orchestral performance was suspended as he passed by the Blodget mansion, Mandy observed him, and so informed her lord and master, who was then at his breakfast. Had Mr. Blodget been aware of the existence of the statute heretofore quoted, it is highly probable that he would have acted with less temerity. Yet, ignorant and audacious as he was, he knew well enough that he dare not defy public opinion out and out. He believed that he might put upon his brother-in-law whatever he pleased, yet he felt that the public in this instance must know, or seem to know, the reasons for his action; so after breakfast he rode to the Bridge, hitched his horse to a rack, and dismounting went into the piazza of the store. Mr. Chivers was emerging just then, having under his arm the purchases he had made wrapped in a bundle. In the piazza were seated two of the neighbors.

"Mawnin', Tommy," said Mr. Blodget. "Saw anything o' old Ryal?"

"Yes, he's at my house. Didn't you know it?"

"Well, yes, I did ruther hear he were thar. But I want it understood that I never sent him thar, an' I ain't responshible fer him in no ways."

"Yes, sir, the old feller come thar yistidy, a-lookin' ruther gaunt in the jaws, an' I, er ruther 'Ria, she give him some victuals. He said you driv' him off."

"Did he tell you—the impident, deceitful old hound!—what it wus fer, and that it wus fer his impidence in wantin' to dictate to me about my dimestic business, like he owned me, 'stid o' my ownin' o' him? Did he tell you them?"

"No. I never ast him, ner he never told me nary word about that ner them."

"Well, right here, in the presence of Mr. Bivins and Mr. Lazenberry, I want it understood that I never driv' that nigger off complete; but that as he have meddled with my business, an' which by good rights I ought to of give him the cowhide, I told him, an' I told him mild, that he would git no rashins from me 'ithout he went to work an' kep' his mouth shet; an' I want it understood, far an' squar', that I never sent him to your house, that I got nothin' to do with him a-abein' thar, an' that I ain't to be hilt responshible fer it ner him."

"All right, Mr. Blodget."

Mr. Chivers puckered his lips, but he was too polite a man to whistle in company except upon request.

"Tommy," said Mr. Lazenberry, noticing the bundle, that had not been wrapped very cunningly, "'pear like you got more flannin than needed fer female purpose. Young, healthy man like you goin' to war flannin?"

"Never you mind, Jim. The almanic say we goin' to have a many a cold spell of weather this comin' winter. Mawnin' to you all, gent'men."

"What chune do he call that he's a-whistlin' now, Jimmy?" asked Mr. Bivins.

"I hain't," answered Mr. Lazenberry — "I hain't never got complete the run o' Tommy's chunes, they so many an' warous; but my believes is, Mr. Bivins, that Tommy a-whistlin' at the present is what he call 'The Thrasher.' You know he always in genil make his chunes hisself an' name 'em arfterwards, an' as a common thing he name 'em arfter defferent birds an' sech. Yes, sir, I'm toler'ble shore in my mind that whut he's a-puttin' up now he call 'The Thrasher.'"

"Well, Tommy's a ruther musicky little feller," said the old man, kindly.

"That boy's whistlin'," said Mr. Blodget, with rather compassionate regret, "an' his indulgin' an' humorin' o' his niggers has kep' him from getherin' anywhar nigh the prop'ty he ought to of gethered before now, by good rights. That flannin he's a-movin' off with, I'll lay it ain't fer him, an' my doubts ef it's fer 'Ria er the childern. 'Twouldn't surprise me ef 'twas fer some o' his niggers that has laid claim to have the rheumatiz like old Ryal."

When he had left the store Mr. Lazenberry said,

"Mr. Bivins, you older man 'n me. Can a man, jes' so, palm off his broke-down niggers on t'other people that way? Is they any law fer sech as that?"

Mr. Bivins was a man of very moderate means and information; but he had a widowed daughter with a respectable property, and her plantation joined Mr. Blodget's; so he answered,

"I don't know, Jimmy, as they is any *law* fer jes' sech a case — that is, in them words; but you hear Mr. Blodget say with his own mouth that he never sent the nigger too Tommy, ner palm him on too him. They's a deffer'nce right thar, Jimmy, betwix' one thing an' another."

"Yes, sir; but Tice Blodget know mighty well that Tommy Chivers not goin' to let no old broke-down family nigger be sufferin' anywhar about him."

"That all may be so, Jimmy. I got nothin' to say, you know I hain't, agin Tommy; fer he is a nice, clever, accommodatin' little feller, an' as good a whistler, ef not the best whistler, I ever knowed. But, Jimmy, we has to 'member that white folks is white folks an' niggers is niggers; an' not only that, but that corntracks is corntracks, an' it's for them reasons that I never feels agzactly like it were my business to bother myself ner meddle myself with what people that owns niggers does with 'em er does not with 'em."

"Well, *I* call sech conduct a blasted shame, I do."

"I can't go to that lenkt, Jimmy, it not a-bein' none o' my business."

"It ought to be somebody's. No man ought to be allowed to fling off his old niggers that's broke theirselves down a-workin' fer him, an' 'special' on sech as Tommy Chivers."

After this retort the subject was dropped.

II.

Under the new régime Ryal seemed to improve so in health that Hannah, shortly after his coming, returned to school. The main trouble with the old man was the thought that he had ceased to be of value. He was a type of that sort of slaves who in simple, humble faithfulness have never been outdone in this world. Any sort of white man, except such as Cato the Elder or Ticey Blodget, would have felt shame to know that in the breast of this dependant, once so prized, now discarded, was not only no resentment, but a continued solicitude for his master's interests. He had been a noted maker of baskets for cotton-picking, and when, in answer to repeated requests to Dr. Park, he was allowed to do some of that work, and he had finished the supply needed on the place, he asked Mr. Chivers if he might make some for his master.

"Bercause, Marse Tommy," he urged, "dey ain't no nigger over dar ken make bastets sich as marster want. Marster were always mon'sous pitickler 'bout de cotton-pickin' bastets."

Just then Dr. Park came up, and when the request was made known to him, said,

"Look here, Uncle Ryal, Mr. Blodget got nothing to do with you now, and the less you have to do with him the better. You belong to the Inferior Court of this county now."

"De Lord hep my soul an' body, Marse Doctor! I thought I b'longed to marster yit, ef I ever gits so I ken be any use to him."

"No, sir."

"Den don't I b'long to Miss Harnah?"

Tears came into his eyes, and there is no telling what Mr. Chivers might have done if he had not rushed off to his cornfield. As it was, no cat-bird that ever lived on any occasion indulged in more passionate utterance than that which now poured hotly from his mouth.

"No, sir, you belong to the Inferior Court of the county and State aforesaid, in such case made by the law and provided," said the doctor, with much emphasis.

"Does you—does you mean de shaiff, Mister Parks? Is I got ter go on de block? De Lawd hep my soul *an'* body!"

"I don't mean that, Uncle Ryal. The sheriff got nothing to do with you. No telling what he may have to do with some other people before long. But you belong, for the time being, to the judges of the Inferior Court. You know Mr. Ivy—Mr. Ephraim Ivy? He's one of 'em. They're five in all."

"Den I got five marsters! De Lord in heb'n know I never 'spected to come to dis! Den I s'pose Marse Ephom an' dem will have to 'wide de bastets twix' deyself. Well, well! I did hope I mout not go out de fambly tell I died."

"Look here, Ryal," said the physician, rather impatiently, "don't you bother yourself about that. Your Marse Tommy an' I will see that you don't go out of the family for good. Fire away on your baskets, if you must work. But you be particular. Whenever you get tired, do you stop. Hear?"

"Yes, sir, Marse Parks; but dat little work I do ain't wuff nothin', not to one marster let alone—"

"Uncle Ryal," said the doctor, softly, as he rose, "I don't think the time is very far off when you will have but one Master, and it will be one who will always be good to you. By-by."

He turned away, and with his handkerchief tried to press back the tears that rose to his eyes.

It was not long before there was a glut in the basket business; and several of the neighbors, instead of stopping their hands to have them made at home, supplied themselves at the dirt-cheap prices set on his work by Ryal. His master heard of all this and of his supposed rapid improvement. One day, as he was riding past, the old man, with a hammer in his hand, was standing by the front gate, to which he had been doing some simple repairs.

"You miser'ble, deceitful scounderl—" began Mr. Blodget.

"Uncle Ryal," called Mrs. Chivers, appearing that moment on the piazza, "it's time for you to quit and come for your medicine and your tea and toast. How do, Mr. Blodget?"

"Howdy, 'Rin! Ruther curous piece o' business, Tommy harb'rin' o' my nigger, an' havin' him workin' fer him in the broad open daytime."

"Sooky," called the lady, "blow the shell for your Marse Tommy."

"Oh, never mind, Sooky, never mind! I jes' only make the remark that it look ruther curous."

"Mr. Blodget, you knew that Uncle Ryal was here as

well as you knew that you had driven him off from home. I'm thankful to believe that you are the only man in this neighborhood that would have used such words as 'harboring negroes' to a woman when talking about her husband, especially one who he knew wouldn't and couldn't do such a thing."

"Why, he! he! 'Ria, I thought, as the sayin' is, the gray mar' were the better horse in this case."

Without another word she went to the gate, took the negro's trembling hand, and led him to his cabin. Mr. Blodget looked at them in silence for a few moments, then rode on.

This demonstration, as Mr. Chivers at length was convinced by his wife and Dr. Park, had been made for the purpose of diverting some part of the odium that Mr. Blodget must know had attached to himself for Ryal's being there.

"Mrs. Chivers is perfectly right, Tommy," said Dr. Park. "You ought not to notice his words, mean as they were, at least for the present. It's right hard, I know; but when such a fellow as Blodget is bent on hanging himself it is well enough to let him wind his own rope, which he's doing fast. Take it out in whistling, my dear friend. Encourage him to whistle, Mrs. Chivers, if you find him needing it. I need not tell you both to continue your gentle care of poor old Ryal. He isn't long for this world."

"What, Doc!" exclaimed Mr. Chivers. "Why, he look better, and he's a heap activer."

"Yes, that's owing to the good nursing he's had here; but the thing is leaving his limbs and is now after his heart. When it gets there the jig's up."

"The good Lord have mercy on us all!" said Mr. Chivers. Then, sobbing as he went, he rushed away to the field where his hands were at work. Tears were in the eyes of the others.

"They don't make any better men these days, Mrs. Chivers, than that little fellow rushing along yonder."

"Dr. Park," answered the wife, "he's perfect—he's just simply perfect. I didn't tell him all the words of Ticey Blodget; for as it was, I could hardly keep him from going over there to see him about it."

"I'm glad he didn't go. The thing is coming to a head fast, and it needs no other forcing except what he does himself."

"But have you no hope about Uncle Ryal?"

"Almost none. My opinion is that he will not live six weeks longer."

"Then I must try to get him to send for Mr. Sanford."

"A good idea! An excellent idea! Mr. Sanford can do him more good now than I can."

III.

Two weeks afterwards Mr. Chivers set out one morning to the Bridge for the purpose of getting another supply of tea and loaf-sugar for his boarder. The Rev. Mr. Sanford had been to see Ryal on the day before, and after a very satisfactory conversation with him it was understood that at the next conference of Long Creek meeting-house Ryal, if pronounced by Dr. Park able to get there, would apply for membership. Though not a church-member himself, Mr. Chivers was gratified in his mind. He was proud of the high standing that his wife held in the Long Creek fellowship, and he sincerely hoped that the day would come when he might venture to knock at that door himself. Thus far he had remained convinced in his mind that a man so fond of whistling tunes that were entirely carnal was not fit for such solemn communion. He moved along on this morning—a lovely one it was in that season, the fall of the year—with a less sprightly step than usual, and in comparative silence. Among the multifarious muses of his oft invocations there was not one avowedly nor mainly nor even slightly religious, and he was not a man to desecrate solemn themes with songs of the joree, or sapsucker, or others of a thoughtless and mere worldly choir. He moved along thoughtfully, Bobby the while depending low from the arm from which, in all moods of his master, he seldom, unless that master was asleep, was separated.

"Hello, Tommy! Mawnin'. How come I don't hear you whistlin' this fine mornin'? Fambly troubles, I suppose. I see you suin' your br'er-in-law."

The salutation reached him not far this side of the grove in front of Mr. Blodget's residence. It came from Mr. Wilcher, the sheriff.

"Mawnin', Mr. Wilcher. What? I reckin not."

The officer drew from his coat-pocket a bundle of writs, selected one, and handing it down, said,

"If that ain't you, I don't know who it stand for."

The paper was indorsed thus:

EPHRAIM IVY *et al.*—*Justices, etc., use of*

THOMAS CHIVERS }
vs. } *Assumpsit, etc.*
TICEY BLODGET. }

"I didn't—that is, I didn't expect, Mr. Wilcher.—Dr. Park never told me—well, well! Why, Dr. Park—"

"I got one agin him from Dr. Park, too, an' a bigger 'n yourn," interrupted the officer.

By this time, having reached the grove, the latter turned

in, and Mr. Chivers in yet more serious rumination went on. Several men, Mr. Ephraim Ivy among them, had come to the store on this the first after Return-day for suits at the fall term of the Superior Court (knowing that the sheriff would be along), in order to ascertain who among the neighbors had been sued. Half an hour after Mr. Chivers had gotten there Mr. Blodget rode up with the sheriff. His face, as he walked up the steps to the piazza, was red with passion. He had never been sued before.

"Mawnin', Mr. Ivy. Glad to see you. Mawnin', gent'-men."

Mr. Chivers, as was his wont whenever there were fewer seats than persons to be seated, was squatted on his haunches near one of the piazza-rails. As while bargaining with Dr. Park in the matter of Ryal's board, his mouth was upon the head of his cane and his fingers were silently performing a tune of extraordinarily quick movement. Mr. Blodget looked down upon him with most angry contempt for some moments, and seemed as if he were revolving how to begin an assault upon one who, however contemptible as an adversary, had inflicted upon him a wound more painful than any that he had ever endured. He really believed that he had every advantage. The writ of *assumpsit*, as all know who have even a slight experience in judicial proceedings, implies and so alleges on the part of the defendant a promise to pay the debt claimed on a certain day therein named, and repeated refusals of demands therefor. He sincerely thought, therefore, that Mr. Chivers had sought to malign and otherwise injure him.

"Tommy Chivers," he said, at length, with what mildness he could command, "I want to ast you, in the presence o' Mr. Ivy an' these other gent'men, if I ever put my nigger Ryal at your house as a boder."

"No, sir; you did not," answered Mr. Chivers, not resting, possibly hastening somewhat, in his music.

"So fur, so good. This paper that Mr. Wilcher, the sheriff, have served on me say I did, and that I promussed to pay you nine dollars a munt, an' that time an' time agin you has made the 'mand on me fer the money. Is them so, er is they not so?"

"They is not, sir," answered Mr. Chivers, his large gray eyes opening wide and twinkling as the unheard music of his clarinet increased in rapidity. "Ticey Blodget," he continued, "I don't know what that paper says, but I never told *nobody* that you had promussed to pay me one cent fer takin' keer o' poor old Uncle Ryal. He come to my house a-sayin' that you had driv' him off, an' I sheltered him an' fed him. I think myself the bode's high, but Dr. Park—"

"Never you mind about Dr. Park. Less git through with the balance o' your false chargin's." He turned a page of the writ and laid his finger on another allegation. The while the music ceased, the loop of Bobby was drawn slowly over Mr. Chivers's wrist, and his right hand took hold of the handle. The defendant resumed, "Here's another itom, an' which, ef it ain't as big in amount o' money, it's the meanest and the biggest lie you've told in the whole con—"

He had gotten thus far in his last speech when Mr. Chivers, even in the act of rising, inflicted with his cane a blow upon his head that felled him to the floor. Immediately he puckered his lips and opened upon "The Game Rooster." Pausing a moment, as Mr. Blodget, after momentary stunning, was preparing to rise, he cried,

"Cler the way, gent'men! Cler the way, ef you please! The chune me and Bobby got on hand now have to have a plenty o' room an' a plenty o' ar."

No mortal eye could have followed that baton as, after a multitude of gyrations, all apparently coexistent, it came backhanded, producing another prostration, when louder yet rose the crow of the exultant chanticleer.

"Hold on, Tommy, hold on!" loudly cried Dr. Park, who at that moment, having ridden there in full gallop, leaped from his horse, rushed up the steps, and drawing away Mr. Chivers, turned, waited for Mr. Blodget to rise, then said,

"Mr. Blodget, I don't know what special provocation you gave Tommy for striking you; but, knowing you both as I do, I suspect it was sufficient. I hoped you might meet me first after being sued about old man Ryal, and you would, but that on my way up the road I was detained with him some longer than I expected."

"Dr. Park," said the man, in rage ungovernable, "I've got to have satisfaction for all of this oudacious business."

"All right, all right, Mr. Blodget. Any sort you want from me that's at all reasonable you can get, if you haven't had enough. The fact is, Mr. Blodget, whatever satisfaction you are entitled to, if any, is due altogether from myself, as *I* had the suit instituted in Tommy's behalf and without his knowledge, knowing that if he could be induced to sue you at all he would insist upon putting his claim at less than it ought to be. But before you go any further on that line, let me give you a message Ryal sent you by me less than an hour ago. He said to me, 'Marse Doctor, tell marster when you sees him, I allays tried to do de bes' I could fer him.' What do you think the old fellow did then? Mr. Blodget, Ryal is *dead!* Mr. Ivy," turning, he said to that gentleman, "the poor, dear old man was very anxious to join you all at Long Creek, and I tried my best to make him hold out at least for that, but I couldn't.

Don't you suppose that in such a case they'll take the will for the deed?"

"I hain't a doubt of it, doctor—nary a doubt," answered the deacon.

When Mr. Blodget recovered from the stupefaction into which he had been thrown, he looked round as if he would fain say something appealing, but could not find what, and after a few moments rode away. Mr. Chivers, going to the farther end of the piazza, wept for several minutes like a little child. Then he rose, and accompanied by Dr. Park, left for his home.

IV.

These were on a Friday. That afternoon one of Mr. Blodget's men came and said to Mr. Chivers that his master had sent him in order to take the measure of the corpse for a coffin, and that two others would soon follow for digging the grave.

"Go back, Joe, and tell your master that I and Dr. Park have sent for Mr. Humphrey, and that we'll attend to all. Tell him he won't be put to any more expense about Uncle Ryal."

This message cut Mr. Blodget deeply. For the first time in all his life he would willingly, gladly have taken a responsibility that others had assumed. He felt that he could scarcely dare to attend the funeral on the following Sunday afternoon, at which he had heard that the Rev. Mr. Sanford was to officiate, and he had an indefinable dread of the words that this devout, courageous man might employ.

On this occasion a large company of white and black were present; for the deceased had been well thought of by all, and indignation, not loudly avowed but decided, was felt in view of the circumstances in which his master had allowed him to die. The coffin was borne and rested on two chairs placed upon the ground in front of the piazza. The visitors—a few in the house and piazza, mostly in the yard and the space beyond—listened respectfully to all the services. A hymn was sung, at which few eyes were without tears; for the negro's voice, especially in multitudinous choir, has a pathos than which I have never heard any music more touching. After an introductory prayer the preacher rose, now an old man, with long white locks; he had gotten little education from schools, but a life of virtue, of reading, particularly of close, prayerful study of the Bible, and a natural eloquence cultivated throughout more than twoscore of years, had made him an eminent leader in his profession. Persons of all the religious denominations spoke of him with greatest respect. To-day it was evident that he was deeply moved, and that he was more studious of his words than usual. Sometimes his feelings, profoundly stirred, transported him, not into anything like denunciation, but into passionate appeals that carried with them solemn and awful warnings. After some observations on the certainty and solemnity of death and the importance of due preparation for the Judgment, he spoke of the lowliness in which the life just closed had been led; of its contentment with a lot that excluded all chances of rising above it in this world; of its faithful, cheerful performance of work from boyhood to an age that perhaps had been made prematurely old by that work's excess from uncommon zeal for the interests of its master; of its touching regret for the failure of the strength of its prime for that master's sake, not its own; of its appeals during its very last days for permission to continue at work—appeals that the physician who tended regarded it more humane to grant than to refuse; and then of that dying message, showing that thoughts of duty were its very last.

"And now, my friends," he said, "I feel constrained to say a few words on a subject that, delicate as it may be, it is equally important that it be well understood. I am thankful that as far as my acquaintance extends, in the main the dependent beings who in the providence of God have been cast among us are reasonably fed, clothed, and housed, and that they are not overworked to a degree that may be called inhumane. Any single exception to that rule is a great wrong, both in a business point of view and especially in the matter of moral obligation. Of all creatures whom the good God has made, man can most easily overwork himself and be overworked by others. Yet whenever this is done it is followed by disaster — disaster that is always painful, sometimes piteous to contemplate. The premature decay that is sure to follow costs in the end more than the value of the extra work done in the period of unimpaired strength and activity. Therefore, it is bad economy in the case of a horse or an ox; but how much more in the case of a man, who, when he fails, is of all creatures most helpless, most useless, most troublesome! The aged or overworked beast may be turned into the pasture and crop a scanty living with little expense until he falls, when short is the delay of death. But in such condition a man needs constant care, dainty food, tender ministrations, and these often throughout periods of many years. To a selfish man these needs seem burdensome; and you and I know some—I am thankful they are not many—who provide for such cases too poorly, and who, I fear, would do more so but for public opinion in the community and the public law of the State. It always seemed to me strange that with any man, Christian or heathen, aged and broken-down servants, human or lower animal, after long-continued, faithful, too laborious service, could be neglected by their owners, or even be parted from by them, when able to provide for those peculiar needs that only remembrance and gratitude can make a man fully competent to supply. Now, among us, my friends, who live in the light of the Christian faith, there is not one who, even in childhood, has not learned that to exact of any dependent creature more of service than it can reasonably perform is a sin against GOD, and the refusal to take care of one thus reduced to prostration is a GREATER; and when that creature is a human being, I tell you, what you already know, that every dollar thus gotten and thus saved is the price of BLOOD!" Pausing an instant, he ended that theme in low but more appalling tone, "And those who have thus gathered will see the day when they will feel like going to some holy place, and, like the wretched Judas, in shame and remorse cast it upon the ground."

He looked upon the congregation in silence for some moments, then said, "On the subject of religious instruction for the colored people in our midst, I often feel much painful embarrassment. I have never known nor heard of a man who wilfully hindered his servants from receiving such as could be rendered without inconvenience to his business and work, and as one whom, as I humbly trust, God has called to be a minister of the Gospel, I feel ashamed to confess that some of the most willing in this respect, besides being among the best, honorablest, and usefulest citizens, are themselves members of no religious denomination. I have often seen such a man lean and weep over a coffin as if its occupant were a dear friend or kinsman, when neither the dead slave nor the living weeper had ever been baptized; and I have witnessed a like scene when only the master had received this sacrament, and he could then only vaguely hope that a most merciful Creator would not drive from His presence the soul of him who had gone without it. How such things can be, I have many, many times asked of myself. The causes, hidden somewhere in our state of society, are known to God, and it is every Christian's, it is every citizen's, duty to pray that he will discover them to us and lead us to make haste for their removal. I have never had a doubt that God means in His own good time to work out the destiny of this dependent people, created like us, in His image, so that they may equally contribute to His glory. As it is now, I say, in all proper respect and fear, that the master who sets before his slaves evil examples, especially he who hinders them from knowing and pursuing good, is guilty before Heaven of a heinous crime; and I verily believe that in that great Day of Account the condemnation of the sinning slave will be far less awful than that of the sinning master."

After some other remarks under this head he referred again to the deceased:

"There lie the decaying remains of what once was the best example of strength, activity, and endurance that I and you have ever known. I say nothing of the causes that laid him there sooner than you and I might have expected. The issues of life and of death are ever with God, and no man can say of another that he died before his time. But oh! my friends, how prostrate now he lies! If that lifeless body were all that was left of such a man, how much more would we shudder when gazing upon it! But the all of that life was not to live in this world and toil and grow old, and end and be no more. That poor slave had an immortal part, distinct as that of any among us who are most conscious of immortality. I firmly believe that it is now beyond suffering or peradventure; for, though hindered from becoming a member of the Church of Christ by circumstances not to be controlled by himself nor the kind Samaritans into whose hands he came by the way-side, I cannot doubt that the God of mercy accepted the will in that behalf of one who, in his humble sphere, had been found more than faithful to all the duties that he had been led to understand. It was like him, and it was a most becoming end to the earthly life of such a man, to send with his dying breath to the master whom he had served that farewell, which, when I heard it, filled my heart with admiration and my eyes with tears. Believe with me, that now, even now, among the throngs whom no man can number, Ryal, once a poor slave, is clothed in garments whose dazzling whiteness no mortal eye could endure to look upon."

He paused, and few present did not join in the weeping in which for a brief time he indulged.

He concluded thus:

"I am sure that none of my hearers can justly fear that anything that has been said by me on this occasion will do harm to the colored people—at least in the way of inciting them to acts or feelings of insubordination. They well know the necessity to keep faithful to the duties of their condition. To my mind never was a ruling race more secure in the possession of control over one in subjection than the white people of the South; secure not only in the means of defence against insurrection, but, and chiefly, in the love and affection of their dependants. They submit, uncomplaining, to punishments, even when greater than what is merited by their wrong-doings; and I solemnly believe that nowhere can be found another people so affectionate, so grateful for kindness, so free from resentment. My friends and fellow-citizens, the very security in which your families live, lying down at night, both when you are at home and when away, with doors unlocked and windows unbarred; the very impunity with which to a degree you may oppress the humble beings who are your own chiefest safeguards, have made the best and bravest among you most forbearing to them, least exacting of unreasonable service, most considerate to their old age and other infirmities. It is only the coward—but I have said enough. I pray God that all of us, white and black, may learn well whatever this lesson was intended to impart. Go in peace, and may the blessing of God be among you and abide always!"

V.

Mr. Blodget would never have exposed himself to the lawsuits, if he had known of the existence of the statute under which they had been instituted. Although he would have readily given, penurious as he was, a far higher sum than that sued for to avoid the exposure to which he had been subjected, yet, ignorant, resentful, combative, and believing himself to have been outraged, he repaired to a lawyer for counsel. Nothing could have astonished him more when informed that defence would be useless and would subject him only to greater mortification.

"What! Can't a man do what he pleases with his own niggers?"

"Oh no, Mr. Blodget! Far from it. There are many things he cannot do with them; and one of them is what you lately attempted."

He left abruptly and went to the office of the court clerk. There his resentment, instead of being abated, rose higher when he was informed that both suits had been withdrawn by the plaintiffs' counsel, who had paid in the costs that had accrued.

"The devil you say!" he exclaimed, as he put back his pocket-book, which he had taken out for the purpose of paying the whole. "Ah! ha! they found they couldn't git it, did they, Mr. Kitchens? I thought so when I come here, a-not'ithstandin' what that lawyer said. He told me 'twa'n't worth while to 'fend it. I believe now they hired him to tell me so, to keep me from prosecutin' 'em fer the merlicious prosecutin' o' *me*."

"You speakin' about Lawyer Chanler, Mr. Blodget? I see you comin' out o' his office."

"Yes, he's the feller."

"Well, I don't hardly think Lawyer Chanler would of give sech opinions onless he helt to 'em; an' my expeunce of all lawyers is that they ain't apt to adwise a man to go an' pay up a debt he's sued fer 'ithout they feel ruther cert'in in their mind that it ain't worth his while to 'fend agin it; and as fer Mr. Chanler, I'd about as soon trust to him fer good, solid adwices as any lawyer I know."

"What you s'posen' they stopped the suit for, then?"

"Well, I did hear Dr. Park say him an' Tommy had brung the suits mostly to let you understand that you couldn't drive off a' old broke-down nigger jes' so, an' fer other people to have to take keer o' him 'ithout payin' fer it. And he said, Dr. Park did, that *he* never intended from the off-start to make you pay *him* fer his serverses, because he have promuss your wife on her death-bed that he'd do all he could fer the old man Ryal; but he have jined along o' Tommy in fetchin' suit, because he say it were a shame fer Tommy to have to be put to the expense of takin' keer o' your niggers an' not get paid fer it."

"Umph, humph! he's mighty official about Tom Chivers, the little whelp! You know Tommy got a uncommon han'some wife, Mr. Kitchens, which she's the ekal o' two sech as that insignificant—"

"What you drivin' at now, Mr. Blodget?" said the clerk, laying his pen on the table, turning round, and looking his visitor squarely in the face.

"Oh! well, Mr. Kitchens, you know they is many an' warous kind o' wheels in this world, an' 'special' in this country."

"Yes, sir, they is, an' some of 'em has got nother hub, ner spoke, ner feller, ner tire; an' that's the case 'ith the one that's on top o' your mind now."

"Oh! now, Mr. Kitchens, a man oughtn't to kick before he's spurred. I ain't a-insinooatin' but what 'Ria Chivers (she's my sister-in-law, you know)—"

"And she's my wife's cousin, an' which I got no idee you did know that, sir."

"That so?" he answered, in some embarrassment. "I did know it, but I may had forgot it when I said the little joke I said jes' now. Fer it *were* a joke, an' a-meanin' jes' only that Dr. Park, like other men that has good conwersonal power, is natchel more obleegin' to people whar the females is interestin' like 'Ria is."

"That's all you meant, is it, sir?"

"All, every bit, Mr. Kitchens. You didn't hear how come Tommy to drap *his* case, ef you know? Tommy Chivers ought to know that they's a off-set on *my* side o' his case."

"Mr. Blodget, I did hear Dr. Park say (for Tommy hain't ben here sence the old man Ryal's buryin') that even ef Tommy had of wanted your money, an' which he didn't, Tommy say them licks he give you more 'n offset his account agin you."

"I — think — it — did, Mr. Kitchens. Good-day, Mr. Kitchens."

"Good-day, Mr. Blodget. You cert'n you meant nothin' wrong what you said about Cousin 'Ria?"

"I got nothin' to do 'ith 'Ria Chivers, Mr. Kitchens. *Tommy* Chivers owe me *some* sort o' settlement."

After he had left, the clerk, looking at him as he moved, said,

"You mean foul-mouth! I don't know wher er not to tell Tommy an' Dr. Park o' your cussed insinooashins. I ruther think I won't, but let you go on makin' your own rope."

The sense of humiliation must be intense in the breast of a man like Ticey Blodget when, grasping and miserly, he is made to keep in his pocket money that he would far have preferred to pay. He felt himself yet lower degraded in public esteem by having been thus made to submit to waivers on the part of the two men, both of whom he now thoroughly hated. As he rode on his return past the dwelling of Mr. Chivers, who with his wife was sitting in his piazza, he did not salute them, but looked straight before him.

"Tice is riled, 'Ria, as I knowed he'd be. I'm sorry I had to hit him," said the husband.

"I'm not," answered the wife. "Even Mr. Ivy said he couldn't see how you could have done different. You got to watch that man, Tommy."

"Oh! I not goin' to be bothered about Tice Blodget. I got my eye on him. I jes' can't help from bein' troubled about it on account o' Hannah."

"Yes, that *is* the pity of it; but Hannah has the sense of a grown woman now, and it isn't going to hurt you with her. She'll know it oughtn't, and it won't. She'd a heap ruther, if it *had* to be done, for it to have been done by you than Dr. Park."

"Think so, 'Ria?"

"I think nothing about it. I *know* it."

Hannah had not attended the funeral, as it was believed advisable not to send for her.

VI.

As Mr. Blodget rode on homeward, the events of the last few days were partially dismissed from his mind, whose thoughts were now being concentrated upon a new domestic trouble. When he had reached home, alighted, and entered his house, not finding Mandy, he came out, and standing in the porch tending towards the kitchen, called her several times. Receiving no answer, he cried in a loud voice to the cook,

"You Hester! Are you all deef? Don't you hear me callin' Mandy? Some of you'll have to have your yeares picked with a fence-rail, er a cowhide, er a somethin' else that'll open 'em. Whar's that gal?"

"I 'clar' I don't know, marster," answered Hester from the kitchen door. "I see her goin' out de gate 'bout a half-hour ago, er sich a marter. She didn't tell me whar she gwine."

"What! Whyn't you keep her back, you fool you? Which way did she go?"

"Law, marster! I can't do nothin' wid dat gal. She went todes whar de hands was a-ploughin'."

"Whar's Luke? Is *he* gone, too?"

"Oh! no, marster; I reckin not, showly. He dar wid de plough-hands, I no doubts."

Going back into the house and getting a cowhide, he set out on foot for the field of which the woman had spoken.

Even before the death of her father Mandy had become dissatisfied with her position. The unswerving devotion of Luke, and consciousness of the dislike and suspicion in which she was held by the other negroes, had begun an overcoming that at her father's death was consummated. At the funeral she sought a private interview with Mrs. Chivers, who was much gratified by her change of mind, but counselled the use of as much prudence as was possible to a purpose to perform her duty. It was not until Mr. Blodget had mounted his horse on that morning to begin his journey to the county-seat that she informed him of her wish, if he would please give his consent, to be married to Luke on the following Saturday night. He was greatly surprised, and hesitated whether to dismount or proceed on his journey. Concluding upon the latter, he said,

"It shows whut thanks a man gits from any of you when he's tryin' his best to be good to you. You tell Luke, a infernal scoundrel— But never mind. I got to go to town to-day; I can settle with him when I git back. I did think *you* knowed whut were best fer your own intrusts. I knowed *he* didn't have the sense fer that, but it can be larnt him, I reckin."

It was not a very prudent movement in Mandy to thus leave the house; but with all her faults she had much of the simple straightforwardness of her father, and she did what she thought to be best, or at least the safest, for Luke. She had gone to the field once before on that day, and urged him to join with her in leaving the place; but Luke, knowing the entire impracticability of such action, refused, and continued at his work with much dread for his master's return.

The hands were ploughing in a field near a body of woods that belonged to Mrs. Harrell, the widowed daughter of Mr.

Bivins, whom a few persons suspected that Mr. Blodget might wed some day. He, instead of going directly across the field (a thing, indeed, that he seldom did), made first for the woods, which he skirted until he came opposite the laborers. When he had reached the fence he quickly scaled it, and walking rapidly to Luke, who was turning his plough and mule to begin on another furrow, said,

"Drop on your all fours, sir, and shuck yourself!"

The negro fell instantly to his knees, but at that moment a woman's voice, loud, piercing, frantic, coming out of the woods, cried,

"My Godamighty, man! that's my husband! You goin' to beat him to death for nothin' but *that?*"

The prostrate man sprang to his feet. Driven to madness, Mr. Blodget, dropping the cowhide and drawing a dirk-knife, struck. Luke seized his wrist, and, wrenching, pushed the weapon, yet in the hand of his assailant, to the hilt in his body.

"Take me back home," he said, before falling, to the other negroes, "and send fer your Marse Tommy and Mr. Sanford. Not worth while to send fer Dr. Park."

Bold, reckless as he had been, he could not meet the last enemy without endeavors to atone. The clergyman did not reach there in time to hear his confession, but to the two men whom only a few hours before he had regarded his worst enemies he uttered, in what time was left, expressions of anguishing, most abject remorse. He had sent for them mainly, he assured them, that they might hear his dying admission of Luke's freedom from all guilt in his death.

The fall term of the Superior Court came on the next week. The Grand Jury were disposed to take no notice of the homicide at first, but afterwards, upon suggestion of some of the most thoughtful that Luke ought to have the benefit of a trial of the facts before the county, brought forth a presentment. The triers, after hearing the testimony, without delay rendered a verdict of "Not guilty."

Not long afterwards Hannah was sent by her uncle and Dr. Park, whom her father, by nuncupative testament, had appointed executors, to a boarding-school in Augusta. After remaining there four years she left off, and a few months afterwards was married to Dr. Park. The Blodget place, according to appointment by the will, had been sold three years before.

Changes came over the being of Mr. Chivers, but with less constant, decisive movement than he could have wished after the solemn scenes in which, though far contrary to his previous expectations, he had acted prominent parts. It was almost touching to notice sometimes how he tried to be remorseful because, with all his efforts in that behalf, he could not part as fast as he believed he ought from the light-heartedness that had followed him from childhood. To his cane his behavior was somewhat peculiar. This dear companion of so many years he had loved, and so had acknowledged many a time. But proud as he had been of its auxiliary service in the matter of Bill Anson's *Rattler*, yet now he reflected that in a moment of passion it had been wielded with equal violence and effectiveness against the head of a human being, in fact his own brother-in-law, and him now in his grave. It would not do, of course, for Hannah to ever set eyes on Bobby again, even if it was not a lesson due to Bobby that he should be retired from his public career. He rather thought so, and so he laid him away at the bottom of the chest in which his wife kept those things that she most seldom took therefrom for domestic or other uses. From a remark made one day by that lady to Mr. Sanford, that another lady thought she overheard, it was believed by some that in that act of consignment Mr. Chivers shed tears.

The successor to Bobby (for gloomy as Mr. Chivers tried to become, he could not force himself when on his travels to utter destitution of companionship) was a young hickory, slender, cut long, as if to warn possible assailants with apprehension of being pushed away, or in the last resort punched, if not speared. His musical essays strove (whenever they could think of it) throughout a long period, with varying success, to descend from the exalted *presto* to which only they had been accustomed, and they ceased altogether long before the *adagio* to which they had felt it a duty to fall. It was many years before he could be gotten into Long Creek, and then not without earnest disclaimer of fitness for the solemn step.

"Well, well, Tommy," said Mr. Sanford, in consoling tone, "the brethren are all satisfied that you'll try to do as well as you can. More than that even the good Lord demands of nobody."

MOLL AND VIRGIL.

"Pattern of old fidelity."—*Lady of the Lake.*

"To follow with allegiance a fallen lord
* * * * * *
Doth earn a place i' the story."
Antony and Cleopatra.

I.

FOND, even in boyhood, of the study of heraldic devices and family descents and nomenclature, I would have liked, if it had been possible, to know how it came about that of two children of the same parents one was called Moll and the other Virgil. But both had passed by some years the periods of their majority when they first came into our neighborhood, and so I had only to speculate upon a disparity that was so much in favor of the male.

Although brother and sister, they were not alike. The former had, for an African, a reasonable face and figure, was lithe, and would have been active but for a lameness in one of his legs, which had been permanently bent at the knee-joint. This infirmity had been caused, as he said, by an attack of white-swelling in his boyhood and unskilful treatment by his physician. In spite of this he was a light-hearted man apparently, and he had a jauntiness that was manifested even in his gait. The sister, who was probably ten years his senior, was singularly ill-favored. Though not regarded plainly deformed, her great breast protruded over the rest of her comparatively small, short body, and her head, with its broad, flat face, as if from regard to this notable prominence, instead of sitting upright above her shoulders, was inclined backward several degrees.

Their advent was in this wise: As they were passing afoot through Dukesborough, southward bound, the woman with a bundle under one arm, the man with another hanging from a stick across his shoulder, the latter inquired of a knot of men sitting in the piazza of Bland's store the way to the plantation of Mr. Sangwidge.

"The plantation o' who?" answered the sheriff, Mr. Triplett, who happened to be there on a visit to the friends around his old home.

"Mister Sangwidge, sir."

"Know no sech man. Know every man in this county too. No sech man in these parts."

"Yessir, marster; he 'bleeged to have plantashin not fur b'low here, beca'se he told us so, and sont us thar."

"Who did you say he were?"

"Mr. Sangwidge—Mr. Sangwidge, de lawyer."

"Oh! ah! that, indeed. You mean Mr. *Sandidge*. Sandidge we calls him about here, not Sangwidge. What you want to know the way thar for?"

"We b'longs thar, marster."

"B'longs thar? How come you don't know the way thar, then, if you belongs thar, an' 'in seb'n mile of it, an' the main, straightforrards public road a-leadin' spang up to the very gate? Bersides, I know Squire Sandidge's niggers toler'ble well, an' I'm pooty cler in my mind that I don't 'member as ever I see two sech as you among 'em. I ain't perfec' shore in my mind in course, but my s'picions is you two niggers is other free niggers, er else you've runned away from somers."

"No, sir, marster; no, SIR!" quickly answered the man. "We ain't. Sis Moll an' me (she's my sister, an' I'm her br'er), we ain't no free niggers; ner we hain't no runned away, we hain't. We b'longs ter Mr. Sangwidge de lawyer, an' he tole us to go ter his plantashin somers b'low this here town whar we is now, an' dar's whar we makin' fer, ef we ever lives to git dar."

"Why, whar you ben so fur an' ben gone so long, you done clean forgot whar your homes is?"

The woman, who had not turned her face from the direction in which they had been travelling, spoke a few words to her brother in a low tone.

"Ya'as," he exclaimed, "dat's so! I cler forgit it. Here's our pass, marster."

Mr. Triplett having read the paper handed to him, said,

"That's so. Squire Sandidge's own name, an' in his han'write. I know it good as I do my own—better, in fac'; fer I got sech a little chance o' schoolin' in my day that I never learnt to write a good solid han'write, an' my han'write mos'ly in gener'l 'pends on the kind o' pen I got, an' them's so warous that sometimes I can't allays read what I've writ 'ithout takin' time. Yes, sir; yes, sir; here's a regular pass to Moll an'—what's that tother name?"

"Werg'l, marster, Werg'l."

"Yes, that's so, an' writ away yonder in Lincoln. I knowed he were in cote thar this week. But yit, my friend, I can't yit see how it is that you don't know the way to your own home, as clos't as you are thar at the present."

The woman gave an impatient step forward, but stopped instantly, as her brother began to satisfy Mr. Triplett's last doubt.

"Well, you see now, marster, we ain't not—I mean me

an' sis' Moll—we ain't nuver ben dar, an' dat what make me 'quir'n' de way dar. Beca'se, you see, marster, we ain't ben b'longin' to Mr. Sannidge, exceptin' sence day befo' yistiddy."

"Ah, that, indeed! Now we gittin' to the merit o' the case, as them lawyers says. Mr. Sandidge bought you two, did he?"

"He not zackly bought us, marster, out an' out, jes' so."

"How then—traded fer you? swapped fer you?"

"No, sir; no, sir. You see, marster, our marster—I talkin' 'bout de one we had fer marster up to-day 'fo' yistiddy. That was in Linkin County, down dar close by Owl Ferry. I reckon you know whar dat is."

"Oh yes, thar er tharbout. I've heerd of it; go ahead. You're all right. This paper make you that. But I jes' natchel has the curiosity to know how Squire Sandidge got holt o' two jes' sech niggers as you two is, an' that not a-buyin' of you, ner a-tradin' fer you in no sort o' fashion."

"You see, marster," answered the man, lifting the wallet from his shoulder, advancing his sound leg forward, and supporting the other with his stick, "here de way it come about, nigh as I could gether from whut dey all said. My marster, his name were Marse Billy White; dey said dat he tuck two o' Mr. Freeman's hosses one night onperknownst to him, an' k'yard 'em down in Clumby, an' sold one o' 'em, an' were gwine sell de tother when dey cotch him. An' den dey tuck marster, dey did, an' dey fotch him to town, an' dey flung him in de jail, an' de jedge he come dar, an' he called de cote, an' Lawyer Sannidge an' a ner lawyer dey come to de cote-'ouse too, dey did, an' dey diwided me an' sis Moll an' de lan' twix deyself, de ter lawyer he takin' de lan', an' Lawyer Sannidge he a-takin' me an' sis' Moll, an' den dey sont Marse Billy to de pentenchwy."

"'SIS MOLL AN' ME (SHE MY SISTER, AN' I'M HER BR'ER), WE AIN'T NO FREE NIGGERS, NER WE HAIN'T NO RUNNED AWAY, WE HAIN'T.'"

Loud laughter followed this account, in which Virgil looked as if he would have joined, but that his sister glanced towards him with warning.

"The lawyers made a clean sweep, did they?" said Triplett, wiping his eyes. "What become o' the stock an' plantation utenchuls, an' the housle an' kitchen furniture?"

"I reckon they went to the judge, Virgil?" suggested Mr. Bland, a rather pleasant man.

"Dat whut I sposen, marster, dough I doan know dat, case I nuver heerd. Dey warn't so mons'ous much o' dem, noways, 'case de mos' o' dem was done sol' fur debt."

"Well, my good people," said Triplett, kindly, "it was a right hard case."

Then he gave them the needed instructions, and they proceeded on their way.

"That's jes' like Squire Sandidge: take fer his fee all a poor feller's got, ef he can git it. I s'pose he thought, bein' in the pentenchuwy, he wouldn't need 'em. An' in fac' I know nothin' about the walue o' the land, but them niggers don't 'mount to no great shakes; one lame, an' tother lookin' like a heathen idle. But he got the 'vantage of her in thar names. Look at him as he sa'nters. He walk like he knowed he were name Virgil or some other big man. As for the 'oman, she look like she jes' as soon be Moll as anything else. But ef I ain't mistakened, the poor thing have got feelins. I don't know how come Squire Sandidge not to sell 'em in thar neighborhood, a-knowin' no sech creeters as them could make any friends in a strange place. Howbeever, I don't sposen he could of got nothin' fer 'em."

II.

The overseer on the plantation having reported that the negroes newly arrived were of little value in such work as was there required, and Virgil claiming on his own part to be something of a carpenter, and for his sister that she was a good cook and washer, Mr. Sandidge removed them to his own residence, which was the last at the western end of the village containing the county court-house. A few days after the removal the guard who had been sent from Milledgeville to bring the convict to the penitentiary passed through the village on his return. Virgil, who was working on the front gate, recognizing his former master in the van, called to his sister. She came forth, and both saluted the unhappy man, simply, and apparently without uncommon sympathy. The guard having dismounted in order to readjust some parts of the harness, the woman, placing a foot on the step, raised herself and spoke a few words in a low voice. As they moved away, both shook hands, and said, "Godamighty bless you, Marse Billy!"

Tears were in the woman's eyes. The guard said, "Looks like them niggers, 'special' the 'oman, think a good deal o' you."

"She nursed me," he answered; "and her brother and I, being of about the same age, were playmates. They were all I had, and I might say I was all they had. They'll get over it. I hope their new master will treat them well."

His sentence was for fourteen years, the full limit of the law. He was a widower and childless, his wife and two children having died a year past. He had been reduced to the estate that he held at his arrest by having been forced to pay a surety debt for one of his neighbors, and it was the latter's property ostensibly which, on failure by some legal turn to subject it to execution, he had taken.

"It will be right hard for a man at forty to begin again, with nothing to start with, won't it, sir?" he asked.

"Right hard. What made you pay your lawyers so much? They got about all you had, didn't they?"

"Everything. The lawyers said they could clear me, and that they'd let me have the property back by my giving a mortgage for three hundred dollars apiece. If the trial hadn't been forced at this court I could have cleared myself, for the hofse I took was mine by good rights, and the other I didn't take, but it followed its mate, and I was carrying it back home the night they arrested me. But it's too late; it's too late. Please don't ask me anything more about it."

Though not a church member, Moll was considerably addicted to the singing of hymns, especially in periods of mental depression. She and her brother repaired to the kitchen, and for some time their conversation, conducted in low tones, was interluded with snatches of songs on a proportionately elevated key:

"'I thank my God I ain't afeard to die.'

Dey sont him for fo'teen year, didn't dey?"

"Yes, 'm, beca'se you know, sis' Moll, dey was two un 'em."

"'In hopes of dat immorchil crownd
I now de cross sistains,
An' glad-lie wanders up and downd,
An' smiles at t'ils and pains.'

Well, whut 'll dat make me an' you den? Mistiss tol' me las' year 'fo' she died dat I were forty-six year old. Dat fetch me to forty-eight, doan it?"

"Yes, 'm."

"An' whut do it fetch you, an' whut 'll it fetch bofe on us, when Marse Billy time up?"

As Virgil was making his calculations she almost screamed,

"'How wa-rie, how ti-yud my Laws.'

Me an' you, boy, got to make an' lay up—we got to make an' lay up, I tell you.

"'I hain' got nothin' 'tall to do
But wange Je-woosalem.'

H—sh—sh!"

"I didn't know you were such a singer, Moll," said Mrs. Sandidge, coming to the kitchen door, evidently gratified by the apparent want of painful concern at the parting. Virgil returned to his work.

"I no gweat singer, miss. I were jes' a-hummin' a few himes, a-thinkin' o' ole times."

"Did your poor master have much to say to you?"

"No, ma'am; jes' howdye and goob-by."

"I've no doubt you all felt right bad."

"Ah, well, miss, dem dat goes agin de law, as dey say Marse Billy done, dey has to pay fer it. I nussed him, an' I 'bleege to feel solumncholy in my mind when I see him gwine 'long wid all dem chains on him, and nuver spects to see him no mo'."

"That's so; and I think you and Virgil perfectly right in feelin' sorry for him. I feel sorry for him myself. Still, the law, you know, Moll—"

"Yes, 'm, yes, 'm; oh, yes, 'm," she answered, quickly and cordially, as if sympathy for the unfortunate was already gone. She turned to her task, and the two had no further conversation touching their late master until late at night, when all others were asleep. They, especially the woman, fully believed in his innocence; yet, whether innocent or guilty, the affection she had for him was of a kind that in such a spirit as hers endures throughout life, and counts not the sacrifices that it can render. Virgil, under a somewhat flippant exterior, carried much resolution, but this was not to be compared with his sister's; and though her understanding was more limited than his, he was entirely under her control. She loved him well, but not like him whom she had borne in her arms in childhood, and who now in misfortune and disgrace—both to her mind undeserved—seemed to her to be ever making appeals for help.

III.

Considering the apparent difference in the locomotive powers of Moll and Virgil, it was soon remarked how deliberate was the gait of the former compared with the alertness of the latter. He never used a cane. A habit, formed originally, perhaps, from indulging his weaker member, had imparted a jauntiness that seemed to ignore any special infirmity as he swung alternately forth and back his sides while stepping briskly along. He was studiously polite, especially to white people, and among those of his race commonly bore himself as if in fairly favorable circumstances he might become somewhat of a beau, whereas down to this period both he and his sister had remained unmarried. Moll, though diligent at work, elsewhere was deliberate, and for a woman, especially a negro woman, uncommonly reticent. Whenever she appeared on the street—at first seldom, afterwards frequently—she usually walked with her hands folded across her capacious bosom, and her eyes looking, if at anything, at objects quite above those within anything like horizontal range. She was slow, whereas her brother was quick, to make new acquaintances.

"Why don't you walk with a stick, Virgil?" asked Mr. Pucket, a young lawyer not yet engrossed in a large practice.

"Dem may walk wid sticks whut need 'em," he answered.

"I ain't one o' dem ar. Sticks wuz made fer ole people an' sickly people. I not one o' dem."

It was remarked how soon and with what slight regrets he had become domiciled in a community hitherto unknown to him. For the negro, like the white man, loves his native home, and in his way dreams of it when absent, especially in circumstances like those which had driven these into virtual exile.

"Bad business that of your master, eh? He paid a high price for them horses, and lost them in the bargain."

"Yessir, oh, yessir. Miss Sannidge an' dat ter lawyer 'min'stered on him. Same ef he been dead; jes' lack *he* 'min'stered on ole marster when he died. Dey settled him up in short; but you see, marster, dem dat flings rocks mus' spec to git flung at an' hit deyself some time."

"He keers not a continental for his master being in the penitentiary," said Mr. Pucket, as the negro walked away.

"*He* mayn't," answered Mr. Triplett, who was standing near, "but his sister do. I see it in her eyes when I overhauled 'em in Dukesborough on thar way here. From all I can gether, it's a right hard case. Most people say the fellow never meant to take but one horse, which wouldn't of been but fer six year at the outside, and that the tother horse, follerin' his pardner, struck him fer fourteen; and there's them that says that ef he could of proved it, the one he tuck were his'n by good rights, and that the feller that he stood security fer knowed it. But that's jes' the way 'ith some people. Arfter they done ruined you by your helpin' of 'em, they despises you an' want to git you out o' their sight. They say Jedge Mike charged p'inted agin him through an' through. But that ain't oncommon fer him. Take it up an' down, by an' large, from whut people tells me, it's a toler'ble hard case."

Mr. Sandidge soon became well-satisfied with a fee that at first seemed to him below the value of his services, however unsuccessfully they had been rendered. Virgil was found to be even more adroit in the use of carpenter's tools than he had represented himself, and having finished what work was needed on the premises, he found that he could earn about seventy-five cents a day outside. The collection of bills, not always solvent, becoming troublesome, his master one day said to him that he might hire his own time, with the understanding that he brought to him every Saturday night, without fail, three dollars. Whether he was pleased with the offer did not appear. He seemed to reflect a space, then answered, "It's—it's jubous business, marster. White folks is mons'ous oncert'n 'bout payin' o' niggers."

The master was sitting in the rear porch, and the man standing on the ground. At that moment Moll, passing by the latter (it was nigh dusk), without pausing, whispered, "Take it, you fool!"

"I'll do de bes' I kin fer you, marster," he then said. Henceforth it seemed that for the first time he had begun to take proper views of life, as if hitherto he had been sowing wild oats, and had become satisfied with reaping their crop. Not that he abated his respectful deportment, or the ready, sometimes merry repartee to the jocose remarks of others; but in these pleasant exercises he did not linger now, as had been rather his wont. When saluted he would take off his hat, dip his head, throw forth the hearty reply, and proceed on his way with a carriage which, since his allowance of independent responsible action, was enhanced almost to a swagger.

On the first Saturday night he was a quarter of a dollar lacking in his returns.

"But you see, marster, I 'ain't quite got my han' in in

de knowin' o' people an' findin' out who to truss. Den I think ef I could spread out mo' it 'd come easier."

"What do you mean by spreadin' out?"

"Spreadin' out over de country furder like, to'd Geechee, an' Buff'lo, an' Islant Creek, an' Town Creek, an' all down in among dar."

"I don't care how fur you *spread*, as you call it, provided you fetch the money every Saturday night."

"Jes' so, m' marster. An' sometimes when I can't drap my work twhell night, an' doan git home twhell Sunday, will dat do? And den sometimes when I gits here of a night arter you gone to bed, an' haf ter leave 'fo' you gits up, ken I leave de money wid sis' Moll, marster?"

"Certainly. However, that would look rather hard on a lame man. In that case you might fetch the money every two weeks. But don't you forget that it will be six dollars then instead of three; and if I or your mistress is asleep when you have to start back, you can leave the money with Moll. She's as honest as you are, I reckon, if not more so."

"Dat so, marster," he answered, gayly. "She ought to be, 'case she older'n me."

"All right. That'll do. Off with you."

"Thanky, marster."

"You see dar now whut I tol' you? Ef you hadn't 'a' hilt back dat quarter fer de fuss week dah man 'd 'a' said you made it too easy, an' 'a' riz on you," said Moll, at their usual night conference. "I'm gwine make some money too, ef de Lord spar' my life an' dah man doan hender me. He wife white 'oman wid some feelin's fer niggers. Well, she is dat. *He* keer no mo' fer niggers un he do fer hound dogs. I'll do dar work ef dey don't press on me too hard, but I gwine make some money fer—fer Aunt Peggy. You hear, Werg'l?"

"I hear, sis' Moll."

"Well, g'long off to bed. You tired in dah sick leg. I ain't. G'lang to bed, an' git some sleep, an' allays 'member whut I tell you."

He went to bed. She sat up many hours later.

IV.

Mr. Elam Sandidge had been joked a good deal about his fee for sending, as Virgil had awkwardly put it, a client to the penitentiary. But now the time had come when he could answer his jokers with other than the silent smile with which he was wont to listen to conversation that he suspected was meant to be regarded humorous.

"Why, gentlemen," he remarked on the street one morning after a hearty breakfast, "when I took the confound things I didn't think they were worth, both put together, as much as a hundred and fifty dollars, and I didn't think so powerful well o' the 'sociate counsel for palmin' 'em off onto me. But as I had no use fer the feller's little piece o' land away so fur off over thar, I let Nellums have it his way. But I'll be confound if now I'd take five hundred dollars apiece for them niggers, shabby as they looked and does yit. I'll be confound if I would; and everybody knows that I don't make a practice o' cussin'."

Mr. Sandidge, indeed, seldom "cussed," as he conscientiously called the imprecation just uttered; and whenever he did he wished it understood that he knew what he was talking about, and that he was in the habit of studying his words before using them. "Yes, gentlemen, five hundred dollars apiece; and that's more'n three times what the land would sell for. For the man, with all his lame leg, fetches me more'n the intrust on a thousand dollars cler o' expense o' both collectin' and feedin' hisself; and as for

25

Moll, well, I don't say t'other people, but *I* never set down to sech victuals as she fetches to my table. I positive hate —it is positive hard—to git up from the biscuit and fried chicken she fetch to my table, long as any's left and ain't eat up. I'll be confound ef it ain't."

It did almost seem as if Mr. Sandidge was in some danger of ignoring his high professional position and becoming a mere profane gourmand.

And Moll—poor old Moll White, as they styled her at first, she seemed so lonely and forlorn, so silent, so resentful for the sudden change made in her condition, so unfit, so undesirous to make new acquaintances. Yet she had never been fully understood. Doubtless no pains had ever been taken to understand such an inconsiderable item in the good God's creation. If any had been, in all probability they would have miscarried. For the psychologist, the phrenologist, the physiognomist, the biologist, or any of the other great men who make it their business to study life with views to the establishment of definitive sciences, would have found Moll White hard to classify, even harder to individualize satisfactorily, I don't care in what habit they found her, whether around the kitchen fire, alternately silent, soliloquizing, humming her hymns, or upon the street, courtesying abstractedly to all whom she met, or otherwise employed. Now this "otherwise" comprehended many simples, increasing in numbers continually. For a change had come over her lately. She manifested willingness, even wish, to know better the people around her, white and black. To this end she grew talkative, visited, when her mistress and her business occupations permitted, the kitchens or backyards of the villagers, not so much to know as to become known, for a purpose she had on her mind. This was generally understood to be the getting a little money for what extra work she might find, for the comfort of an old aunt Peggy, who had been left behind. The pious thought was much commended. Then her cooking and other kitchen and house service were so satisfactory that her mistress was quite willing for her, in what was termed Moll's own time, to work on hire for others. A plain woman was Mrs. Sandidge, who had married her husband before there was any special promise of the success which he was destined to attain, but who, notwithstanding, had not parted from her simplicity or goodness of heart.

"I do think, on my soul, Missis Triplett," she said to that lady one day, "that that nigger's the industriousest creeter I ever knowed. When they first come to our house I couldn't but laugh, and even git sort o' fretted 'ith Mis' Sandidge fer sendin' 'em there. But they've both showed theirselves to be as vallible niggers as they is any in this whole town. Virgil brings or sends Mis' Sandidge three dollars every single Sat'day night of his life, and Moll, besides cookin' and keepin' a cleaner kitchen than ever *I* had before, picks up *I* don't know how much in warious ways. She do up nice things fer Missis Joyce, the Taylor girls, and I don't know who all. She wash and irons fer several people, white and black. She mend and patches fer nigger men who their own wives is too lazy and good-fer-nothin' to do them fer 'em; and here lately she been goin' out before day, and between times, and getherin' old field plums, and arfter always givin' me the pick, sellin' the balance fer what she can git. And *as* fer sleepin', if that nigger git any o' that, you know when she git it as well as I do; fer no matter what time o' night you call her, she not only answers, but she come a-scootin' with her frock an' all on, just as if it was the broad of sun daytime. I laugh at her sometimes, and tell her she must expect to git rich, or make her aunt

Peggy rich. She laugh back, she does, well as she know how to laugh, at such a joky idee; for she's a heap more conversonal creeter than she were at first, and look more contented like. I couldn't help from bein' sorry fer her when she come here ef it had been to of saved my life. Fer ign'nt as the poor creeter is, she's got feelin's. Mis' Sandidge don't b'lieve it, he say, any more than a cow, but I tell him he's mistakened. Why, Missis Triplett, I could set there in the house an' tell her mind were oneasy when she'd be tryin' to sing a hymn from the *Cluster*, and which they's no more music in her woice hardly than in the m'yowlin' of a cat, and it sound like she felt bad *as* a cat, and went to m'yowlin' because she couldn't help herself. And then the tryin' to scrape up a little somethin' for her old aunt—Peggy, as she call her—show she *have* natch'l good feelin's. And as fer spendin' any of what she make on herself—*stingy?* Why, Missis Triplett, stingy ain't the word, ner I don't know what *is* the word to tell how that nigger lay up what she can gether. I try to be good to her as I can, a-seeing of her so wobesolemncholy, so to speak, and I do think the poor thing have got over some of it. And stingy as she is—and I tell you now that she make flour go further than any cook ever *I* had in all my born days since I been house-keepin'—she's honest as the days is long, to my opinion. She keep her own soap and starch siparate from mine; but somehow I will 'casion'ly put some o' mine along with hern jest to encourage her like, and show her honesty is the best policy, as the almanac says."

Yet even Mrs. Sandidge knew not all the ways adopted by Moll to scrape bits of silver together for her aunt Peggy, though she did know of some besides those mentioned. From the flour at times received instead of money she made ginger-cakes. She was never without beer, made of dried

apples, until the season of persimmons and honey locusts.
She cobbled shoes with great skill for a woman—so the
negro men said. She physicked, on a limited and extremely
cheap scale, man and beast, haired and feathered tribes. She
always kept a little tar in a keg sunk in the ground behind
the kitchen, and retailed it to wagoners whose wheels, incoming or outgoing, needed lubricating. She sharpened cutlery,
and put blades and rivets into dilapidated knife-handles.
And she did many other things. She soon became known
as a money-getter in all ways possible to one in her condition, and some that would have been thought impossible.

"Who you goin' to leave your propt'y to, Moll, when
you conclude to remove from this mortal sphere?"

This inquiry was made by young Mr. Pucket, who thought
that one way to get the practice that he had not yet was to
walk about the streets, sit before the tavern and stores, and
make pointed remarks.

"When I do whut, Mis' Puck?"

"When you git ready to shuffle off this sublun'ry quoil,
and—as the saying is—peg out?"

"Never you mind whut's to cum o' whut little I ken
scrape up fer my ole aunt. You gimme dat ter thrip. You
know dem brackberries is wuff more'n seb'npens."

The young men, after pretended chaffering, used to pay
her charges, which were quite as high as she felt safe in
naming. Although not a church member, and seldom attending religious service, yet she abstained on Sundays from
all work on her own account. In the afternoons she sat
quietly in the kitchen, or, putting on her nice frock, sallied
forth upon her calls. The white ladies of the town always
had some words of kindness for her, and it was in these
visits commonly that she made engagements for the coming
week. Within less than a year she had become as well

known in the town and through a circuit of several miles as any native negro. Believed to be entirely harmless, she was never molested in her wanderings, night or day, even after the hour when the race, by corporation regulations, were expected not to wander from their homes except with written permits.

"There goes a nigger yonder," one might say to the marshal, as a form would be descried moving softly along after bedtime.

"Nobody but old Moll White," would be the answer. "She's made at least a quarter, I'll stake my hat, some'rs to night, an' I'll take another bet she'll make another quarter twix' this an' day. That nigger can live 'ithout sleep, I b'lieve. If she ever go to bed I don't know it, though I pee-ruses an' pre-amberlates this town good part an' warous parts o' ev'y single blessed night. It don't hardly seem like to me she's folks. I come up 'ith her sometimes of a night, and her eyes — for you can in gen'l see them a-shinin,' make no odds whut kind o' night it is—they'd skeer me ef I hadn't got usened to 'em. She don't agzactly seem to me like she's folks. She don't look much like folks, day ner night, an' her actions is outlandisher than her looks. Jes' betwix' us here, not to go no furder, I wouldn't be surprised not so powerful much ef somethin' oncommon was to happen to that nigger an' to that Werg'l too; fer he come an' go at all hours o' night too, though he do git some sleep, beca'se I've saw him a-noddin' hard an' strong, an' which I hain't yit saw that o' Moll."

Mr. Sandidge was not well satisfied with the condition at home. "That nigger goin' to break herself down, Betsy," he said to his wife, "ef she don't stop some o' her everlastin' settin' up o' nights, an' projectin' with her var'ous trades. Then she'll be fit for nothing, but a dead expense."

"Now, Mis' Sandidge, don't you bother about Moll. I've been a-studyin' that nigger. She ain't like other niggers. She tells me she git all the sleep she want, and she say that not from a child could she ever go to sleep when anybody try to make her do it. She's one o' that kind that a body have to humor her to some extents or have trouble 'ith her. She's never took as much as a pin from this house since here she's been, nor a dust o' flour, and you know yourself that *we've* never had such cooking, nor nothin' like it."

"That's what I'm a-talkin' about, and I don't want to give it up. And as fer that Virgil, I ain't sure but that he's got about as much business as me. Next time I see him I'm going to tell him to fetch me or send me five dollars stid o' three a week. I hain't a doubt he makes six."

"Law, Mis' Sandidge! do, pray, don't make that po' one-legged nigger do any more'n he's a-doin' already. He's payin' you well. You know you tried to sell 'em when they first come fer a hundred dollars apiece, and I heard you tell Mr. Perkins last week that a thousand wouldn't buy 'em. You let me an' them manage it, an' you 'tend to your law."

"Go ahead, steamboat—er I should ruther say, steam*boats*."

Mr. Sandidge was about to start on the fall circuit, and he thought he would not then insist further upon those points. Indeed, he was a reasonable family man, and on occasions which he was conscious of not being able to control, was wont to yield with as pleasant, merry words as he could think of.

V.

Meanwhile the career of the brother was marked by yet more notable, if not more various, activities than that of the sister. Before his master's pecuniary ruin he had been known as rather shiftless, sometimes suspected of avoiding or slighting work quite within his capacities on the plea of his lameness. Since then he had taken on a better development. At this juncture especially it is doubtful if any other negro in the State of Georgia ever found a greater variety of ways for getting the weekly sum exacted of him and a trifle for himself, or, as he always put it, for his aunt Peggy. Independent action, great responsibility, and a tender regard for the aged relative left behind near Owl's Ferry brought forth powers which even himself had not suspected that he possessed. He made and mended fences, dairies, milk-houses, wheelbarrows, shoes, harness, reels, winding-blades, warping-bars, looms, spinning-wheels, children's cradles, and these not by the day, but by the job, for he worked at them night *and* day. At night also he waited on young men, blacking their shoes, fetching water, going upon errands, and doing other, if there were other, things. He abjured the use of tobacco, except as he could beg it. He usually went to bed before Moll, but this was rarely before midnight, and both were known to be, by at least an hour, the earliest risers in town, the sister always calling the brother.

"Didn't love to sleep so much," she would say sometimes, "could make some'n wuff some'n fer — fer Aunt Peggy. But I s'pose yer short leg make you tired."

For the first few months his operations were confined within the town or its close neighborhood, but as his acquaintance became enlarged, he circulated more and more widely. If his day's work took him not more than three or four miles from home, he returned at night, and spent the waking hours on whatever jobs he or his sister had on hand. He was ever punctual with his weekly three dollars, always slowly making up the last dollar with small coins, giving a grunt of thankfulness for being able, as he styled it, "to squeeze thoo." Gradually he moved on southwardly to Island Creek, Town Creek, even the hither bank of the Oconee. The very week that Mr. Sandidge started on the fall circuit, Virgil, now calling himself "Werg'l Sanwidge," crossed that river with the view of seeking employment in the capital city of Milledgeville.

"Hello! Whose nigger are you?" asked the principal keeper of the penitentiary, as he walked one morning by the new-comer, who was working on some fence palings in the neighborhood of that institution.

"I'm Werg'l Sanwidge, marster. I b'long to Mis' Sanwidge, de big lawyer. You know o' him, I speck." Then he drew out his pass.

"Cert'n'y. Know him well. Wonder he let niggers hire their own time that way. But s'pose you fitten fer nothin' 'bout home. What you ast fer your work?"

"I in gen'l works by the job, marster, an' dey pays me by de job."

"What can you do?"

"Mos' anything come to han', marster, bofe a-makin' an' a-mendin'."

"Why don't you mend that short leg, then?"

"Ah," he answered, gayly, "such as dat beyant even white folks, let 'lone niggers."

"I want a little work round and in the penitentiary, but these confound nigger workers charges too high."

"Ain't it dangersome, marster, bein' 'bout dem white men you got penned up in dar? Beca'se ef it ain't, I'll do your work, an' on livin' pay."

"Dangersome? Thunder! Who you s'pose want to hurt such a lookin' creeter as you? and them men know they couldn't if they wanted to."

After some further parleying, Virgil was engaged, and his work was speedily acknowledged by his employer to be satisfactory.

At noon on the Saturday then ensuing he left off, saying that as he had not reported at home in two weeks, he must do so now, but would be again on hand the next Monday morning. He reached home late that night, finding his sister in expectation of him. They had a talk of many hours. They seemed at times quite cheerful; at others anxious. Moll set before him a good supper, and after their conversation was over, let him sleep some hours. An hour before day, having already gotten his breakfast, she aroused him. After he had eaten, she ripped the shuck mattress that lay on his bed, took out a bag some two inches in diameter and twenty in length, with stout cords attached to either end, and handed it to him, saying,

"You be keerful wid dat. Dey's twenty dollars an' quarter and seb'npens in dar. I got ten dollars and thrip persides, but maybe I better keep dat twhell we see how dat do. Now you go. It's danjous, but it's wuff tryin'. Ef I wuz a man *I* could do it, an' I hope Godamighty will let you do de same. Go 'long. Goob-by."

When he was gone she sat the remainder of the night, her hands alternately folded over her bosom or resting upon her knees. When it was dawn she rose and went to her usual work.

"Where's Virgil at work now, Moll?" Mrs. Sandidge said, Monday morning, when Moll handed in the avails of his two weeks' labor. "He must be some distance off to be gone two weeks, and have to go back the same night he comes."

"He workin' down to'ds de 'Conce River, miss. I think dah whut he call it."

Virgil's work became so satisfactory to the penitentiary authorities that his first engagement was extended. His occupations were so various that he was often thrown among or near the prisoners, sometimes attending upon a squad that, under an armed guard, were detailed for work outside the walls. In this while he had never mentioned even the name of his late master, and was never heard to address a remark to any of the convicts except when it seemed becoming the character of his and their several or joint employments. On one afternoon in particular he moved about with noticeable alacrity. It had been raining all day, and the night promised to set in early and black. In spite of the weather he would not withdraw from his work, and although for hours and hours his clothes had been wet through and through, he lingered until the dusk, when he was called by the gate-keeper, who cried that he was about to shut up for the night. The convicts had been remanded to their cells some time ago.

"Comin', marster, comin'," he answered, cheerily; and whistling the while, he walked from a remote corner, where he had been engaged, along the lower tier of cells.

"My!" he exclaimed, when he was emerging, "dish here day bin like one o' dem days we used to hear ole people talkin' 'bout when we wuz boys."

"You or your marster, one must love money, Virgil, not holdin' up from work sech a day as this have ben."

"Ah, marster, when Sa'day night come dis nigger got to k'yar home de money, rain or shine."

"Well, sir," said the man to one who was standing near, as Virgil moved away, "there go the industr'ousest creeter, white *er* black, I ever come up with. Ef he was my nigger, a thousand dollars might buy him, but not nine hundred and ninety-nine."

"Yet," answered the other, "he cost his marster, so they tell me, jes' one speech, an' a mighty poor one at that, for that feller that was sent here from Lincoln for stealin' horses."

"Is that so? Why, he never much as peached, as I know of, that he even knowed the name of anybody here."

"Oh, I s'pose he were ashamed o' his old marster, an' didn't want it knew that he ever 'sociated with such low-flung white folks. Some niggers is mons'ous proud, an' he's one of 'em. Jes' look at him as he go yonder. He swaggers hisself like he want it knew that ef he *is* one-legged, he b'long to the astockersy, he do."

"Umph! humph! I'll ast him 'bout his fambly connection to-morrow."

The promise of the coming night was fulfilled. The rain slackened not, and the darkness was intense. The town clock sounded eleven beats. One of the guard had just passed his patrol from one of the sentry-boxes. A few moments afterwards a smothered cough sounded from the wall at a spot which he had passed, and was answered by one on the ground outside. Immediately afterwards a ladder was applied to the wall, and a man rapidly descended by it.

"Tang God! tang God! Here, quick! take dis bag o' money, an' go fer life arfter we git down dis larther. Hoss hitch by de big white-oak by de State-'ouse. Sis' Moll waitin' fer you all de time."

This was said in a loud, passionate whisper.

"Who goes there?" sounded from the wall.

The two men dashed away, and immediately afterwards a musket-shot was fired.

"Run, Marse Billy, run!" Then the negro dropped slowly to the ground. After a few moments the guard, attended by another bearing a lantern, descended by the ladder, and walked rapidly to where he lay, one shot having entered his loin, and another perforated the artery beneath his lame knee-joint. When the men came up he raised his head, peered with anxiety around for a brief period, then smiling, lay down again, and into his eyes came a darkness deeper than that upon the bosom of the night.

VI.

"Somethin', I can't but think, is the matter 'ith Moll to-day, Missis Triplett," said Mrs. Sandidge, as the latter, after a brief visit on the next forenoon, rose to leave. "Hear that mum'lin'? She'd be goin' it strong exceptin' she know you're in the house. She ben a-singin', or what you may call it, all day, and sech wailin's as she make sometimes couldn't come from folks's ner nothin' else's mouths, to my opinion, 'ithout they had somethin' on top o' their mind. They'd skeer me sometimes ef I hadn't got uset to 'em, an' know they ain't no harm in nother her ner them. I ast her this mornin' ef anything troubled her, an' she said she were jes' sorter oneasy about her aunt Peggy. Poor thing! I ben thinkin', Christmas come, I'll git Mis' Sandidge to let 'em both go an' see their old aunt, they think so much of her."

Mrs. Triplett had hardly gone when a guard of the penitentiary, accompanied by three other men, rode up, and calling out Mrs. Sandidge, informed her of the death of Virgil, the enlargement of the convict White, and the fact that the latter had been traced as far as within a few miles of the town.

"Dead!" exclaimed Moll, coming from the kitchen door, where she had heard the news, "Werg'l dead! Who kilt him?" When they had repeated the story, she said, "How come Werg'l to be dar? Tole me he were on 'Conee River. I tole dah boy be keerfuler wid hisself, an' not be meddlin' wid business doan b'long to him. My laws! my laws!"

She turned, and was moving towards the kitchen, when the guard called to her: "Hello, my good 'oman, hain't saw anything o' your ole marster, has you?"

"Whut—whut you talkin' 'bout, white man?" She turned and looked him full in the eye, her great round nostrils dilating and contracting.

"I'm a-talkin' about your marse Billy, that your br'er Werg'l holp to git out o' the pentenchwy last night, an' got shot fer doin' of it, an' which it mout of ben better, or leas'ways look more deservin' like, ef it had of ben him stid o' that po' nigger. But an' which that feller are hid away some'rs 'bout; because it stan' to reason that ef he'd 'a' aimed to go furder, he'd 'a' other not got off the hoss he rid twenty mile from Milledgeville, er he'd 'a' tuck a fresh 'n' an' kep' on a-scootin'. An' which it's plain to my mind that he ain't wery fur from this wery place whar we all air at the present. An' which furthersomemore," he said, more and more slowly, as he closely watched her face, "I'm authorized to make an offer, in good silver money, o' fifty dollars to them that's other a-harb'rin' him, er can p'int to the same, that 'll give him up to me an' take the money."

Folding her arms across her breast, she said, "I can't tell dat I knows nothin' 'bout. Dey kill my br'er, de ownles I got—God know he were—an' now dey come atter me."

The officer looked at her steadily for some moments, she as steadily returning his gaze.

"'Tain't oftin you find 'em as coold an' cunnin'," he said, smiling to those around him. "But don't you see that she's a-thinkin' more 'bout her ole marster this minute than she is 'bout her own brother that's dead?"

"Oh, my poor Werg'l! oh, my poor br'er!" she almost screamed.

"She know no more about that man than I do. What

you want to be tormentin' the poor thing so for?" said Mrs. Sandidge, reproachfully.

"Beg you pard'n, madam," the man answered, while dismounting, and ordering his followers to do likewise; "I shell have to s'arch these princrses, but I shell try to do it with little trouble as I can help."

Moll turned and walked with her accustomed step to the kitchen, followed by the hunters. She stared wildly at them as they pursued their search, but she spoke not a word.

"He have ben here," said the leader, while standing by Virgil's bed, "fer these bedclose, don't you feel they're damp whar he ben a-layin'?"

When they had searched the rest of the premises in vain, and were proceeding to the mansion, Moll turned from the door where she had been watching them, entered the bedroom that once had been her brother's, and throwing herself upon the floor, said, in a low voice, her eyes seeming ready to burst from their sockets, "My Godamighty! ef dey takes dat chile, I want ter go atter Werg'l."

Instantly she rose again and returned to the kitchen door. Hearing a merry ejaculation in an upper attic room of the mansion, she raised her hands, their fingers widely extended, and thus stood until the party descended, with their prisoner again in chains.

"Hello! Molly pnt the kittle on," said the guard, holding up the bag of money. "Ef I'd 'a' knowed you so rich, I'd of knowed better 'n to make such a' offer as jes' a little fifty dollars."

She uttered a laugh, loud, prolonged, hideous in the extreme, and her understanding, limited as it had been, was forever gone.

The recapture of an escaped convict under the law resulted in an addition of two years to the term of his imprisonment. The case had created some sympathy, partly on account of the uniformly good conduct of White before his attempted escape, partly from a rising opinion in his native county that his intention had been, as he had pleaded, to take only one of the horses. Mrs. Sandidge was deeply affected. What her husband's feelings were none knew precisely, as he was accustomed to keep his feelings and his counsel, when not necessary to be expressed, to himself. The negroes had already paid him at least what he had appraised them at, and people said he ought not to complain, if he did.

Moll's insanity took a curious direction. She imagined herself a young girl, whose chief business was that of nurse to her "marse Billy," who was again an infant. She made a sort of doll out of old clothes, continually carried it in her arms, or sat and sang by an unfinished cradle in which she laid it. They could not get her out of the kitchen into an out-house until they had moved her cradle there at a time when she was walking with her baby in the yard. At that time there was no asylum for the insane in the State, and as she was entirely harmless, they let her do commonly whatever she fancied. Her physical health gave way rapidly, and it soon became obvious that her life was tending to a speedy end.

In spite of Mr. Sandidge's general imperturbability, one thing gave him an annoyance that he did not attempt to conceal, at least from his wife. I let the latter tell of it, as it was the only bit of fun that excellent woman could indulge in a case wherein her sympathies led to the shedding of many a tear:

"An' you think, Missis Triplett, that the poor thing hain't got it intoo her head that me an' Mis' Sandidge is the child's parrents, an' whenever she see Mis' Sandidge she other run an' hide her baby, er cry an' beg me to not let his pappy whip him? *I* don't mind it, not one single grain; but Mis' Sandidge—werried. Why, you don't know how it *do* werry him. Havin' o' no children o' our own, he say people 'll laugh an' make game of us. He even got so, Mis' Sandidge have, that he dodge her same as she dodge him. Ah, well!" she seriously resumed, "I do think it's the pitifulest case. One poor nigger shot down onprepar'd, an' the tother run mad, an' all a-tryin' to help the marster they raised with. As fer me, I can't but honor their feelin's, an' I mean to humor that poor creeter an' be good to her as I can while she last."

"Good woman," said Triplett, when his wife repeated to him this conversation—"one o' the best an' feelin'est in this whole town. Squire Sandidge 'shamed o' the bad grammars she use in her talk sometimes; but she's his equil, spite o' her grammars, an' he can't but know it when he think about it. It *are* right funny, the idee o' him bein' the father o' nothin' but a rag baby. A curis case, take it all together. Yit it don't s'prise me no great deal. I'm gittin' to be of a old man, an' have knowed right smart o' people in my time, white folks *an'* niggers, an' my expeunce of niggers is that in gen'l, whar a man treat 'em right, an' have ben raised 'ith 'em, they ain't a more thankfuler ner 'fectionate creeters than them, ner them that'll take bigger resks fer 'em."

Meanwhile other things were going on in Lincoln. The wife of the man Freeman, from whom the horses had been taken, by entreaties and threats at last prevailed upon her husband to make known the fact that the only animal intentionally taken was really the property of White, who had sold it conditioned upon reclamation at a certain date if not paid for, and that the condition had been wilfully violated. The wretch filed his confession in the County Court clerk's office, and absconded to unknown parts. The revelation shocked the community painfully; a petition for Executive pardon was rapidly and universally signed, and within a month after White's second incarceration he was released. As soon as this was done he started for his home. On reaching the village in which he had been recaptured, he stopped at the residence of Mr. Sandidge (who was at his office), and asked permission of his wife to see Moll.

"Cert'nly, cert'nly, sir," she answered; and leading the way, she whispered, "The poor thing have lost her mind an' run distracted. She's mighty weak."

"Yes, ma'am; so I heard."

The invalid was lying with her face to the wall, her baby upon her arm.

"Why, Moll," he said, "turn over. Howdye. You ain't forgot me, have you?"

She turned herself, and looked first at him, then at Mrs. Sandidge, then at him again, as he knelt by the bed. Slowly, laughing, she said, "Well, I jes' do declar'! *Ef* I 'ain't been a-dreamin' Marse Billy war a baby, an' me a-nussin' him! An' *show* nuff here him, a gweat big boy! *Dee* Laws bless my soul!"

After another moment she looked from him pleadingly to Mrs. Sandidge, and said, "Miss, please, ma'am, doan' scole Marse Billy fer dat. He not went to do it; did yer, honey?"

But Moll did not wait for the answer. Laying back upon the pillow the head that she had raised, she immediately expired.

Tears were in the eyes of her new mistress; her old master wept, as years before, at the departure of his mother.

THE END.

By R. M. JOHNSTON.

OLD MARK LANGSTON. A Tale of Duke's Creek. 16mo, Cloth, $1 00.

DUKESBOROUGH TALES. Illustrated. 4to, Paper, 35 cents.

American literature can fully care for itself when it contains such a novel as this. ... The plot is not the usual one, nor are its details worked out in the ordinary manner. The prominent characters are veritable creations.—*Hartford Post.*

The characters are strong, and the Southern dialect piquant and amusing in its interpretation.—*Boston Post.*

In our opinion, there is nothing in contemporary fiction to match the portrayal of human character to be found in this book. It is vivid, keen, and unerring.—*Atlanta Constitution.*

The story is full of a quiet humor, with touches of deep pathos, and will well repay the reader for the time spent upon it.—*Christian at Work, N. Y.*

The "Dukesborough Tales" of Colonel Johnston have already rendered that Georgia village real and typical to us. The homely wit and simplicity of its inhabitants have won our ready sympathy. ... He has created, founded, and erected into a regular borough the town with whose early history he is quite at home.—*Baltimore Sun.*

They are among the best character studies that we have ever seen, the characters in this instance being such as are native to Middle Georgia in recent and ante-bellum days. Mr. Johnston has a keen sense of humor, and understanding of the adaptability of common incidents to the purposes of story-telling. He is a good story-teller, and is at his best when he is not inventing, but remembering; for it is a peculiarity of these tales that they read like veritable pages from the real life of their actors. ... There are tales in the collection which any American writer, even the greatest, might be proud to have written.—*N. Y. Mail and Express.*

PUBLISHED BY HARPER & BROTHERS, NEW YORK.

☞ *Either of the above works sent by mail, postage prepaid, to any part of the United States or Canada, on receipt of the price.*

By CONSTANCE F. WOOLSON.

EAST ANGELS. pp. 592. 16mo, Cloth, $1 25.

ANNE. Illustrated. pp. 540. 16mo, Cloth, $1 25.

FOR THE MAJOR. pp. 208. 16mo, Cloth, $1 00.

CASTLE NOWHERE. pp. 386. 16mo, Cloth, $1 00. (*A New Edition.*)

RODMAN THE KEEPER. Southern Sketches. pp. 340. 16mo, Cloth, $1 00. (*A New Edition.*)

There is a certain bright cheerfulness in Miss Woolson's writing which invests all her characters with lovable qualities.—*Jewish Advocate*, N. Y.

Miss Woolson is among our few successful writers of interesting magazine stories, and her skill and power are perceptible in the delineation of her heroines no less than in the suggestive pictures of local life.—*Jewish Messenger*, N. Y.

Constance Fenimore Woolson may easily become the novelist laureate.—*Boston Globe*.

Miss Woolson has a graceful fancy, a ready wit, a polished style, and conspicuous dramatic power; while her skill in the development of a story is very remarkable.—*London Life*.

Miss Woolson never once follows the beaten track of the orthodox novelist, but strikes a new and richly loaded vein, which so far is all her own; and thus we feel, on reading one of her works, a fresh sensation, and we put down the book with a sigh to think our pleasant task of reading it is finished. The author's lines must have fallen to her in very pleasant places; or she has, perhaps, within herself the wealth of womanly love and tenderness she pours so freely into all she writes. Such books as hers do much to elevate the moral tone of the day—a quality sadly wanting in novels of the time.—*Whitehall Review*, London.

PUBLISHED BY HARPER & BROTHERS, NEW YORK.

☞ *The above works sent by mail, postage prepaid, to any part of the United States or Canada, on receipt of the price.*

By W. D. HOWELLS.

MODERN ITALIAN POETS. Essays and Poets. With Portraits. 12mo, Half Cloth, $2 00.

APRIL HOPES. 12mo, Cloth, $1 50.

A portfolio of delightsome studies among the Italian poets; musings in a golden granary full to the brim with good things.... We venture to say that no acute and penetrating critic surpasses Mr. Howells in true insight, in polished irony, in effective and yet graceful treatment of his theme, in that light and indescribable touch that lifts you over a whole sea of froth and foam, and fixes your eye, not on the froth and foam, but on the solid objects, the true heart and soul of the theme.—*Critic*, N. Y.

A more companionable, entertaining, stimulating work than this book has not been printed for many a day. It is a book to be studied privately, to be read aloud, to be cherished and quoted and reread many times, and every reader of it will cry for more translations from the Italian by the same delight-conferring pen.—*Chicago Tribune*.

This is a noble volume, the fruit of studies begun twenty years ago in Italy.... The subject is discussed with all the rare fascination of style and thought which Mr. Howells is so well qualified to bring to it, and the volume will be treasured by every lover of poetry of whatever period or clime.—*Christian at Work*, N. Y.

No living writer could give us this picture of a literary movement with such delicacy of appreciation and discrimination. The period embraced is about a century; the names selected comprise all the poets which a survey of the movement, now over, distinguishes as principal factors in it.—*Hartford Courant*.

In culture, the critical power, and in literary art these essays possess qualities reached by no American, and made more brilliant and pleasing by no foreign essayist.—*Boston Globe*.

"April Hopes" is a specimen of Mr. Howells's well-known consummate art as a delineator of young men and maidens, and a chronicler of all the fluctuations of love affairs. From the life-like description of Harvard Class Day and its participants, in the opening chapters, to the conclusion of the story, Mr. Howells is at his best.—*N. Y. Journal of Commerce*.

Mr. Howells never wrote a more bewitching book. It is useless to deny the rarity and worth of the skill that can report so perfectly and with such exquisite humor all the fugacious and manifold emotions of the modern maiden and her lover.—*Philadelphia Press*.

PUBLISHED BY HARPER & BROTHERS, NEW YORK.

☞ *Either of the above works sent by mail, postage prepaid, to any part of the United States or Canada, on receipt of the price.*

TOWARDS THE GULF.

A Romance of Louisiana.   pp. 316.   16mo, Cloth, $1 00.

"Towards the Gulf" is a tale of unusual power, whether considered with regard to its literary or artistic merits. It is a picture of a phase of New Orleans life, at once dreamily poetic and vividly realistic, rich in curious and felicitous illustrations of personal, social, and local traits. The dramatic situations are strong, and are skilfully developed. The Creole dialect is well handled, and life at a cotton plantation is portrayed with a fidelity which is both charming and picturesque.—*Observer*, N.Y.

The story is told with a great deal of skill and many touches of just sentiment. . . . The sketches of society and manners in New Orleans, of life on a river plantation after the war, of negro peculiarities, etc., are striking, and the book is distinguished throughout by delicacy of tone.—*N. Y. Tribune.*

A novel full of genuine interest. The pictures presented are varied, and light and shade are well blended. The descriptive power of the author is strongly marked. . . . The story dwells forcibly upon the prejudices and evil doings of the men.—*Philadelphia North American.*

"Towards the Gulf" is a story which we have taken real delight in reading.—*Hartford Daily Courant.*

The tale is simply yet powerfully told. . . . The book is certainly one of the strongest romances lately published, and will gain for its talented and unknown author no small meed of praise.—*Springfield Union.*

The scenes are well pictured and the characters are well drawn.—*Troy Daily Press.*

Of that exceedingly small number of novels having a flavor of its own. . . . It pulsates with life. There is color and motion, and not only all the charm of individuality, but of locality, and of a picturesque locality at that.—*Chicago Herald.*

It is something to rejoice over that another star has been added to the growing galaxy of Southern writers; for it is impossible to suppose that any one not Southern-born and bred, and imbued with all the distinctive elements of Southern culture, could ever have written this volume.—*New Orleans Picayune.*

PUBLISHED BY HARPER & BROTHERS, NEW YORK.

☞ *The above work sent by mail, postage prepaid, to any part of the United States or Canada on receipt of the price.*

THE ENTAILED HAT;

Or, Patty Cannon's Times. A Romance. By GEORGE ALFRED TOWNSEND ("Gath"). Pages x., 566. 16mo, Cloth, $1 50.

Neither Hawthorne nor Dickens ever painted their characters more vividly than has Mr. Townsend those of Vesta and Milburn, the owner of "Steeple Top." The events which led up to the fatal night when Vesta was informed of the true condition of affairs are the creation of genius. The entrance of Milburn into the aristocratic home of Judge Custis, to plead his own case, and his manner of doing it, is an artistic piece of literary work which will excite the admiration of the critical reader.—*Chicago Inter-Ocean.*

The book is remarkable in its local color, its vigorously drawn characters, and its peculiar originality of treatment. The interest is exceedingly dramatic, and there is enough of incident to furnish a half-dozen ordinary novels. . . . The story is so well told, and with such picturesqueness of effect generally, that the reader is carried unresistingly along in the skilfully stimulated desire to know the final fate of the actors in the exciting drama. This romance is a remarkable one in many respects.—*Saturday Evening Gazette,* Boston.

Vesta Custis and Rhoda test the power of the author in drawing feminine characters, and he has more than met the demands made upon him. They stand out from the pages like flesh-and-blood creatures. Equally successful is the delineation of Patty Cannon and the life of the negro kidnappers. The story moves rapidly, and the unflagging interest of the reader is maintained almost to the end. It entitles Mr. Townsend to a high place in the ranks of American novelists, and it would not be surprising if the "Entailed Hat" held a permanent place in American literature. We know of no story in which the details of American life have been so skilfully used, except in the novels of Hawthorne and Bayard Taylor.—*Philadelphia Press.*

It would be difficult to find in recent fiction a lovelier woman than Vesta, or a more touching one than the exquisite slave Virgie, or a stronger one than Milburn, or better portraits of the common life of the time and place than Levin Dennis and Jimmy Phœbus and Jack Wonnell. . . . The story has decided power and originality, and is a marked contribution to our really native fiction. —*Hartford Daily Courant.*

PUBLISHED BY HARPER & BROTHERS, NEW YORK.

☞ *The above work sent by mail, postage prepaid, to any part of the United States or Canada on receipt of the price.*

BEN-HUR: A TALE OF THE CHRIST.

By LEW. WALLACE. New Edition from New Electrotype Plates. pp. 560. 16mo, Cloth, $1 50; Half Calf, $3 00.

Anything so startling, new, and distinctive as the leading feature of this romance does not often appear in works of fiction.... Some of Mr. Wallace's writing is remarkable for its pathetic eloquence. The scenes described in the New Testament are re-written with the power and skill of an accomplished master of style.—*N. Y. Times.*

Its real basis is a description of the life of the Jews and Romans at the beginning of the Christian era, and this is both forcible and brilliant.... We are carried through a surprising variety of scenes; we witness a sea-fight, a chariot-race, the internal economy of a Roman galley, domestic interiors at Antioch, at Jerusalem, and among the tribes of the desert; palaces, prisons, the haunts of dissipated Roman youth, the houses of pious families of Israel. There is plenty of exciting incident; everything is animated, vivid, and glowing.—*N. Y. Tribune.*

From the opening of the volume to the very close the reader's interest will be kept at the highest pitch, and the novel will be pronounced by all one of the greatest novels of the day.—*Boston Post.*

It is full of poetic beauty, as though born of an Eastern sage, and there is sufficient of Oriental customs, geography, nomenclature, etc., to greatly strengthen the semblance.—*Boston Commonwealth.*

"Ben-Hur" is interesting, and its characterization is fine and strong. Meanwhile it evinces careful study of the period in which the scene is laid, and will help those who read it with reasonable attention to realize the nature and conditions of Hebrew life in Jerusalem and Roman life at Antioch at the time of our Saviour's advent.—*Examiner,* N. Y.

It is really Scripture history of Christ's time, clothed gracefully and delicately in the flowing and loose drapery of modern fiction.... Few late works of fiction excel it in genuine ability and interest.—*N. Y. Graphic.*

One of the most remarkable and delightful books. It is as real and warm as life itself, and as attractive as the grandest and most heroic chapters of history.—*Indianapolis Journal.*

The book is one of unquestionable power, and will be read with unwonted interest by many readers who are weary of the conventional novel and romance.—*Boston Journal.*

PUBLISHED BY HARPER & BROTHERS, NEW YORK.

☞ *The above work sent by mail, postage prepaid, to any part of the United States or Canada, on receipt of the price.*

www.ingramcontent.com/pod-product-compliance
Lightning Source LLC
Chambersburg PA
CBHW020543300426
44111CB00008B/773